Contemporary F
African Writers a... ...
Burden of Commitment

MW01284332

Contemporary Francophone African Writers and the Burden of Commitment

Odile Cazenave and Patricia Célérier

UNIVERSITY OF VIRGINIA PRESS *Charlottesville and London*

THIS BOOK IS MADE POSSIBLE BY A COLLABORATIVE GRANT
FROM THE ANDREW W. MELLON FOUNDATION.

University of Virginia Press

Printed in the United States of America
on acid-free paper

First published 2011

9 8 7 6 5 4 3 2 1

Library of Congress Cataloging-in-Publication Data

Cazenave, Odile M. (Odile Marie), 1961–
    Contemporary Francophone African writers and
the burden of commitment / Odile Cazenave and
Patricia Célérier.
        p.   cm.
    Includes bibliographical references and index.
    ISBN 978-0-8139-3095-4 (cloth : alk. paper)
    ISBN 978-0-8139-3096-1 (pbk. : alk. paper)
    ISBN 978-0-8139-3115-9 (ebk.)
    1. African literature (French)—History and
criticism.   2. Politics and literature—Africa, French-
speaking—History—20th century.   I. Célérier,
Patricia, 1956–   II. Title.
PQ3980.5.C39   2011
840.9′96—dc22

                                  2010042426

To Andreas and Ogemdi
To Simone and Roger Degait

CONTENTS

PREFACE

This book project was born of several years of collaboration through a series of roundtables and participations in panel discussions we co-chaired at the African Literature Association (ALA) and the Congrès International des Etudes Francophones (CIEF). These include "Littératures de la postcolonialité" (Sousse, Tunisia, CIEF 2000), "Ecrire le génocide au Rwanda: Réflexions sur le projet Rwanda, Ecrire par Devoir de Mémoire" (Richmond, Virginia, U.S.A., ALA 2001), "Nouveaux regards sur la jeunesse et la ville" (Abidjan, Ivory Coast, CIEF 2002), "Nouvelles formes d'engagement au féminin" (San Diego, California, U.S.A., ALA 2002), "Ecritures de la violence dans l'Océan Indien" (New Orleans, Louisiana, U.S.A., CIEF 2003), "Figurations mémorielles et histoire dans le roman africain francophone contemporain" (Boulder, Colorado, U.S.A., ALA 2005), "New Voices of Commitment in Francophone African Literature" (Accra, Ghana, ALA 2006).

This is not a work where a single chapter can be attributed to one of us alone; rather it is the result of a careful process of combined readings and long-standing discussions, including on writing. This collaborative process helped us produce, we think, an original piece of scholarship based on a sustained dialogue.

The authors express their gratitude to the following colleagues who generously gave of their time and critically engaged with our ideas: Susan Andrade, Elisabeth Cardonne-Arlyck, Ken Harrow, Christine Reno, David L. Schalk, and Susan Zlotnick. Conversations with the writers and critics Hamidou Dia, Boubacar Boris Diop, Emmanuel Dongala, Cheikh Hamidou Kane, and Lilyan Kesteloot have contributed to sharpen our historical understanding of engagement in its African contexts. Conversations and invited lectures with the writers Mongo Beti, Tanella Boni, Ken Bugul, Tierno Monénembo, Patrice Nganang, Michèle Rakotoson, Sami Tchak, Véronique Tadjo, and Abdourahman Waberi have enabled us to discuss further what it means to be writing as a francophone African writer today, what challenges it entails, and what role and position it may spell.

Many thanks to the University of Virginia Press's Humanities Editor, Cathie Brettschneider, Susan Spilecki, and especially Teresa Jesionowski for their careful editing, Patricia Célérier's research assistants at Vassar, Dan Lupo '09, Caroline Hudnut '08, Janeen Madan '10, and Stephanie Owen '11, and Chad Fust, Vassar College's Technology Training Coordinator, for their help with editorial matters and attention to details. This book benefited from a 2005 Vassar College research grant (Gabrielle Snyder Beck Fund) and a 2009 award from Vassar College's Dean's Discretionary Fund under the Andrew W. Mellon Foundation's Faculty Career Initiative.

Finally, our heartfelt thanks to Kerry Chukwu-Onuoha for his unfailing support, to Ogemdi and Andreas for their patience, and to Théo for being there.

The Burden of Commitment

To those calling for a politically committed writer, I propose an engaging man.

SONY LABOU TANSI, *La vie et demie*

I am not opposed to the principle of social conflict, to civil war or to a bloody revolution. In theory, I am quite favorable to it. In practice, I remain favorable to it. Under the condition that I remain uninvolved.

BESSORA, *Et si Dieu me demande, dites-Lui que je dors*

The very existence of "Engagement," which can loosely be translated from the original French as political involvement of the intellectual class, has come to seem passé. This is true not only in France, widely viewed as the home of the *engagé* intellectual, with Emile Zola's "J'accuse" of January 3, 1898, the foundational document, but also in Europe and the United States. The belief in the transformative ability of literature and in the higher (visionary) power of the writer and of the intellectual has given way to a less idealistic, less dogmatic, and more complex stance.

Critical evaluation of francophone African literature has followed this shift, and few critics today would lend unequivocal credence to Lilyan Kesteloot's 1972[1] assertion in *Intellectual Origins of the African Revolution* that "literary works can accelerate the development of social and political crises" (11).

Working across genres but focusing on the novel, this book takes up the question of renewed forms of commitment in contemporary francophone African literature. It also focuses on new ways of understanding African literature and its voices, such as the diversification of the processes of identification with and belonging to Africa, the different modes of resistance to the old notions of writing as art, the remapping of the theme of African youth and its future, and finally the impact of an increasing conservatism on Europe's urban environment, especially in the context of immigration. By looking at *engagée* literature from yesterday (when the African writer was implicitly seen as imparted with a mission) to today (when authors usually aspire to be acknowledged primarily for their works as writers), this book addresses the current processes of canonization in contemporary francophone African literature. We argue that aesthetic as well as political issues are now at the forefront of debates about the African literary canon as writers and critics increasingly acknowledge the ideology of form.

As we write this book, in the post-9/11 and post-Katrina era, postcolonial theory, one of the predominant analytical tools in literature, is also at a juncture, cast in doubt for its alleged entrenchment in the Euro-American university system, its excessive attention to Western cultural production and practices, and its ambivalent politics. As noted by David Jefferess, Julie McGonegal, and Sabine Milz in "The Politics of Postcoloniality," in *Postcolonial Text* (2006), "Postcolonial theory has provided a valuable critique of the discourses that underwrote the colonial project and that continue to inform neo-liberal imaginings of a unified world (market), including 'civilization' and 'progress'" (2). It has also proposed useful analyses of the legacy of imperialism. Yet, those analyses have often been based on a rejection of preexisting humanist and materialist theories. Although the influence of Jacques Derrida and Gayatri Chakravorty Spivak has been undeniable, postmodernist attacks on "grand narratives," of which Marxism is one, have challenged materialist readings and still-framed Engagement as a simple binary.

Postcolonial studies engage a wide variety of fields of inquiry: postcolonial theory, of course, but also diaspora, ethnic, migration, and globalization studies. Under pressure from scholars in these fields, postcolonial studies are pushed to acknowledge that a "productive understanding of, and resistance to, global processes of oppression must work on the level of both the material and the symbolic" (Jefferess, McGonegal, and Milz, *The Politics of Postcoloniality*, 8). They are drawn away from the "self-fashioning without a subject" model that Terry Eagleton warned against in *Sweet Violence: The Idea of the Tragic* (2003): "A faith in plurality, plasticity, dismantling, destabilizing, the power of endless self-invention—all this, while undoubtedly radical in some contexts, also smacks of a distinctively Western culture and an advanced capitalist world. . . . In a later stage of capitalist production, we are now confronted with the singular spectacle of self-fashioning without a subject. An openness to cultural 'otherness' comes pre-wrapped in ideas of the protean, provisional and performative which may strike some of the cultural others in question as distinctly foreign goods" (xi).[2]

The current crisis of neoliberal capitalism and the ensuing delegitimization of free market ideology have worsened the political and economic climate, bringing about a stronger need for transparency and commitment. The renewed realization that the financial crisis is also a crisis in political leadership has, in turn, raised the issue of intellectual leadership and vision. This is something that Aminata Traoré has been drumming about for quite some time. In *Le viol de l'imaginaire* (The rape of the imagination, 2002), she underscores the urgent necessity for Africans to reevaluate their dependence on foreign aid and the lack of self-determination it has implied. Evidencing a wide diasporic intellectual legacy ranging from such theoretical texts as Aimé Césaire's *Discours sur le colonialisme* (1950; *Discourse on Colonialism*, 1972) and Ngugi Wa Thiongo's *Decolonizing the Mind* (1986), Traoré's work is another marker in the long process of decolonization.[3]

As they are reminded of their postcolonial existence in a world faced by new forms of economic and political domination, postcolonial critics are forced to revisit the models of political participation and analyses elaborated by previous generations of thinkers, especially nationalism and the idea of national liberation, that is, liberation itself. Postcolonial criticism is again grappling with the notion of engagement, thereby proving that it cannot be dismissed as mere rhetoric. Engagement provided a body of work on the nature of oppression and economic marginalization, and theorized practices of resistance. The notion of Engagement has thus not gone away; it has changed its genres and forms.

So, what is Engagement more specifically?[4] In *The Spectrum of Engagement: Mounier, Benda, Nizan, Brasillach, Sartre* (1979), David L. Schalk traces the modern roots of the concept to Paul Nizan's 1932 novel *Les chiens de garde* (*The Watchdogs*, 1972) and broadly defines Engagement as "a political involvement, usually by members of the intellectual class" (ix). Emphasizing the controversial nature of Engagement, he remarks that it has always both "powerfully attract[ed] and repel[led] intellectuals themselves" (xi). Schalk pinpoints Engagement more precisely by adding that it usually involves an element of choice, in a historical context determined by the rise of ideology and the growth of nationalist passion (33): "We may define engagement as the political or social action of an intellectual who has realized that abstention is a ruse, a commitment to the *status quo*, and who makes a conscious and willful choice to enter the arena, never abandoning his or her critical judgment" (25). Expanding on Nizan's ideas after World War II, Jean-Paul Sartre will come to regard that element of choice, and the responsibility related to it, as the condition to exercise one's individual freedom.

Although generally associated with the Left, Engagement is not its exclusive domain (see the far-right intellectuals Robert Brasillach, Lucien Rebatet, and Louis-Ferdinand Céline, for example). Because Engagement links up the idea of politics to that of morality, it poses the question of the role and responsibility of the intellectual. That question is, of course, fraught with tensions. In *La trahison des clercs* (1927; *The Treason of the Intellectuals*, 1969), Julien Benda maintains that an intellectual must rise above the contingent. Nizan, a Marxist, argued that "culture aids in attaining full consciousness of the social reality" (Schalk, 58) and that "engagement provides an ethical ingredient in political life which otherwise would be lacking" (111). The critical and qualitative dissent generated by intellectual Engagement was a necessary and dutiful response to the urgency of the times.

In *Littérature et engagement: de Pascal à Sartre* (2000), Benoît Denis differentiates between a "littérature engagée" and a "littérature d'engagement" (11–12), hereby echoing Schalk's claim that "engagement is both contemporary and universal" (4). In the French context, "littérature engagée" refers to a period in the twentieth century, heralded by the Dreyfus affair, and continuing today, when the principles of a political commitment *in* literature are rethought. "Littérature d'engagement" more generally points to a genre ("littérature de combat et de controverse") that has always existed.

Our analysis posits a third model for contemporary francophone African literatures. Refusing to pigeonhole this corpus in the worn-out dichotomy of committed versus noncommitted texts, we consider it as one where pluralistic aesthetic commitments are an integral part of its elaboration. Many of the current francophone African texts are self-reflective—as opposed to strictly self-referential—in the sense that their writers are generally cognizant of what is being written by their contemporaries elsewhere in the world and have an understanding of the complexities of their postcolonial situation. Furthermore, intellectuals from the United States, Europe, Africa, and India have come back to the forefront of public opinion[5] to address such questions as the war in Bosnia, the increasingly global refugee problem, the Israeli-Palestinian conflict, and 9/11 and its aftermath: the wars in Afghanistan and in Iraq. The renewed involvement of intellectuals in public life has given momentum to the idea that writers can make a difference and that their words can foster action.

Currently, African literatures are being pulled simultaneously in two different directions. Contemporary postcolonial literature has gotten readers used to disillusioned representations of the African continent and at times even turned away from the African continent to focus on Africans in Paris/France/Europe. But more than a sense of disinvestment or rejection, this development shows a desire on the part of the authors to be identified as writers rather than as people from a specific national, cultural, or geographic origin. With the collapse of the apartheid system in South Africa, the early 1990s showed signs of tremendous hope of social change on the African continent. Yet, shortly thereafter, terrible conflicts and atrocities broke out, particularly in Sierra Leone and Liberia, Algeria, Rwanda, the Congo, and Ivory Coast. Francophone writers have been reacting to these different issues and realities from the mid-1990s on.

In his 2000 essay, *De la postcolonie, essai sur l'imagination politique dans l'Afrique contemporaine* (*On the Postcolony*, 2001), Achille Mbembe proposed that the "postcolony" is an age of "entanglement" and "displacement" that "encloses multiple *durées* made up of discontinuities, reversals, inertias, and swings that overlay one another, interpenetrate one another and envelop one another" (14).[6] For Mbembe, the postcolony "cannot be forced into any simplistic model and calls into question the hypothesis of stability and *rupture* underpinning social theory, notably where the sole concern is to account for either Western modernity or the failures of non-European worlds to perfectly replicate it" (16).

Boniface Mongo-Mboussa takes up that notion in *Désir d'Afrique* (2002) and makes a convincing point in saying that francophone African literature's organic "expansion" has wrongly been evaluated by critics as a series of ruptures, thereby preventing a full understanding of the field. In other words, he advocates for a reconsideration of the idea of literary tradition. Yet, the idea of a francophone African literary tradition should not limit the range of interpretative possibilities. The concept of literary tradition works well if one considers

Alain Mabanckou's work in the light of Henri Lopès's and Emmanu-el Dongala's. That concept has geographical, cultural, and linguistic congruence. However, the Djiboutian Abdourahman Waberi's work, for instance, cannot be explained merely in the light of other franco-phone African writers, albeit of his generation and/or living abroad. An understanding of other non-francophone influences must be taken into account, such as the production of Nurrudin Farah, the Somali writer living in South Africa, with whom Waberi shares his nomadic imagination.

Thus, our study questions the critical appraisal of the body of fran-cophone African literature. Currently, the notion of Engagement ar-ticulated by Sartre operates dismissively and paradoxically: engage-ment remains an inevitable theoretical premise, but at the same time it has collapsed upon itself. The new generations of African writers have had to negotiate this exhaustion of the concept of engagement. Both writers and literary critics must now deal with a problem of ter-minology and a context in which certain terms can seem obsolete or be politically manipulated. They are aware of the fact that hanging on to the same terms since independence may prevent a more nuanced understanding and practice of African literatures at the turn of the twenty-first century. Our analysis demonstrates that there are new terms for understanding the political engagement of francophone Af-rican literature and new modes of critical evaluation that are more attentive to the interconnection of politics, ideology, and aesthetics.

This study is divided into four chapters: Chapter 1, "Enduring Commitments"; Chapter 2, "The Practice of Memory"; Chapter 3, "Lifting the Burden? Francophone African Writers Engaging in New Aesthetics"; and Chapter 4, "The Fashioning of an Engaging Litera-ture: The Publishing Industry, the Internet, and Criticism."

In Chapter 1, "Enduring Commitments," we examine the clas-sic parameters of the engagé, that is, the canonical, African novel. African literary discourse developed in a context of historical vio-lence, both institutional and symbolic. Committed to liberation and self-determination, francophone African literature was marked by a self-conscious ideology. Elikia M'Bokolo gives the following defini-tion of the notion of ideology in "Le Panafricanisme au 21ème siè-cle" (21st-century Pan-Africanism): "a system of ideas, representa-tions and social concepts, that conveys the interests of categories and social groups, provides a global interpretation of the world as it is organized, and implies points of view, norms of conduct, and instructions for action" (1). In his 1970 article "Idéologie et appareils idéologiques d'Etat" ("Ideology and Ideological State Apparatuses," 1971) Louis Althusser underlined that "ideology is a representation of the imaginary relationship of individuals to their real conditions of existence" (36) and posited the following equation: "ideology = illusion/allusion."[7]

The nature, function, and reception of francophone African literature have been topics of numerous and frequently polemical debates. These debates revolve around opposing theoretical and political ideas: the origin of Black civilizations, the elaboration of a Black aesthetics, the question of authenticity and tradition, the role of *oralité* and vernacular African languages, the use of French, the function of the writer and the critic, and finally, the categorization of African literature vis-à-vis Francophonie and world literature.

We revisit the notion of commitment traditionally linked to African literatures, particularly the type of commitment associated with some of the pioneering francophone African writers. We show that commitment, however ideologically fitting at some point, was never one-dimensional and that it has evolved along with their writing. We also discuss the ways critics have tied (and institutionalized) francophone African literature to the issue of commitment.

Typically, the socially committed novel has offered a representation of history that hinges on two opposing and parallel narratives: one of oppression, the other of resistance. In this type of novel, time is specific and geographically grounded; characters are propelled by a dynamics of hope for social change and by the possibility of transcendence. Gradually, however, postcolonial novels have become darker, time and location sketchier and more disjointed. The fictional nation-state has taken on a cynically farcical quality, and authors have tended to focus on creating more intricately woven and layered narratives.

Expanding on the works of critics from Africa, Europe, and the United States, we provide a new reading of the works of "enduring militants." We show how they transformed their ideas of political commitment, seminal to their literary productions, in the course of their literary careers, and demonstrate that the generational factor cannot always be used to gauge the (committed) nature of a writer's work. Although there are similarities in the literary crafting of engagement in a specific generation, individual authors have enriched it in particular ways. An author such as Mongo Beti[8] has given ample evidence of his subversive understanding of the literary mise en scène of political commitment. *Ville cruelle* (Cruel city, 1954), *Le pauvre Christ de Bomba* (1956; *The Poor Christ of Bomba*, 1971), *Perpétue ou l'habitude du malheur* (1974; *Perpetua and the Habit of Unhappiness*, 1978), *Les deux mères de Guillaume Ismaël Dzewatama* (1983), *La revanche de Guillaume Ismaël Dzewatama* (1984), *L'histoire du fou* (1994; *The Story of the Madman*, 2001), and his last two novels, *Trop de soleil tue l'amour* (Too much sun kills love, 1999) and *Branle-bas en noir et blanc* (Trouble in black and white, 2000), show a steady problematization of a form of literary engagement grounded in realism.

We extend our analysis to other enduring militants who have had a profound impact on francophone African literature and represent different generations of African youth: Cheikh Hamidou Kane, Ahmadou Kourouma, Aminata Sow Fall, and Emmanuel Dongala. We examine how their writing manifests a continuity and/or a renewal in commitment.

All of these writers have revised the traditional narrative of political engagement so that the African subject is no longer either an active resister or a victim of oppression. Works written by Dongala and Sow Fall from the 1990s on, for instance, offer their readers new possibilities for constructing the African subject. Dongala's distinct forms of engagement display a change in tone and focus that was indeed spurred by the Congolese civil wars but also by his displacement to the United States, looking (back and) at the continent from a distance. Thus Dongala's work has generated new voices that translate his current preoccupation and foremost desire to speak to African youth.

Through her thirty-year career, Sow Fall, one of the pioneer women writers, has demonstrated a preoccupation with Senegal and the African continent that highlights specific social, political, religious, and cultural issues central to her country's current profile. But the span of Sow Fall's literary production, from *La grève des Battù* (1979; *The Beggars' Strike*, 1981) through *L'ex-père de la nation* (The former father of the nation, 1987) to *Douceurs du bercail* (The comfort of the fold, 1998), shows that the nature of her commitment has evolved beyond her country and the continent. Looking at her literary work and also at her influence on Senegal's cultural life, we assess the ways by which this author shows dedication to the broader issue of human rights.

Our second chapter, "The Practice of Memory," examines the central role of memory in the current rethinking of the concept of engagement in literature. Having mapped out the historical context of this gradual shift and discussed key contemporary theoretical issues related to it, we identify the aesthetic transformations the practice of memory has brought about through close literary analyses of significant texts.

In the 1990s and early 2000s, the will to remember, the commitment to the act of remembrance, the (re-)cognition of the past, and the memorialization of its traumatic periods became themes around which to rally political energies. Today, the interest in memory is closely linked to that of history. Historians such as Pierre Nora, Benjamin Stora, and Mahmoud Mamdani and philosophers such as Paul Ricoeur have demonstrated that the relationship between memory and history is at the crux of the notion of collective memory. Such contemporary scholars have reversed the assumption that history shapes memory, underlining the dictates of memory on history in France,[9] in Europe in general, in the United States, in Latin America, and on the African continent. Finally, the study of history has moved from analyzing events to analyzing collective subjectivities.

In the francophone world, the resurgence of the issue of memory and the advent of what Ricoeur has called "the war of memories" was sparked by a series of historical events in the ex-"Métropole." The 1984 Papon trial forced French society to confront its past, particularly the extent of the responsibility of the Vichy regime in the deportation of Jews. It resulted in a desacralization of the national discourse on French history and induced a reinvestigation of France's colonial past. In the 1990s, new literary voices rose to be heard. Maghrebi and sub-Saharan African writers living on the African continent or in Europe confronted history and its mistakes anew.

This chapter considers three particular aspects of this literary appraisal:[10] the recrafting of the heroic figure, the revamping/subverting of the myth, and "Rwanda: Ecrire par devoir de mémoire" (the Duty of Memory Project). We examine the ways in which the hero is related to memory and history and analyze the transformations of the heroic figure in the following texts: Boubacar Boris Diop's *Le cavalier et son ombre* (The knight and its shadow, 1997), Tierno Monénembo's *Cinéma* (1997), Werewere Liking's *La mémoire amputée* (2004; *The Amputated Memory*, 2007), and Patrice Nganang's *La joie de vivre* (The joy of living, 2003).

In analyzing Gaston-Paul Effa's *Tout ce bleu* (1998; *All That Blue*, 2002) and *Mâ* (1999), Tanella Boni's *Les baigneurs du lac rose* (The swimmers of Lake Rose, 1995), Véronique Tadjo's *Reine Pokou: Con-*

certo pour un sacrifice (2004; *Queen Pokou: Concerto for a Sacrifice*, 2009), Michèle Rakotoson's *Lalana* (2002), and Jean-Luc Raharimanana's *Nour, 1947* (2001), we show that the myth operates as a site of aesthetic experimentation. Effa reconnects with Wole Soyinka's definition of the myth as a basis for self-apprehension; Boni and Tadjo interrogate foundational myths in an attempt to understand the mechanisms ruling modern African societies and their potential for change; Rakotoson and Raharimanana resurrect Malagasy myths of precolonial and colonial resistance in an attempt to represent the continuing struggles and replenishment process of a people in the postcolonial context of Madagascar.

The project "Rwanda: Ecrire par devoir de mémoire" is one of the most visible instances of the type of reappraisal mentioned above. Following an initiative by Fest'Africa, ten writers committed their time to writing about the 1994 Rwandan genocide. As a result, an array of literary productions, novels, selections of poems and short stories, plays, and essays were published during the year 2000. Considering some of these texts—*Murambi, le livre des ossements* (*Murambi: The Book of Bones*, 2006) by Diop, *Nyamirambo* by Nocky Djedanoum, *La phalène des collines* (The butterfly of the hills) by Koulsy Lamko, *Murekatete* by Monique Ilboudo, *L'aîné des orphelins* (*The Oldest Orphan*, 2004) by Monénembo, *L'ombre d'Imana: voyage jusqu'au bout du Rwanda* (*The Shadow of Imana: Travels in the Heart of Rwanda*, 2002) by Tadjo, and *Moisson de crânes* (Harvest of skulls) by Waberi—we explore the variety of ways in which these writers have given artistic expression to the genocide. Put together side by side, their works raise a number of questions about memory and testimony, as well as about an epistemology, a literary epistemology, of violence and loss.

We also address the differences between "devoir de mémoire" (duty of memory) and "travail de mémoire" (the workings of memory), "devoir de lecture" (the reader's duty) and "devoir de regard" (the duty to intervene), raising the issue of the reader's responsibility and engagement (and that of the publisher's role). We close this section by looking at the critical reception this project has generated.

Chapter 3, "Lifting the Burden? Francophone African Writers Engaging in New Aesthetics" focuses on the following questions: Where has the need to be emancipated from the old notion of engagement led African writers creatively? Are there new aesthetics of engagement at work in contemporary francophone African literature? Has their search for new forms led francophone African writers to a modernist conception of literature that has produced unconscious phenomena of mimetism/creative assimilation? Would the fact that most francophone African writers publish in France (i.e., that the marketing of their works is controlled by a few publishing houses with a readership mostly circumscribed to its national borders) have enabled such a trend? How much does geography (Africa, France, and, more recently, the United States) influence the quality of their writing?

Through close analyses of relevant texts, we show that contemporary francophone African authors are investigating the ideological implications of narrative while writing new narratives of African identities; these aesthetic experimentations are centered on two main topics: violence and immigration.

Through Isabelle Boni-Claverie's *La grande dévoreuse* (The avid devourer, 1999), Ken Bugul's *La folie et la mort* (Madness and death, 2000), Cécile Vieyra's *Une odeur aigre de lait rance* (An acrid smell of spoiled milk, 1999), Mabanckou's *Bleu blanc rouge* (Blue white red, 1998), Sami Tchak's *Place des fêtes* (2001), and Bessora's *53 cm* (1999), we assess the role(s) and representation(s) of the youth and the city in the francophone African novel at the turn of the century. More specifically, we study the inscription of postcolonial violence in a literary context where children and the young have increasingly become voices of violence, especially in writings by men; see, for example, Dongala's *Johnny chien méchant* (2002; *Johnny Mad Dog*, 2006), Kourouma's *Allah n'est pas obligé* (2000; *Allah Is Not Obliged*, 2007), Monénembo's *L'aîné des orphelins* (2000), J. R. Essomba's *Le dernier gardien de l'arbre* (The last keeper of the tree, 1998), and Florent Couao-Zotti's *Charly en guerre* (Charly at war, 1996).

Looking at works by Calixthe Beyala, Daniel Biyaoula, Mabanckou, Essomba, Bessora, Fatou Diome, Leonora Miano, and Waberi, we examine how they revisit the theme of immigration and construct new literary identities, and how they develop a different aesthetics of struggle to which Nganang's *Temps de chien* (2001; *Dog Days*, 2006) provides a counterview—no longer a collective political struggle, but an isolated, individual, and fragmented process—through the representation of clandestine immigration, the emergence of new protagonists and new heroes. Studying the works of Bessora, Diome, and Beyala, we reflect on the textual implications of humor, laughter, and subversion. Likewise, we analyze how provocation operates as an eye-opener in the books of Sami Tchak and Beyala. Looking at the recent works of Achille N'goye, Bolya, and Mongo Beti, we determine the extent to which crime fiction is part of a new aesthetics in African literature.

Finally, in Chapter 4, "The Fashioning of an Engaging Literature: The Publishing Industry, the Internet, and Criticism," we reflect on publishing politics in France and Africa. We evaluate the impact of the development of new literary series, such as Gallimard's Continents Noirs, Hatier's Monde Noir, and L'Harmattan's Encres Noires. We look at publishing houses such as Serpent à Plumes, Editions Kaya Makhele, and Actes Sud, as well as Nouvelles Editions Africaines and hybrid structures such as Africultures. We examine the granting of literary awards and its role in the recognition of specific authors and texts. Identifying the new forms of publishing that circumvent and/or complement the old structures, we look at the relationship between the growing influence of technology on the dissemination of francophone African literary production and changing commitments.

Having analyzed the implications of these changes, we point to a significant discrepancy between the easier access to information on francophone African literature and authors, and the fact that there is a substantial backlog in the translation of primary sources. Mongo Beti, Lopès, Sow Fall, Monénembo, and Diop have not been sufficiently translated. Conversely, several of Beyala's books were translated soon after her 1992 breakthrough in France with *Le petit prince de Belleville* (*Loukoum: The "Little Prince" of Belleville*, 1995).[11] This means that the field of francophone African literatures is being shaped differently on different continents and in different countries. This has important implications in terms of canon formation, the interpretation and reception of the entire field, and the teaching of African literature in French.

Another parameter in canon formation and the recognition of authors is the granting of literary awards. Some of these awards are specific to francophone letters and go back to colonial times (Grand Prix de l'Afrique Noire, Prix Tropiques, Concours de la Nouvelle Radio France Internationale, etc.); others are part of France's postcolonial literary life (Prix Edouard Glissant, for instance).[12] Awards such as the Prix Fonlon-Nichols and the former Prix Marguerite Yourcenar have contributed to the increasing visibility of francophone literatures outside of France and Africa, in this case in the United States.

Today, the dissemination of African letters goes beyond the publishing houses themselves. Many short stories, poems, and essays appear directly (or first) online. Many websites give readers immediate access to information on literature as well as the possibility of contacting the writer or his or her representative. In doing so, they allow the readers to be engaged differently with African literatures.

Readership is also influenced by the increasingly frequent presence of francophone African authors in the media and by their systematic participation in festivals, particularly in France where the book market pulsates to the rhythm of annual literary book fairs, in Paris, Saint-Malo, Limoges, Lille, among others.

African literature cannot be looked at in isolation anymore. It is part of the larger world of African arts. One of the ways to be politically engaged is to engage in/with popular culture itself. Whereas African literature still reaches relatively small segments of the African population, popular culture—music, videos, movies, etc.—has a wider circulation because it is less exclusive.

We make the point that the disentrenchment of the notion of engagement is not specific to African writers but extends to filmmakers, musicians, and painters. This disentrenchment, of which Ousmane Sembène was the early proponent in the 1960s when he moved from writing to filmmaking, has produced new creative (and political) synergies, particularly since the 1990s. Nganang's novels, *La promesse des fleurs* (The promise of flowers, 1998) and *Temps de chien* (2001), can best be understood in the light of the work of other Cameroonians of the same generation, filmmakers Jean-Marie Teno and Jean-Pierre Bekolo, whose films, documentaries, and videos aim at challenging their country's political establishment. But his fiction and essays should also be traced to his elders, notably Mongo Beti and the writer and filmmaker Bassek Ba Kobhio. Thus, the diverse ways in which recent novels establish a committed relationship to fundamental issues in human rights are to be found in other forms of African art. The artistic fermentation in popular culture, at the turn of the 1990s, has had a profound impact on African literature and is nourishing it. The role and status of the African writer has shifted. Her/his commitment is not necessarily limited to literature. Removed from dogmatism, it is more inventive and encompasses a wider array of social and cultural practices. Contemporary francophone African writers are cultural practitioners who affirm their world citizenship.

The aim of our book is to lay out the terms of a conversation on the meaning of engagement today, fifty years after most francophone African countries gained independence. As we see it, the originality of our work lies not only in our historical analysis of political commitment in literature but also in our reassessment of the burden it has been to writers and the ways it has shaped our understanding of African letters. Thus, in Chapter 1, for instance, we do not construct Mongo Beti as the perfect embodiment of the evolution of the concept of engagement, but as one example of the different, and at times paradoxical, approaches pioneering generations of African men of letters—in this case, those belonging to the "generation of 1928" (Robert Pageard)—provided toward literary engagement.

Our study concerns African authors who write in French, which does not imply that they agree with the politics of Francophonie, or only write or want to write in French. Indeed, a number of African authors writing in French also write in other languages; for instance, Nganang writes in several European languages (English, French, and German), and Lamko's 2007 production of his opera *L'Opéra du Sahel* made use of Bambara, Wolof, and Bamana. We also acknowledge that the term "francophone" African literature delineates an artificial and politically problematic field, with African literatures in other European languages and, more crucially, with African literatures in African languages. The necessity of developing literacy and cultural productions in African languages is discussed through the works of authors such as Sembène, Mongo Beti, Sow Fall, Kane, and Diop, and also explored in Chapter 4 when we look at African intellectual legacies.

Rather than limiting our work to a few specific authors and their texts, we chose to articulate theoretical issues across a variety of perspectives and generations. We deliberately opted not to treat women's literary production as a separate corpus because we feel that women writers have been at the forefront of African literature and participated in the renewal of its politics of form. Lastly, we do not suggest that the dominant theoretical paradigm has shifted (or should shift) from Engagement to littérature-monde or world literature.

CHAPTER ONE

Enduring Commitments

One may wonder if putting literature in the service of a cause, reducing its status to that of a vassal, was not a desperate (and hopeless) way to protect it, when the expression, "Littérature Engagée" [committed literature] is a pleonasm. Forever, since Plato wanted to expel the poet from the city, the mere fact of putting one's quill to the page has been a form of engagement: any new attempt at capturing language in writing necessarily interferes with the tables of the law, the collective myth engraved in marble.

BERTRAND LECLAIR, *Théorie de la déroute*

There is no pat answer to the issue of literary commitment. The difficulty in understanding that notion today is that it is conceptualized differently depending on the location of writers and critics. In the francophone world, literary commitment is equated with Engagement, which, in turn, is quickly associated with Sartre, and has been the subject of long-standing debates. In the United States and the Anglo-Saxon world in general, literary commitment has been explained with other analytical tools and can arguably be considered as appended to postcolonial theory. These different contexts have generated theoretical axes, and paradoxes, that are compounded by the transnational nature of contemporary reality, whereby writer and critic may straddle several geographical and cultural spaces. Last, it can be said that two francophone African literatures exist today: one on the continent and one outside, both essentially published by European and North American publishing houses. Although things are slowly changing, these two literatures tend to ignore each other, with diasporic writing being granted most of the critical attention.

This chapter aims to unpack the concept of *Littérature Engagée* and to reevaluate how it pertains to francophone African literature. We interrogate the relation between politics and literature in the light of the current resistance to the idea that literature should be committed to political goals. We try to reassess the legacy left to contemporary francophone African authors, the ways their visions and styles have been influenced, and how the new generations have come to achieve discursive agency.

DEBUNKING THE NOTION OF ENGAGEMENT

Almost fifty years after the publication of Frantz Fanon's essays "Mésaventures de la conscience nationale" ("The Trials and Tribulations of National Consciousness") and "Sur la culture nationale: fondements réciproques de la culture nationale et des luttes de libération" ("On National Culture: Mutual Foundations for National Culture and Liberation Struggles") in *Les damnés de la terre* (1961; *The Wretched of the Earth*, 1963), the project of national liberation and culture has been derailed. As Neil Lazarus remarked in *Resistance in Postcolonial African Fiction* (1990), "Independence marked the attainment of nationhood, and it threw into sharp relief the differences that existed between nationalists and more radical anticolonialists. The nationalists tended to identify the goal of the anticolonial struggle as, precisely, the attainment of nationhood. By contrast, the radical anticolonialists . . . tended to view the attainment of nationhood in the light of a seizure of colonial state power, a seizure to be followed, in their plan, by a wholesale reconstruction of society in the postcolonial era" (5).

Now that the political parameters established by such theorists as Fanon, Amilcar Cabral, and Albert Memmi, when engagement meant something specific to the first generation of African authors, have changed, how do we rethink political commitment in the light of shifting notions of domination and production? What is the current position of African intellectuals in relation to the debate? Who defines literary commitment today? And can its practices be tied to a given geography? How do we revisit what has often been posited as an opposition between ethics and aesthetics?

In his 1984 essay "Outside the Whale," Salman Rushdie debunked George Orwell's argument against the politically committed American literature of the 1930s as well as his celebration of Henry Miller's "quietist philosophy" (95), affirming that "works of art, even works of entertainment, do not come into being in a social and political vacuum; and [that] the way they operate in a society cannot be separated from politics, from history. For every text, a context" (92). To Rushdie, there could be no willed passivity to the act of writing, and "writing inside the whale" amounted to a failed metaphor for escapism. Rushdie thus judged Orwell's view of the relationship between literature and politics to be flawed, that is, based on the false premise that politically committed literature is necessarily didactic and knows no nuances of style and perspective: "It is a view which excludes comedy, satire, deflation; because of course the writer need not always be the servant of some beetle-browed ideology. He can also be its critic, its antagonist, its scourge. From Swift to Solzhenitsyn, writers have discharged this role with honour" (98).[1]

As seen in our introduction, however, the critical understanding of francophone African literature's "context" has been overly determined by its ties to Engagement. Adding that African literature's political commitment actually predates Engagement, Guy Ossito Midiohouan affirms: "The excessive attention granted to *engagement* by the dominant historiography has not only resulted in obscuring the institutionalization of this literature. It has also led critics to elaborate a mistaken theorization of genres and appreciate the importance, interest, and range of these works through the warped prism of an ideological assumption the heuristic value of which is at the very least questionable."[2]

Benoît Denis signals in *Littérature et engagement* (2000) that the notion of Engagement has become "a vague and catch-all idea, indiscriminately referring to an author's vision, the general ideas running through his work or even the function he assigns to literature" (9). One could argue further that, even when defined in relation to the historical context of its development, as a post-Dreyfus phenomenon theorized around World War II and measured up against the impact of communism on some of its leading proponents, notably Sartre, Engagement was always an elusive concept, most particularly when sustained by an opposition between ethics and aesthetics.

Littérature engagée is a term that is hard to define precisely because it has taken on many meanings. In examining French literature, critics such as Susan Rubin Suleiman and Denis have proposed helpful concepts to reflect on Engagement. Although in *Authoritarian Fictions: The Ideological Novel as a Literary Genre* (1983), Suleiman concentrates specifically on *romans à thèse*, that is, texts that express their ideological message overtly, her analysis provides a pertinent contrast with the *roman engagé*. That contrast is all the more salient as labeling a politically committed novel a *roman à clef* is frequently used to dismiss it. To Suleiman, the *roman engagé*'s status is both ideological *and* fictional, and its "problematic existence is due . . . to the combination of—or more exactly, to the friction between— . . . two modes of discourse. This 'friction' opens up questions regarding the protocols of reading and interpretation, the rapport between realism and didacticism, and between fictional representation and historical reality" (2). Often opposed to modernist writing, politically committed literature tends to be the object of negative interpretations alleging that it violates the realist novel's conventions of verisimilitude and representation.

For Denis, Engagement may be explained according to two perspectives: as a historically situated idea and as a transhistorical phenomenon.[3] He points out that debates and polemics often give the historically situated idea of Engagement a "trans-historical value" and thus that "Engagement translates into a fundamental stance taken by the writer in regard to literature" (26). Yet, because writing is understood and configured by the times the author lives in, the notion of engagement necessarily differs, within the context of what Denis and Jacques Rancière respectively call "the space of possibilities" and "the distribution of the sensible."[4] Thus, each time period confronts writers with a set of specific questions and tensions, such as: What is their vision of literature? What are their roles and responsibility? How personal can that vision be? Is it in agreement with the dominant discourses of their times? What function does their society attribute to literature and the act of writing, and how do they live with it? The meaning of engagement is necessarily influenced by these questions, and we will see later on how it has affected francophone African writers today.

In *Politique de la littérature* (2007), Rancière indirectly echoes Suleiman's point to conceive of the "friction" inherent in literature in non-oppositional terms: "The communicative and poetic functions of language never cease to intertwine" (14). What Rancière, a philosopher, adds to the debate is his view that "politically committed literature *is* literature. It presupposes that we do not have to wonder if writers should be political or rather dedicate themselves to the purity of their art, but that that very purity has to do with the political. It presupposes that there is an essential link between politics as a specific form of collective practice and literature as defined practice of the art of writing" (12, emphasis ours). Although such a theoretical move can arguably be considered as a strategy to do away with the issue of ideology, it unstraps the writer and opens up possibilities for new protocols of understanding.

Yet, the idea of the necessity of a committed literature continues to haunt African literature. It goes back to the particular premise for the interpretation of francophone African literature, that is, the aligning of the value of African writers and their production with the expression of progressive (or revolutionary) politics, dominated by two historical moments, Négritude and Nationalism, both largely influenced by the ideas of Pan-Africanism. This notion of commitment has acted as the foundational criterion for the historiography of African literature and the benchmark for its chronology. As M'Bokolo makes explicit in "Le Panafricanisme au 21ème siècle": "The African history that these radical thinkers and writers unveiled, and which prodded them on, was the history of a fighting Africa, the history of African resistance against foreign domination and exploitation as well as that of the deportation of Africans against their will and their continued struggles" (13). To summarize, this literary commitment is embedded in a specific cultural and historical context, born of the effects of the world wars, the Négritude movement, the Sartrian legacy, the fight against colonialism and the international rise of nationalist movements, and finally the percolating ideas of such anticolonial theorists and pan-African scholars as Cheikh Anta Diop, Césaire, Fanon, and Memmi.

In *Littérature et développement: Essai sur le statut, la fonction et la représentation de la littérature négro-africaine d'expression française* (1984), Bernard Mouralis remarked that the historical context of the emergence of an "independent" African literature rested on three determining factors: "The existence of an elite trained by the colonizer, the introduction and superior status of a European language making for an ambiguous relationship between the writer and his readers, and the lack of adequate structures to ensure a truly independent cultural existence, notably in the realm of information and publishing" (18–19). The canonical idea of francophone African literature, which is identified as *engagée*, is articulated on the conflation of three processes of self-liberation and definition: first, a historical fight against colonialism; second, an attempt to eschew the colonial "littérature de tutelle" (literature of tutelage); and third, the beginning of a critical reflection on the status and function of African literature, drawing on ideas of origin and authenticity. Moving from "littérature de tutelle" to "littérature de protestation" (protest literature), African literature and its discourses have thus depended on ideology and have strategically aimed at engaging readers.

Abiola Irele in *The African Experience in Literature and Ideology* (1981) and Midiohouan in *L'idéologie dans la littérature négro-africaine d'expression française* (1986) have shown that the notion of ideology is at the core of analyses trying to address the specificity of francophone African literature. Both critics, however, underlined the interrelatedness of ideology and myth as well as the ill-conceived perception of a common identity based on the notion of authenticity—notwithstanding of course that identity meant something different in each respective case. "As an ideological movement," said Irele, "Négritude . . . presents itself . . . as a counter-myth. But it is important to note that for Senghor, the answer does not consist in a systematic rejection of Western racist theories, but rather in a modification of the terms in which they are set out, and in a redefinition of the very notion of race" (71). In turn, Midiohouan refuted as myths both the idea of a national literature drawn along colonial borders and written in a colonial language,[5] and Engagement understood as "the necessary condition for the birth and blossoming of a completely autonomous literary movement" (213).

Négritude, like Engagement, is a complex notion. As Irele has also noted, Négritude "has acquired, in the way it has been used by different writers, a multiplicity of meanings covering so wide a range that it is often difficult to form a precise idea of its particular reference at any one time or in any one usage. The difficulty stems from the fact that, as a movement and as a concept, Négritude found its origin and developed in a historical and sociological context whose implications for those whom it affected were indeed wide-ranging, and which ultimately provoked in them a multitude of responses that were often contradictory, though always significant" (67).

Benetta Jules-Rosette has shown in *Black Paris: The African Writers' Landscape* (1998) that Négritude played a significant role in legitimizing African cultures, and particularly African literatures, and "served as a vehicle for developing a viable cultural, as well as commercial, identity for African writing in France during the 50s and 60s" (14).[6] Poetry was the mode of engagement for Négritude writers until the 1950s when the realist novel took literary precedent, and when Négritude was increasingly criticized as a colonial and culturalist discourse. That criticism would solidify to produce counterdiscourses by emerging writers such as Sembène and Mongo Beti, and critical essays such as Marcien Towa's *Léopold Sédar Senghor: Négritude ou servitude?* (1971), Stanislas Adotevi's *Négritude et négro-*

logues (1972), and René Depestre's *Bonjour et adieu à la Négritude* (1980).

Mongo-Mboussa reminds us in "L'inutile utilité de la littérature"[7] (The useless relevance of literature) that by 1969, Négritude was perceived by many, including J. B. Tati-Loutard, as "an inhibitory force . . . leading to a stylistically and thematically conformist text" (7). To Manthia Diawara, the main problem posed by Négritude to the Sembènes, Depestres, and Mongo Betis resided in its a-historicity. Although Négritude successfully advocated for the recognition of black cultures, its universalist stance, based on Western/Eurocentrist notions of the Universal, defused that recognition, the only guarantee of which was the nation-state.[8] With the passing of Senghor in 2001 and Césaire in 2008, Négritude is attracting further attention and being queried anew.

The other defining movement in committed francophone African literature was Nationalism. As mentioned earlier, the initial convergence of progressive analyses of literature as engagement created a seemingly one-dimensional understanding of the field of francophone African literature. The basis for a politically committed literature, that is, a literature that reflected a nationalism tying the political and the national, eroded in time.

As remarked by Awam Amkpa, it is now clear that "the nation-state has failed to speak for Africans, and most African countries are at odds with their governments." Yet, if the vision that sustained the hopes of former generations has not been actualized, "people as social and political actors are still trying to change their reality for the better, and hence remain utopian."[9] The repeated efforts by the State to control the production of knowledge through the educational system and the arts keep African authors and filmmakers in an oppositional stance. Yet, as Amkpa also noted with regard to Sembène's legacy, the ensuing push-and-pull has generated contested spaces in which new creative transactions are happening. In that respect, artistic engagement is providing a body of critical knowledge that informs daily life and opens up new realms of possibility. The African modernity associated with independence has given way to plural modernities, and new exercises in citizenship are reconfiguring the African experience.

In the past thirty years, the critical understanding of the concepts of nation, nationalism, and citizenship has been framed in more global, transnational, and transcultural terms. Edward Said, particularly with *Orientalism* (1978) and *Culture and Imperialism* (1993), and V. Y. Mudimbe, with *The Invention of Africa: Gnosis, Philosophy and the Order of Knowledge* (1988) and *The Idea of Africa* (1994), devised new strategies to free the understanding of the postcolonial subject from essentialisms and racial orthodoxies. They respectively showed that the new realities of exile and diaspora cannot be conceived of as merely alienating because to the many people now experiencing displacement as a form of permanence, it may translate into a measure of freedom from the constraints of "origin" and "home." Benedict Anderson's idea of nations as "imagined communities" (*Imagined Communities: Reflections on the Origin and Spread of Nationalism* [1983]) also demystified the construction of the nation as a natural and obvious site of belonging. Anderson manifested both the inevitability and the benefit of being grounded in a diversity of historical and cultural practices.

Through his concept of "the Black Atlantic," Paul Gilroy explicated the modern transformation in the African diaspora's "relationship to [its] land of birth and . . . ethnic political constituency." He argued that it now rests on a "desire to transcend both the structures of the nation, state and the constraints of ethnicity and national particularity" (*The Black Atlantic: Modernity and Double Consciousness* [1993], 19). In *Nous, citoyens d'Europe? Les frontières, l'état, le peuple* (2001; *We, the People of Europe?: Reflections on Transnational Citizenship*, 2003), and later in his 2007 essay, *Très loin et tout près: petite conférence sur la frontière* (Very far and quite close: a short presentation on the border), Etienne Balibar addressed the meaning of borders and political space as it pertains to Europe and the issue of citizenship.

Just as nationalism, nation, and citizenship are no longer thought of as unidimensional, African literature and the notion of Engagement no longer answer to a "process of unanimity" (Mouralis, *L'oeuvre de Mongo Beti*, 227). The centrality of political commitment in the historiography established by literary critics (Chevrier, Mateso, Midiohouan, and Dabla) increasingly lost its relevance as the form of *romans engagés*, and the types of commitments expressed therein, were paid closer attention to.

As noted in the introduction, the parameters of the *engagé* francophone African novel written before independence include a representation of history articulated on a narrative of resistance and oppression—see Mongo Beti's *Ville cruelle* (1954), Ferdinand Oyono's *Le vieux nègre et la médaille* (1956; *The Old Man and the Medal*, 1969) and *Une vie de boy* (1956; *Houseboy*, 1966), and Sembène's *O pays, mon beau peuple!* (1957). The struggle between these two opposing forces provides the dramatic tension early criticism has tended to reduce the *engagé* novel to. However, Oyono's *Une vie de boy* and Mongo Beti's *Le pauvre Christ de Bomba* (1956) demonstrate, through their subversions of the diary/travelogue genre, that engagement already took on various textual forms. Similarly, Kane's *L'aventure ambiguë* (*Ambiguous Adventure*, 1963), written in 1952 but published in 1961, straddled the pre-independence/post-independence classification. Although it was immediately recognized as a seminal text of African literature, Kane does not come to mind as one of the *engagé* writers. *L'aventure ambiguë* tends to be read in a way similar to that of Kourouma's *Les soleils des indépendances* (*The Suns of Independence*, 1981), written and published in 1968, due to its subversive textual quality.

In the late 1960s, Kourouma broke away from the "model" narrative with a protagonist who is no longer a hero and cannot act on his ideals. In *Le devoir de violence* (1968; *Bound to Violence*, 1971), Yambo Ouologuem connected such notions as colonialism and afrocentrism in a scathing fictional representation of servitude. Ten years later, in *La vie et demie* (1979), Labou Tansi added the grotesque to this literary process of denunciation. From then on, the carnivalesque became part of the canon, including violent representations of sexuality and graphic language.[10] From the late 1970s to the mid-1980s, this dark and sarcastic trend applied itself to the (de)-construction of the socialist nation-state—see Monénembo's *Les crapauds-brousse* (*The Bush Toads*, 1983) in 1979, Henri Lopès's *Le pleurer-rire* (*The Laughing Cry: An African Cock and Bull Story*, 1987) in 1982, and Williams Sassine's *Le zéhéros n'est pas n'importe qui* (The zero-hero is not anybody) in 1985. In the early 1980s, Pius Ngandu Nkashama's *Le fils de la tribu* (The tribe's son, 1983) and *Le pacte de sang* (1984) represent the infernal cycle of ethnic violence, as does Bolya Baenga in 1986 with *Cannibale*.[11] The "committed" novel has thus undergone many aesthetic changes over a comparatively short period of time, among which the multiplication of the mediating processes between literary fiction and its references to history, the creative blurring of the notion of verisimilitude, and the use of subversion are the more striking elements.

The reliance of African literature's legacy on resistance, and its role in shaping both literary criticism and the canon, is established. Mid-iohouan has rightly underscored the risks raised by this type of over-simplification: "Engagement, i.e. the questioning of the established order, should not be the only condition for the emergence of an au-thentic negro-african literature" (10). Although the idea of an "au-thentic literature" is debatable, Midiohouan usefully debunked the myth of *littérature engagée*. Twenty years later, however, the myth remains operative[12] and weighs on the production and reception of francophone African literature in subtler ways.

Francophone African literature suffers from a "burden of represen-tation" that is generic in the sense that it continues, to various degrees, to affect Black arts. Black artists remain largely cast as "cultural rep-resentatives" and their "visibility in the public sphere . . . regulat-ed."[13] There are, however, specific forms to the burden francophone African literature has had to shoulder that can be traced to the colo-nial imposition of the French language and to the development of lit-eracy along those lines. As remarked by Christopher Miller, "Franco-phone literacy arrived in colonial Africa like a Trojan horse, bearing an ideology of collaboration and assimilation, a condition of 'original sin' that the francophone literature of Africa has sought to overcome during the last seventy years."[14] Again, the burden can also be traced to the articulation of francophone African literature on notions of resistance and nationalism that created an ambiguously prescriptive "identity effect," to use Miller's wording. These two historical trends have resulted in the development of a "false consciousness" and fed, albeit differently, into assimilative processes that have also affected critics of African literature (123).

The hope that the struggle for national liberation had helped foster in many Africans collapsed around the 1980s, as the African state de-finitively lost its credibility in the eyes of those who had wanted to re-envision it.[15] This had deep consequences on the writer's imagination and positioning in society. The failure of the nation-state and its loss of legitimacy implied that the writer could no longer be the bearer of truth nor justifiably be part of an enlightened elite. His understand-ing of his role as writer and intellectual was similarly questioned. The "repression of utopia" (Jameson) and the shift from utopia to dystopia were to become central themes to the next mood in franco-phone African literature, often coined as "afropessimist." The larger implication was a rethinking of the responsibility of African intellec-tuals and writers. Many of these writers had been living in exile but had retained an (arguably) organic link to their communities of origin and shared an African imagination, which Irele has described as the "wider scope of expression of Africans and people of African descent, which arises out of . . . historical circumstances" (*The African Imagination: Literature in Africa and the Black Diaspora*, 7). With the failure of the nation-state and the doors of the future seemingly closing, the nature of the writers' participation/estrangement became more complex. From this ferment came new politics of form, a reconfiguration of aesthetics, and thus a rethinking of what *littérature engagée* meant.

We mentioned at the beginning of this chapter that there are two concurrent francophone African literatures: one on the continent where engagement remains pertinent and possibly unavoidable and the other, outside the continent, where writing is seen in individualistic terms. Yet, regardless of the actual place of writing, one always writes from an imaginary location.[16] Furthermore, a writer's identity is tied to a personal history that cannot be reduced to only that of a community. As the poet and philosopher Hamidou Dia has said, "There is no writing without qualifier."[17]

African realist novels started to shape into a canon at a time when, in France, the nouveau roman bore enough aesthetic consequences to derail the conception of literature as engagement. If we follow Phyllis Taoua's argument in *Forms of Protest: Anti-Colonialism and Avant-Gardes in Africa, the Caribbean, and France* (2002) that the nouveau roman is a response to the process of decolonization and signifies a retreat from reality, it could be said that the politically committed and modernist conceptions of the novel merged differently in the case of African literatures. This argument is, however, complicated by the fact that the 1970s were also the time when a postcolonial African literary criticism began to coalesce.

In the 1980s, as African women writers became more visible, and their commitment to expression recast the parameters of literary engagement, novels such as Lopès's *Le pleurer-rire* (1982) and Monénembo's *Les écailles du ciel* (1986) marked another turning point, a move from the neocolonial to the postcolonial novel, and Afro-pessimism. Afro-pessimism took a number of forms, most tellingly a literature of experimentation in the vein of Sony Labou Tansi, provocatively exploring the possibilities of the grotesque and appropriating some of the magic-realist strategies.[18] To Mbembe, this type of literary approach belongs to an "aesthetics of vulgarity" addressing and keeping in check a specific type of postcolonial domination through the portrayal of "the postcolonial subject as a homo ludens." It constitutes all at once a reactive/adaptive/transgressive form of political resistance. "Is it enough," Mbembe asks, "that the postcolonial subject, as a homo ludens, is simply making fun of the commandement [*sic*], making it an object of derision . . . ? To a large extent, the outbursts of ribaldry and derision are actually taking the official world seriously, at face value or the value, at least, it gives itself. . . . In the end, whether the encounter of state and people is 'masked' or not, does not matter. The key point is that, in this specific historical context of domination and subjection, the postcolony neither minces nor spares its words" (*On the Postcolony*, 107–8).

From the mid-1980s on, African writers, especially those living outside the continent, objected to the systematic notion of the African writer as strictly *engagé* and searched for more individually creative avenues. Yet, in his preface to Diop's first novel, Mongo Beti praises *Le temps de Tamango* (1981) as a new moment in politically committed fiction.

The 1990s saw both an emergence of collective endeavors, such as Rwanda: Ecrire par devoir de mémoire, and works written in response to the commemoration of France's abolition of slavery. These marked yet another rethinking of the role and responsibility of the African writer/intellectual. The literary production of the first five years of the twenty-first century shows both a renewed interest in engagement and the proliferation of its aesthetic expressions.

THE "ENDURING MILITANTS": RETHINKING ETHICS AND AESTHETICS

What sustained the literary commitment of writers such as Sembène, Alioum Fantouré, Mongo Beti, Kourouma, and later, Sow Fall, Dongala, and Lopès? To what extent have critics solidified the meaning of engagement attached to their works? To what extent has the quality of their aesthetics been overlooked? These issues need to be reassessed. One can argue that the testimonial quality of these writers' works has been both overblown and oversimplified. The current historiography of African literature is uneven. The intellectual stature of Ahmadou Hampaté Bâ, for example, has been largely unacknowledged by critics when his work, produced at the time of the Négritude movement, provided a useful epistemological anchor to the West

African artist. Conversely, how do we account for Kourouma's *Les soleils des indépendances* (1968), a book hailed for its creative appropriation of the French language when it was published, but the shrewd perspective of which was largely ignored at the time?

Although the late Sembène and Mongo Beti belong to a different generation (they were born respectively in 1923 and 1932), there are shared core beliefs in their oeuvres. The logic of their engagement was pan-African, anticolonialist, and anti-imperialist. Both of these *intellectuels engagés*[19] rejected the notion of an African authenticity and strongly objected to Négritude in its Senghorian definition, that is, "the primacy of the cultural over the political" (Midiohouan, "Le devoir de penser: Mongo Beti et la passionnante aventure de *Peuples noirs-Peuples africains*" [The duty to think: Mongo Beti and the thrilling adventure of *Peuples noirs-Peuples africains*], 2003, 209). Both saw themselves as social critics and spokespersons for their people, and took on the arduous and long-term responsibilities associated with that positioning. Africa and its future can be said to have been their main concern. Their works focus on injustice, economic exploitation, and corruption. They explore the power differentials between colonizers and colonized, the State and the people, the rich and the poor, men and women, and the old and the young generations. After independence, both Sembène and Mongo Beti pointed to the continued social and economic abuse of/in African societies (see, for example, Sembène's *Xala* [1973; translation, 1976] and Mongo Beti's *Perpétue et l'habitude du malheur*, respectively published in 1973 and 1974) and the formation of a new exploitative elite.

In his written work, Sembène, who was an autodidact, always favored clarity, even when he interspersed his narratives with Wolof. Conversely, Mongo Beti's style aimed to challenge the reader through multiple references to French history, the Enlightenment, Latin and Greek classics, and so on. His books contain allusions to, and in, the vernacular until *Mission terminée* (1957; *Mission to Kala*, 1958). But that vein was not fully explored until after he retired from his job as a professor of classics and wrote *Trop de soleil tue l'amour* (1999) and *Branle-bas en noir et en blanc* (2000). Sembène grew increasingly weary of writing in French. Mongo Beti brushed the question of language aside and likened French to a car one needs to use to go where one wants to go. As noted by Richard Bjornson in *The African Quest for Freedom and Identity* (1991), "[Mongo] Beti had no objection to retaining French as a primary vehicle of expression for Africans, but he insisted that they must be free to adapt it to their own purposes rather than merely serving as receptacles for the cultural assumptions embedded in it when it is used in France" (329).

The question of language was central to the first generations of African writers. Like Sartre, the "enduring militants" believed in the utilitarian function of language (see *Qu'est-ce que la littérature?* [1947; *What Is Literature?*, 1949]). Yet, while their poetics of oppression[20] was articulated on a social use of language denunciatory of abuse and "truth-revealing," the authors were aware of the consequences of producing literature in the language of the former colonizer.

As Alioune Tine has underlined, Sembène identified the problematics of writing in French when he returned from France, after twelve uninterrupted years during which he had written *Le docker noir* (1956; *The Black Docker*, 1987) and *O pays, mon beau peuple!* (1957). Back in Senegal in 1960, he became conscious that the readership of francophone African literature was restricted to a small elite. Given his political objective of reaching the masses, he moved away from writing to filmmaking. Language was thus one of the battlegrounds of Sembène's engagement. While all his books were written in French, his literary production underwent a steady process of Wolofization. In 1968, he filmed two adaptations of his short story *Le mandat* (1965; *The Money Order*, 1972), one in French and the other in Wolof, making this latter version the first film to be produced in an African language (Tine, "Wolof ou français: Le choix de Sembène," 46). His later films, especially from the 1990s on, would be in Wolof and other African languages, and subtitled in French or English, displaying the dynamics of the interactions between French and Wolof in Senegal, highlighting which language is spoken when, where, and in what context.

The question of language and writing in French by francophone African writers is tied to that of readership. In francophone African literary criticism, the issue of the double readership of African literature has also been constructed as central. Taken up by Mohamadou Kane in *Sur l'histoire littéraire africaine* (1992), readdressed by Mongo-M'Boussa in *Désir d'Afrique*, and vehemently rejected by Nganang in "Ecrire sans la France,"[21] that concept is, however, not original to African literatures. It was, among other instances, a major point of contention between Harlem Renaissance writers, notably Langston Hughes, W. E. B. Du Bois, and James Weldon Johnson.[22] On the one hand, Hughes affirmed: "We younger Negro artists who

create now intend to express our individual dark-skinned selves without fear or shame. If white people are pleased, we are glad. If they are
not, it doesn't matter. . . . We build our temples for tomorrow, strong
as we know how, and we stand on top of the mountain, free within
ourselves." On the other, Du Bois believed in the artist as propagan-
dist and truth-sayer, and proclaimed: "I do not care for any art that is
not used for propaganda."[23] Weldon Johnson thought that "Negro"
writers had two readerships/audiences (black and white) to address,
and that the task of successfully writing for both of these was too
great. He raised the following questions: Who should be the intended
audience of black artists? Whom should they speak for? Should they
speak for "Negroes" and/or as "Negroes"? This problematic remains
a reality for African writers today who, in an often uneven editorial
landscape, still have to contend with the question of being African
writers or writers from Africa. That dilemma is often indicative in itself of their stance toward engagement.

The understanding of Sembène's work remained uneven until fairly recently.[24] To some, he still is the *engagé* author of *Le docker noir,
O pays, mon beau peuple!* and *Les bouts de bois de Dieu* (1960;
God's Bits of Wood, 1962); to others, he is first and foremost the filmmaker of *La Noire de . . .* (1966; *Black Girl), Emitai, Ceddo, Xala,
and Camp de Thiaroye,* and as such remains a militant and the father of African cinema. To others still, his filmmaking evolved into
a more entertaining vein, especially with *Faat Kine* (2000), although
his last production, *Molaade* (2004), focused on female circumcision and returned to more socially committed material. Interestingly,
however, his stance in *Molaade* remains indirect. For the first time
in Sembène's career, one of his films takes place outside Senegal, in
Burkina Faso. That location and the predominant use of Bambara de-
flect the delicate issue of female circumcision. In the end, the viewer
can lose track of the fact that it remains an issue in Senegal. Since
Sembène's passing in June 2007, renewed critical attention has been
paid to his life and work, including Samba Gadjigo's *Ousmane Sembène: Une conscience africaine: genèse d'un destin hors du commun*
(2007; *Ousmane Sembène: The Making of a Militant Artist,* 2010)
and Diop's "Ousmane Sembène ou l'art de se jouer du destin" (Ousmane Sembène or the art of dodging destiny).[25] The libertarian side
of Sembène's personality, his place in Senegalese culture as well as the
contradictions he sometimes displayed, are examined more closely.

Mongo Beti, who was at times regarded as the embodiment of

a self-righteous militancy, produced a wide-ranging and polymor-
phous literary corpus. With Odile Tobner, he founded *Peuples
Noirs-Peuples Africains (PN-PA)*,[26] "one of the few independent
progressive journals with a focus on Africa" (Bjornson, 326). He
produced eleven novels, three essays, a *dictionnaire*, and many articles published under his pen name, and in collaboration with a variety of people. The form and language of his literary commitment
developed accordingly. Each of his essays contributed to refining his
vision of Cameroon and gave new impetus to his fiction. As analyzed
by Bjornson, "the process of writing *Main basse sur le Cameroun:
Autopsie d'une décolonisation* (The seizure of Cameroon: autopsy
of a decolonization, 1972) represented a turning point in Mongo
Beti's career as a writer because it encouraged him to formulate the
neo-colonialist concept that undergirds everything he ha[d] written
since 1972" (330).[27] Despite his absence from Cameroon for over
thirty years, from 1958 until 1991, Mongo Beti's production cannot
simply be construed as literature of exile nor interpreted as a testimonial narrative.[28] It can be said that the prevailing mode of Mongo
Beti's writing remained first and foremost denunciatory, but the textualizing of that denunciation was recrafted over time. Although his
work has always featured the "petit peuple," his move back to Cameroon in 1994 reinvigorated his fiction, informed by an inside vision
of that country. His construction of dialogues became less classic,
more dynamic, and infused with the vernacular language of Yaoundé where he opened his bookstore, Librairie des Peuples Noirs.[29]
His contextually sharper understanding of the possibilities and limits of oppositional politics in Cameroon was mediated differently
in the two novels he wrote after his return home, *Trop de soleil tue
l'amour* (1999) and *Branle-bas en noir et blanc* (2000). His use of
irony took on a different shade, simultaneously less classical and
more personal, and yet it retained the Chester Himes flavor Mongo
Beti had always been fond of. From the *Dzewatama* cycle through
L'histoire du fou (1994), to his last two novels, the figure of the mili-
tant/hero gradually hollowed out. In *Les deux mères de Guillaume
Ismaël Dzewatama* (1983) and *La revanche de Guillaume Ismaël
Dzewatama* (1984), the father of the family, Jean-François, once a
militant in an African students' movement in France and now a public prosecutor, loses his heroic status to his adolescent son, Guillaume Ismaël. In *L'histoire du fou*, the only character that could re-
motely resemble a hero, the lawyer, speaks at cross-purposes, often

in Latin, and is in short a figure reminiscent of Don Quixote.[30] Finally, in Mongo Beti's last novels, there are no heroes.

Aesthetically, the driving force in Mongo Beti's work, novels, and essays is the conspiracy. Well before *Trop de soleil* and *Branle-bas*, two books with a definite detective novel feel, his narratives, from *Remember Ruben* to the *Dzewatama* cycle[31] hinged on the ideas of denunciation and investigation. The dynamics of conspiracy, although contextually specific, are the result of an aesthetic choice; they reflect the continuing morass of neocolonial politics in francophone Africa.[32]

Since Mongo Beti's passing in 2001, critics have turned to the "bigger picture" and the interconnectedness of his writing and his life. Waberi who positioned himself as part of "a generation bereft of a collective engagement" declared that reading Mongo Beti's work was key to his understanding of "the African writer's destiny, its fortunes and misfortunes" ("Mongo Beti: Si près si loin," 22). In *Lettre à Jimmy* (2007), Mabanckou establishes a parallel between James Baldwin's opposition to Richard Wright's literary stance and Mongo Beti's famous indictment of Camara Laye's *L'enfant noir* (1953; *The Dark Child*, 1954). To contextualize, *L'enfant noir* was written with the support of the Ministère of France d'Outre-Mer and celebrated by the French literary establishment when it came out. That view was not necessarily shared by all African intellectuals. In his article, "Afrique Noire, littérature rose" (1955), published in the literary magazine *Présence Africaine* under his real name, Alexandre Biyidi (Mongo Beti) denounced what he saw as an unacceptable lack of political commitment and a stereotypical and tame rendition of Africans, at a time when Africa remained under colonial domination.[33] We should also remember that Alexandre Biyidi had just published under the pseudonym of Eza Boto, *Ville cruelle* (1954), one of the first narratives to represent colonial abuses. Beyond the historical issue of colonialism, however, Biyidi's attack raised the question of the moral responsibility of the African writer and the nature of literary engagement (as addressed by Ambroise Kom in "Mongo Beti and the Responsibility of the African Intellectual"). Since then, critics such as Eustace Palmer, Sonia Lee, Christopher Miller, Adèle King, and Abiola Irele have reappraised *L'enfant noir*, carving more space for an appreciation of its aesthetic qualities and cultural relevance.[34] Miller, for instance, sees it as "subversion," stating: "Times have changed somewhat. In the postcolonial period and context, particularly to outsiders, the 'betrayal' seems less important than the revelation and preservation.

What appeared to be a repression of politics in the 1950s now looks like a subtle subversion of colonial domination from within. Camara's handling of outsiders—with diplomacy and tact—can no longer be dismissed as a form of either naïveté or simple 'alienation'" (*Theories of Africans*, 179).

Although *L'enfant noir*'s authorship (and that of Camara's subsequent novel, *Le regard du roi* [1954]) was cast in doubt by such critics as Kesteloot and King, today this novel is considered one of the canonical works of African literature. In the preface he wrote for Plon's 2006 edition of *L'enfant noir*, Mabanckou asserts its unique literary longevity: "Published in 1953, the Guinean Camara Laye's *L'enfant noir* has not aged a bit. Few African narratives published around the same time display such freshness. They often seem dated and moralizing. They are devoid of the magic that is the condition for a text's longevity across several generations and for its smooth sailing towards the future."[35]

Today, Mongo Beti remains for some the embodiment of engagement against which, or with which, the different generations of his fellow writers have come to define themselves. In "Mongo Beti et nous," Boubacar Boris Diop acknowledges that "with Frantz Fanon and Aimé Césaire, [Mongo Beti] was among those who helped us to better understand the causes and mechanisms of our alienation" (88).[36] In *Les petits de la guenon* (The female monkey's litter, 2009), Boubacar Boris Diop's own translation of *Doomi Golo* (2004), the narrator recalls Mongo Beti as one of the significant African political and intellectual models. Yet, through this evocation, Diop also admits that the ideals his generation had fought for have not materialized: "Cheikh Anta Diop. Amilcar Cabral. Mongo Beti. Samory Touré. Thomas Sankara. Lumumba. . . . Each one of them has, in his own way, been a rebel. We dared to say no but that was not enough. We missed something. I still do not know what it is" (218–19).

The basic quality of Mongo Beti's commitment is that it endured through his years in exile and when he came back to Cameroon in the early 1990s. Tobner remarks in *Négrophobie*, the book she authored with Diop and the late François-Xavier Verschave in 2005, that Mongo Beti had a keen knowledge of African politics and spent a lifetime studying the effects of neocolonialism on the continent. As pointed out by Célestin Monga in "Economie d'une créance impayée" (the economy of an unpaid debt), his oeuvre has articulated "a logic of a collective memory of dissent" (162), all the while seeking to keep at bay "an unquestioned valorization of the oppressed as subject" (Spivak, "Can the Subaltern Speak?" in *The Post-colonial Critic*, 255). As such it has inspired other important analyses on democracy, such as Monga's *Anthropologie de la colère: Société civile et démocratie en Afrique* (1994; *The Anthropology of Anger: Civil Society and Democracy in Africa*, 1996), and following generations of African intellectuals.

Mongo Beti's engagement translated into several phases of renewal, including in his novels. As a whole, his diverse body of work constitutes a "place of awareness" (212) and contributed to redefining the concept of African culture (as shown by Midiohouan in "Le devoir de penser," 121). Deconstructing conventional European and African discourses on Africa, Mongo Beti's fiction and essays converge in revealing the intricacies of neocolonial fantasies and in searching for a counterhegemonic voice.

There were no women among the early generations of committed writers. Largely because engagement was tacitly associated with male writers, the production of Sow Fall has not been analyzed in relation to political commitment. Although not politically radical, Sow Fall is among the handful of francophone African women who started writing in the 1970s,[37] publishing two novels during those years: *Le revenant* (The ghost, 1976) and *La grève des Battù ou les déchets humains* (1979; *The Beggars' Strike or the Dregs of Society*, 1981). Unlike the other women writers of the same period, Sow Fall never used the autobiographical or semiautobiographical vein, and gender was but one of the components in her writing. From the very start, however, she imposed herself as a Senegalese citizen and author. Among other things, she founded a publishing house, Khoudia, and since the end of the 1990s has been instrumental in developing an annual poetry festival in local languages, including Wolof, Serere, and Pulaar. Again, although she cannot be considered a revolutionary, her novels are strong indictments of the ailments of her society. *La grève des Battù*, published in 1979, revisits some of the questions raised by Sembène in *Xala* (1977), but in an innovative manner. In *La grève*, Sow Fall represents Dakar's beggars on strike and the Muslim followers deprived of the possibility to perform their duty of charity.[38] This was quite provocative thirty years ago, and still is today. In *L'appel des arènes* (The call of the arenas, 1982), Sow Fall examines the tensions between modern and traditional education in Senegal, and the changes happening within Senegalese families with respect to foundational values. With *L'ex-Père de la Nation*, published in 1987, she produces a narrative that articulates the centrality of the theme of power in African literature, addressing that issue head-on. *Le jujubier du patriarche* (The patriarch's jujube tree, 1993) goes back to some of the themes of her earlier books, notably the reaffirmation of the grounding quality of Senegalese traditions. Sow Fall's later novels continue that theme but give it more breadth. *Douceurs du bercail* (1998) features African immigrants and the humiliation they suffer in their attempt to enter France. That theme is not new in itself, but its central importance in the narrative is. Urging Africans to reexamine their dreams of an elusive El Dorado, this novel proposes a return home as key to self-fulfillment and a new social departure. This was all the more crucial as it highlighted a turning point in the global politics of immigration, starting with the Pasqua laws in France. In 1986, in an alleged effort to curb illegal immigration to France, Charles Pasqua, the Minister of the Interior, accelerated the legal procedures to deport people illegally residing in France. In 1993, he pushed for the Réforme du Code de la Nationalité, which made it much harder for undocumented immigrants to work or to find housing.

In several ways, Sow Fall's work and cultural engagement echo Kane's. Similarly to Kane's *L'aventure ambigüe* (1961), Sow Fall's *L'appel des arènes* reevaluates the question of choice of education for the young generations and the difficulties in balancing two sets of cultural beliefs. Inasmuch as *L'appel des arènes* focuses on Senegalese wrestling (*Laam*, in Wolof), a sport that is essential to Senegalese culture, traditional and current, rural and urban, this book can be said to anchor the narrative from within.[39] Both *L'ex-Père de la Nation* and Kane's *Les gardiens du temple* (The temple's gatekeepers, 1995) converge in their fictional representations of the first years of independence in Senegal. Both works link the idea of Engagement and that of ethics, inviting their readers to position themselves against the corruption of the political world depicted by the narrative. They encourage readers to return to "ancestral"/core values in order to recapture their lost dignity and honor.

As Irele has noted, Kane saw *L'aventure ambigüe* as "a *récit* (not a *roman*), thereby calling attention to the objective significance of this drama for the men of his generation" (Irele, *Lectures africaines*, 7). Some of the principles heralded by Négritude, such as authenticity, the valorization of blackness, the reappropriation of African history and the validation of the richness of African civilizations, permeate

Kane's work. Using "the novel as a vehicle for expressing [his] vision of an African mode of existence," Kane can be "considered traditionalist in the sense in which [his] work [is] meant to promote a sense of the integrity of the African self amidst the flow of change" (7).[40]

Both novels and their authors posit the values of dignity and integrity as necessary conditions to the exercise of democracy. They interrogate the notion of political power, particularly in the context of nation formation, and place the ideal of Pan-Africanism on the horizon. Today, Sow Fall and Kane have a special place in Senegalese society. They are regarded as core members of that country's intellectual life and as models to emulate.

Lopès and Dongala, both Congolese, belong to the same generation and have been confronted with the same historical context in the Congo. An Homme d'Etat (diplomat and politician) and a writer, Lopès represents an exception to the norm set by his generation of writers in that he has steadfastly published while occupying official positions. As Dominic Thomas remarks in *Nation-Building, Propaganda and Literature in Francophone Africa* (2002), the "ambiguity" of Lopès's "biographical identity . . . designates and underlines his belonging to both sides: on the one hand the postcolonial nationalists, and on the other, the non-official resistance authors. . . . Lopès's literary and political careers are inextricably linked, and the relationship between the two has helped shape both the man and the writer" (91).

Thomas further underlines that "the relationship between literature and politics, and between fiction and reality, is of uppermost concern to any critical reading of Lopès's literary productions" (92). Interestingly, *Le pleurer-rire* (1979), a cornerstone of the genre, is the last of his explicitly *engagé* books. From then on, he would publish more personal novels, exploring the issue of métissage culturally (*Chercheur d'Afriques* [The seeker of Africas, 1990]) and historically (*Le lys et le flamboyant* [The lily and the flamboyant tree, 1997]). In "Le corps politique d'Henri Lopès," Romuald Fonkua considers métissage to be Lopès's central theme and obsession, and shows that it is explored in its relationship to Africa and history, the key question being: how does a métis (biracial) intellectual negotiate the political? How does he address Africa's treatment of métis?[41]

Constantly straddling the lines between literature and politics, Lopès has refused to be boxed in a clearly identified position. In a 1993 article titled "My Novels, My Characters, and Myself," he skillfully justified his meanderings by laying claim to "mentir-vrai" (lying truthfully) as aesthetic principle: "Every real author is a liar. Anyone who takes up a pen and straightforwardly records the truth is at best a good reporter or sociologist. An author's task should not be to tell the plain truth; on the contrary, he should proclaim his own truth, that no one else sees clearly but which he himself feels intensely during his fleeting moments of insight. To do so, he must be a good liar, a fine illusionist. He must succeed in creating what Louis Aragon once called the 'lie-truth'" (86).

Both Lopès and Dongala, because of the historical circumstances surrounding post-Independence Congo, have been diffident vis-à-vis political activism. Lopès has even referred to it as "feverish activism" (23). In a section of *Ma grand-mère bantoue et mes ancêtres les Gaulois* (My Bantu grandmother and my Gaul ancestors, 2003) titled "Débat avec les masses," Lopès addresses the current fatigue of some young African authors regarding that type of militancy. In *Dossier classé* (A shut case, 2002), he reflects, through his characterization of Bossuet Mayélé, on the dreams, beliefs, and denials of the anticolonial generation. Papa Samba Diop has argued in "Ecriture et décentrement"[42] (Writing and decentering) that the lack of dogmatism in Lopès's writing (with regard to race, nation, and language) translated into the development of characters likely to go through metamorphosis. Insisting on their instability enabled Lopès to express doubts about political ideologies and the centrality of language. Therefore, in saying, "I have no fixed identity" (248), Lazare Mayélé embodies the writer's quest for identity and querying of métissage.

Early on, Lopès exhibited his criticism of, and demarcated himself from, a collective vision of African "victimhood." Although his work features the African "martyrologue" (martyrdom) during the colonial period and the struggle for independence, and *Le pleurer-rire* denounces what he would call later in *Ma grand-mère* "tropical nazism" (42), Lopès has been overwhelmingly dismissive of the notion of Engagement. In *Ma grand-mère* and *Dossier classé*, he repeatedly objected to the novel as being informative and to the writer being regarded as a journalist, a pamphleteer, or a sociologist. Because of his age and stature, Lopès can be said to have caused both a shift toward an aestheticization of francophone African literature and a distancing from the classic understanding of African literature as *engagée*. Another interesting difference from the other "enduring militants" quoted above is his position on Négritude. In an interview with Jean-Luc Aka-Evy,[43] Lopès says the following on the topic: "I do not reject Negritude; I would even say that it is one of the breasts I suckled on and the potion I continue to take on occasion. Negritude can be compared to the fathers of the church: they had thought everything out before the fact. Métissage is already a notion at work in Negritude. Césaire, Damas, Tirolien . . . these three characters, being Antilleans, are therefore métis, and at the same time, they praised Negritude. Edouard Maunick has said: 'I am a métis, preferably *nègre*.'"[44]

Although admittedly ironic, this statement is muddled. The ideological construction of Antilleans as *métis* seemingly creates an amalgam between a cultural and a political understanding of Négritude. On closer analysis, it becomes evident that Lopès proposed a reading of Négritude that enabled him to theoretically ground his own argument on métissage, which is central to his oeuvre from *Le chercheur d'Afriques* to *Le lys et le flamboyant* and *Dossier classé*. In "Humour, érotisme, royaume d'enfance: trois stratégies de libération du sujet chez Henri Lopès" (Humor, eroticism, and the kingdom of childhood: three liberation strategies in Henri Lopès), Mongo-Mboussa interprets these three strategies as a way for Lopès to free himself of the burden of Négritude. Mongo-Mboussa insists that, while placing himself within a genealogy, Lopès has always been conscious of the dangers of a militant literature and that even *Le pleurer-rire* can be understood as an intersection of playful voices.[45]

If one considers the entirety of his production, métissage is indeed the notion at the core of Lopès's engagement. With *Le chercheur d'Afriques*, and more particularly with *Le lys et le flamboyant*, Lopès inscribes métissage in its relationship to history. From Abdoulaye Sadji's *Nini, mulâtresse du Sénégal* (1954) to Sembène's *O pays, mon beau peuple!* to Sassine's *Mémoire d'une peau* (Memory of a skin, 1979) and Mongo Beti's *Dzewatama* series, the theme of métissage had been approached (and continues to be approached today) from different angles.[46] Lopès's contribution resides in the continuity of his historicization of that topos.

When he attempts to articulate the notion of commitment theoretically, Lopès does two things. On the one hand, he rejects the historical construction of the African writer as a "voice for the people" and reminds his readers of the political appropriation of such notions as national liberation and identity; on the other hand, he advocates for a stronger expression of individual commitment on the part of the African artist/intellectual. In doing so, Lopès paradoxically disengages from and reengages with engagement:

> Today, on the other hand, and at any rate more than yesterday, the writer from the southern hemisphere has the duty to tap his inner resources and speak in his own name.
>
> Before, each time we were slightly tempted to denounce the manipulation of the notion of national identity or the dictatures hidden behind the country's banner, we held ourselves in check, for fear, or so we thought, of playing the game of the former colonizer or of imperialism. . . .
>
> In the name of the rights of the people, we have stifled human rights. Today, we must observe the cult of individuality, which has nothing to do with selfishness . . . and implies two things: setting limits on our freedom and the duty of tolerance. (18–19)

Dossier classé is quite telling in that respect. Through Monsieur Babéla, the protagonist's old teacher, Lopès refocuses his readers' attention on the generation of the "évolués," a generation contemporary to Négritude that had fallen by the literary wayside: "They had struggled to have some of their basic rights recognized. Demanding the country's independence had not even crossed their minds. At that time, they only aspired to becoming French citizens" (168). Monsieur Babéla illustrates how colonialism created a situation whereby, with respect to traditional oral culture, writing was fetishized and how, in turn, that gave power to the colonial historian (and critic). Through a layered narrative featuring three generations, that of the "évolués," that of the "enduring militants" with the characters of Bossuet Mayélé and his friend, Goma, and that of the protagonist, Lazare Mayélé, Bossuet's son, the author gives us a panoramic view of the values historically at work in Congolese society. In doing so, he contextualizes the "enduring militants'" generation and, in the process, posits African writing and literary criticism against the idea of rupture. In a conversation with Lazare, Monsieur Babéla gives him the following advice: "If you are setting about writing a novel, Lazare, please avoid the stumbling block most writers have come against this past decade. They want to convince, they want to inform, they want to. . . . The novel, he went on, does not aim at informing but at training. I read to grow, to mend my ways. Reading is my prayer. . . . He had only spoken for a few minutes, but I drew from his words the core of what I believe in as a writer" (245).

Topically, the three generations are also a pretext for Lopès to criticize other forms of black commitment. Lazare, who lives in the United States, serves to critically highlight African American activism, particularly Black Power, and to refute, or even mock, an artificial and anachronistic vision of Africa as an ideal land of origin and black authenticity. Here, as in *Le chercheur d'Afriques* and *Sur l'autre rive* (On the opposite bank, 1992), the author displaces Africa and invites his readers to think of an Africa elsewhere, in the United States, in the West Indies, and in France. In that regard, Lopès has been instrumental in representing the francophone diaspora and part of diasporic writing *avant l'heure*. These questions participate in Lopès's self-avowed wish to "change attitudes" (*Dossier classé*, 223) and to reflect more broadly on the relationship between engagement, memory, and history. The following exchange between Babéla and Lazare is indicative of Lopès's stance and can be read as a direct rebuttal of Rwanda: Ecrire par devoir de mémoire:

> —You don't mean to say that there should not be a duty of memory, that impunity is to be encouraged?
> —No. We need a memory, but an appeased memory. The serious memory of historians. Our society is still the aporia of emotions dating back from Homeric times. A savage society where the rules of life and ethics are not those of the modern western world. Passions have to subside. We need to pause and put ourselves together. Economically, socially, culturally, morally. Emotionally as well. Emotional education is essential. (222)

This dialogue is symptomatic of the virulent debates regarding the nature of the African intellectual's engagement vis-à-vis history that have traditionally taken place in African literature and that are resurfacing today with a new acuteness. This is a question that Dongala tackles in his novels, and that we will discuss further in Chapter 2.

Dongala's novels cast a particular light on the question of commitment as a dominant model of African literature because they simultaneously illustrate and elude that model. Dongala's commitment has both an obvious quality and a more complex one; it goes with and against the grain of the African literary canon. His novels manifest his humanistic stand against injustice while they are predicated on a reflexive literary consciousness that keeps dogmatic interpretations in check. They systematically confront the immanence of the Political with the transcendence of Being and Knowledge. They appeal for change in the here and now as they call for a more profound, more metaphysical, change in Man. Of the same generation as Sow Fall, Sassine, Monénembo, and Labou Tansi, Dongala stands out because of his refusal to make oppression the main paradigm of his novels. Whereas the dramaturgy of oppression is central to his theater,[47] it is only a fixture of his novels inasmuch as it is mediated by irony and humor, and it portrays characters lifted up by their common humanity.

Generally speaking, Dongala has had a nuanced approach to the question of engagement. This does not mean that he stayed away from the cultural politics of his times—or that he was able to do so. The beginning of his literary career is interesting in that regard and can be considered a preface to the type of literary engagement he would practice later on. From 1977 to 1982, after he had published a novel, *Un fusil dans la main, un poème dans la poche* (A gun in the hand, a gun in the pocket) in 1973 and as he was writing *Jazz et vin de palme* (Jazz and palm wine), to be published in 1982 and subsequently banned, Dongala wrote a number of articles in which he articulated his position on then contemporary issues. Three of these articles are discussed hereafter.

In 1977 Dongala published, under the name of Boundzeki Dongala, a passionate op-ed piece in the French daily *Le Monde*, titled "Appel aux intellectuels africains" (A call to African intellectuals), in which he raised the question of human rights in Africa, and in his country in particular. He accounts for the betrayal of "the craving for freedom and dignity [that] was the main impulse behind African peoples' struggle against the colonial regime." He indicts his country's rulers by saying: "Marxist and Leninist Congo drags on the street the corpses of its political enemies." He appeals to the moral conscience of his fellow African intellectuals: "African intellectuals, this is an appeal to you! Let's unite and talk! Let's defend human rights in Africa! Only our voices are strong enough to be heard, right now." He elicits their sense of responsibility in denouncing "the fundamental reality of daily life on the continent: the absence of respect for human rights, not to say of any rights" (10). We already see here that Dongala's political argumentation is tied to the broader concept of human rights and that, while it clearly mentions the Congolese reality, he stays away from party politics. This will be a constant feature of his aesthetics of commitment.

His other articles were published between 1978 and 1982, under the name of Emmanuel Boudzéki Dongala, in *PN-PA*. They are interesting for a number of reasons. They display a range of interest that goes from Africa, to the diaspora, to France and the United States; they inscribe Dongala in a radical, third world, and internationalist

intellectual tradition;[48] finally, they raise the question of Dongala's relationship to Mongo Beti (his senior by nine years) and to the type of
activism he symbolized.

Published in 1978, in the fifth issue of *PN-PA* and in the first year
of its existence, "Coucou, revoilà les tirailleurs sénégalais" (Hello,
the Tirailleurs Sénégalais are back) is in line with the type of historical, investigative, and denunciatory analyses Mongo Beti produced.
Its approach is reminiscent of Mongo Beti's in that Dongala's textual
unraveling of oppressive neocolonial structures is similarly grounded
in a reinterpretation of African history and is the object of a passionate intellectual probing. This preoccupation with a reinterpretation of
Africa's history will later serve as a bridge toward fiction writing, as
Dongala's first novel, *Le feu des origines* (1987; *The Fire of Origins*,
2001), demonstrates.

"Coucou, revoilà les tirailleurs sénégalais" addresses the aftermath
of the French Légion's military intervention on Kolwési in May–June
1978, officially to free the thousands of Europeans working in this
main mining city of the southern province of Shaba in then Zaïre
from the hands of the "Katangais" rebelling against the government
of Mobutu. This episode ended in widespread killings and torture of
both Africans and Europeans and in the creation of a "force inter-
africaine d'intervention" backed by the West and by Senghor, Omar
Bongo, Bokassa, and Mobutu. What concerns Dongala in the article
is not only the creation of this inter-African force but the fact that
it was sent to Shaba "to be the first line of defense for western interests" (53). With the younger generations of Africans in mind, the
writer reminds his readers of the role traditionally played by "black
troops" and the ways they were instrumentalized by colonial France.
Taking the example of the so-called tirailleurs sénégalais, Dongala
underlines the perverse characteristics of their recruitment and their
mission, in Algeria, Tunisia, Morocco, Cameroon, Madagascar, and
Asia. As Sembène does in his 1987 film *Camp de Thiaroye*, Dongala
features France's ingratitude and social neglect of the "tirailleurs sénégalais" very critically. He ends his article on the following note:
"Things have come full circle; again black legions will be the first line
of defense, this time not to 'defend the cause of liberty in the world,'
but to defend France's and the western world's rights to economic se-
curity" (59).

Also published in *PN-PA* in 1979, "Littérature et société: Ce que je
crois" (Literature and society: what I believe in) is the better known,

and the more frequently quoted, of all these articles. It is prefaced by a letter from Dongala to Mongo Beti explaining the circumstances in which it was written. Originally intended to be part of a special issue on Congolese literature commissioned by a local newspaper, *La Semaine Africaine*, "Littérature et société" was censored by the Congolese government. In his letter to Mongo Beti, Dongala consequently asks him to publish his text in *PN-PA*. "Littérature et société: ce que je crois" lays down ideas and values that are still at the core of Dongala's production, and others that have fallen to disuse. Both of these categories of values and ideas shed light on the evolution of Dongala's literary commitment, or at least on the ways he has conceived of it.

In "Littérature et société," Dongala positions himself defensively as someone outside the circle of writers patronized by the Marxist-Leninist government in power. He characterizes his creative process as a "need to write" (58), as an individual act implying "a measure of autonomy" and an "irreducible individual freedom" (61). In that sense, he is not that far from Lopès's stand. Dongala further explains his creative urge by a preoccupation with "enhancing our appreciation of our human quality" (63). While affirming his priorities toward his compatriots and the continent, he invokes his "right to indifference" (62) and makes a strong claim for his right, as man and writer, to change his mind (64). Thus Dongala tries to eschew a forced political participation and programmatic use of language by carving out a creative space beyond the confines of a literature strictly couched in the discourse of nationalism.

Having lived in the United States as a student during the time of the Civil Rights and the Black Panthers' movements, Dongala's perspective on African nationalism is informed by his concrete experience of Black political and cultural nationalism. As previously mentioned, *Jazz et vin de palme*, a volume he would publish three years later, fictionally represents that diasporic vision.

In "Littérature et société," Dongala makes semantic distinctions that are still relevant today, notably between the notions of engagement and revolution. Pointing to a "confusion between engagement and revolution," he remarks that political commitment does not automatically reflect a revolutionary standpoint, that "to be politically committed means to choose one's causes, good or bad" (60). Going further, Dongala qualifies the accepted understanding of the term "revolutionary" by saying that what is revolutionary is in fact what allows for a reconceptualization: "A revolutionary book, novel or poem is a text that shatters the structures of literary tradition, that brings about a new sensibility, a new way of seeing, of conveying, of understanding things" (59–60). He closes his argument by stressing that engagement and revolution do not necessarily converge and pronounces himself a committed but not revolutionary writer, that is, someone who may have chosen to fight for a cause but has not (yet) proposed a rethinking of literature.

Thus, Dongala's enduring will for change is anchored in a cautious sobriety that dates back to the personal and professional circumstances of his life. Although he acknowledges a sense of solidarity with his people and the oppressed peoples of the world, he vehemently refuses to be cast as their spokesperson: "I do not delude myself, I do not write for the 'people,' a historicized and categorized people. . . . I am no one's messenger and I have neither guide nor heroes" (63). In this text, Dongala contrasts the idea of *écrivain populaire* with that of *écrivain du peuple* while also insisting on his "right to be indifferent." This is an interesting and provocative view of literary commitment given the context of the times, particularly if we recall that such works as Mongo Beti's *Main basse* and *Perpétue et l'habitude du malheur*, two books which certainly did not make room for indifference, had appeared respectively in 1972 and 1974, and that *La ruine presque cocasse d'un polichinelle* (The almost laughable ruin of a buffoon, 1979) was due to come out the same year as "Littérature et société." Clearly, the publication of this article in *PN-PA* showcases the types of broad dialogues Mongo Beti and Tobner fostered in their journal.

CRITICISM AND ENGAGEMENT: REASSESSING THE TOOLS

The theoretical understanding of francophone African literature and its situatedness at the time of the "enduring militants," and to this day, has paradoxically remained constant and yet changed. As Mouralis reminded us in *Littérature et développement*, francophone African literature was constructed simultaneously with its criticism, often by the writers themselves: "Contrary to what usually happens elsewhere, African writers are not content with producing texts of fiction—poetry, theater, novel—; parallel to that production they constantly elaborate a discourse, the main function of which is to voice what an authentic African literature must be. The articulation between the production of fictional texts and the elaboration of a discourse on literature that could be termed a 'literary consciousness,' appears to be one of the essential characteristics of this literature" (12–13). Just as African literature was read as "naturally" committed and supposed to reflect social reality, the criticism of African literature was largely channeled and atrophied by the same expectations. In "Comment appréhender la 'sagesse des barbares?'" (Grasping the "wisdom of the barbarians"), Fonkoua stresses this idea as follows: "Until the beginning of the 1980s, the themes of Engagement, the topos of realism, and the status of the popular hero caused writing to be a necessarily signifying act. The literary text as well as the writer were in the service of the Other."[49]

Furthermore, as we pointed out earlier, and as Justin Bisanswa highlights in "D'une critique l'autre: la littérature africaine au prisme de ses lectures" (From one criticism to another: African literature through its critical readings), the contradictions of French literature and its criticism appeared when francophone African literature started to become visible on the French literary scene. According to Bisanswa, these contradictions stemmed from the fact that French literary criticism was heavily influenced by structuralism and semiotics, and that the Nouveau Roman became dominant and emphasized the death of the author and of the subject. Meanwhile, the critical approach to francophone African literature was still grounded on an anthropological perspective pointing out Africa's distinctive features.[50] This raises the question of whether criticism was reduced to mimetism and nothing else.

In that respect, Sewanou Dabla's Nouvelles écritures africaines: romanciers de la seconde génération (2000) was a turning point in criticism, providing a different reading grid that allowed for a more flexible approach, in line with the textuality of the work. Dabla's essay broke away from the previous vein of African literary criticism where the emphasis remained on the sociopolitical testimonial value of the work, and critics paid only scant attention to form.

In "La littérature en miroir. Création, critique et intertextualité" (Reflecting literature: Creation, criticism and intertextuality), Mongo-Mboussa shows that the 1980s marked a time when intertextuality became more prominently explored. This is evident in Diop's Le temps de Tamango and Lopès's Le pleurer-rire and Le lys et le flamboyant, where the author takes issue with form and raises questions about fiction and truth. Thus, the writers themselves take on the realist novel and what had been seen as the implicit mission of the writer:

to be a voice (or a countervoice) for her or his people. "The intertextual play at the heart of the text," adds Mongo-Mboussa, "is above all a way to elicit a debate, to posit oneself with or against the grain of certain critical interpretations and labels" (50). In that context, Mongo-Mboussa sees Labou Tansi and Kossi Efoui as representative not only of an iconoclastic writing, but also of a way to reinvent oneself as a writer. It is then also a way to parody certain writings and to mock critical approaches, particularly the ways they lock in both the writer and the text; it signals a new relationship to literature and what it can do.

Because of this new tonality in writing, literary critics pushed back to the periphery texts that were clearly identified as *engagés*. However, as will be discussed in more detail in Chapter 2, the 1980s also witnessed a historical process whereby France had to confront the depth of its responsibility and amnesia during the Vichy regime. The Papon trial was a catalyst for this and the beginning of a reexamination of its recent history by French society. As Benjamin Stora has shown in relation to Algeria, such unveiling of the national "subconscious" results in the refashioning of national history and in the creation of new (or displaced) historical representations.[51] The 1990s saw the emergence of texts in reaction to several international conflicts and tragedies, such as the 1994 genocide in Rwanda and the civil wars in Algeria, Liberia, and Sierra Leone. These texts put the question of the relationship of the writer to his text and readership back on the agenda. It forced the writer to think about her or his ethical position and to raise the question of a "moral imagination" (Thomas, *Black France*, 143). As Catherine Coquio underlines in *Rwanda: Le réel et les récits* (Rwanda: the real and the told, 2004): "The writer's political commitment in regard to genocide leads to the elaboration of a language and a form capable of translating a reality that goes beyond the categories of perception and understanding. It does so without bypassing any of the issues: neither the collapse of mental balance and moral boundaries nor the evidence of political responsibilities. This translation must be apt to re-integrate the non-sense of genocide in a construction that is meaningful without being conservative. The writer is free to choose her/his structure within these contractual limits" (142).

In 2000, following a period of political demonstrations for increased democracy, two books came out that may be said to represent a transition in the critical understanding of oppression and resistance, at least from the standpoint of Cameroonian post-independence reality. In *La malédiction francophone: défis culturels et condition post-coloniale en Afrique* (The francophone curse: cultural challenges and the postcolonial condition in Africa), Ambroise Kom underlines how neocolonial calcifications continue to block Africans' daily lives in francophone Africa. Although from a younger generation, he situates himself within the continuum of Mongo Beti and his denunciation of Francophonie.

In *De la postcolonie*, Mbembe, from a younger generation still, revisits Fanon's and Memmi's analyses of violence and dependence, pointing to the social embeddedness of the "authoritarian imaginary" (43) and the internalization of oppressive structures.

> [A]t any given moment in the postcolonial historical trajectory, the authoritarian mode can no longer be interpreted strictly in terms of surveillance, or the politics of coercion. The practices of ordinary citizens cannot always be read in terms of "opposition to the state," "deconstructing power," and "disengagement." In the postcolony, an intimate tyranny links the ruler with the ruled. . . . If subjection appears more intense than it might be, this is because the subjects of the *commandement* have internalized authoritarian epistemology to the point where they reproduce it themselves in all the minor circumstances of daily life. (128)

Mbembe proposes that there is no "before or after" (15) to oppression and resistance and that they can best be described as a complex "entanglement" (17).[52] To him, "th[e] authoritarian imaginary, consolidated during the colonial and independence period, also had a considerable impact on the way social movements emerged, the framework in which they acted, the forms of mobilization they adopted, their chances of victory, and the possibilities of their defeat" (43). In *L'occident décroché: Enquête sur les postcolonialismes* (The West unhinged: study of postcolonialisms, 2008), Jean-Loup Amselle sums up why Mbembe's overriding concept of the "authoritarian imaginary" and analysis of violence have received mixed reviews, "essentially attributing Africa's difficulties to Africans themselves and forgetting to mention the historical and social causes of their dereliction, he may have seemed to blame the victims" (92).

CONCLUSION

The notion of engagement endures and has a legacy. Diop, who belongs to the generation of post-independence far-left militants, highlighted that trend when he said about Mongo Beti: "Even if Africa has never lacked in theoreticians, especially at the time of the nationalist struggles, he is among the few, with the Kenyan Ngugi Wa Thiong'o, to have fully carried out his calling as a novelist and a political thinker. Through his novels, his essays and the courageous positions he took, Mongo Beti had come to symbolize for us the free intellectual, willing to pay the price of his convictions and answering to his conscience only" ("Mongo Beti et nous," 89).

In turn, Mongo Beti's preface to Diop's *Le temps de Tamango* raised the question of the existence of a new generation of *engagé* writers. Diop's revolt against France's involvement in the 1994 genocide in Rwanda radicalized him anew and placed him in Mongo Beti's lineage.

Diop's decision to write a novel in Wolof, *Doomi Golo* (2003), manifests a rethinking of his role as a francophone African writer. In his essay, "Ecris et . . . tais-toi" (*L'Afrique au-delà du miroir* [Africa beyond the mirror], 163–72), he subsequently addressed the question of language and what it meant to be writing a novel in Wolof: "The writer does not play his part by telling others what they should think or do but, much more modestly, by speaking to them about themselves, if need be through his own fantasies. He does not only use language, he creates it, thus contributing to changing society. Writing in Wolof, I feel I take my place in a literary history that is being constructed" (171).[53]

With Verschave and Tobner, Diop also participated in *Négrophobie*, a book written in response to the journalist Stephen Smith's *Négrologie: Pourquoi l'Afrique meurt* (Negrology: why Africa is dying, 2003), in which he protests against revisionism and the instrumentalization of memory.[54] For Diop, "what is at stake in the ideological commotion one can witness lately is the memory of Europe's past crimes. At work is an effort to convince the entire world—Africans included—of Europe's innocence" (73). With Verschave[55] and Tobner, Diop argues that the current international context is rife with double-speak, with policies and attitudes aiming to recolonize countries in the name of democracy and freedom. They believe the Foccartist politics of Francophonie in Africa are still at work but have been redesigned, with the 1994 La Baule summit, the 1994 genocide in Rwanda, and the civil war in Ivory Coast marking different adaptations of the evolving reality experienced by "francophone" Africans, and the shifting nature of France's economic hold on the *Pré Carré*

(private preserve) that no longer says its name.[56] They signal the doctrine of Francophonie as constitutive of contemporary French political life and culture, across its political spectrum. They consider that
the French Parisian media elite has not broken away from old Africanist habits, lacks the courage to coherently disavow the successive
French governments' continuing clientelist policy toward its former
colonies, and thus prevents the French public from understanding the
reality of the continent.

From Boni and Tadjo, to Moussa Konaté, and the younger Nganang and Raharimanana, several francophone African writers have
claimed an "enduring" lineage, one that considers the elaboration of
a literary consciousness as indissociable from a reflection on Africa's political situatedness. In parallel to their fictional texts, these authors[57] publish essays that inform the field of francophone African literature as well as contemporary African (world) politics. As was the
case with Mongo Beti, Nganang and Raharimanana are producing
works that hinge on both creative and expository writing.

Whereas for many writers of the older generation, engagement
was a necessary *prise de parole* in a world where radical change was
deemed possible, today's literary commitment is less idealistic, more
tentative, and more dystopic than utopic. It is often expressed to disturb rather than transform. Engagement has gone beyond duality.
Postcolonial literature in general has developed textual homelands
that do not correspond to previous definitions, moving away from the
national to the transnational. The oppositional discourses sustained
by literary critics, according to whom the accent is either on social
reality or on aesthetics, have lost much of their credibility. As underlined by Miller in *Theories of Africans*, "the whole notion of what
is 'political' has changed in the postcolonial era: political vision and
symbolic representation are no longer held to be mutually exclusive"
(124).

When, in 2002, at the festival Etonnants Voyageurs in Bamako,
Mali, Efoui provocatively (and by now, famously) enjoined critics to
leave African writers to their writing and proclaimed that African
literature does not exist, he was indicating his refusal that his creation be racially or historically bound and voicing an artist's need
to be free to explore the form she or he will give his or her creation,
away from the expected sociological or anthropological scripts: "African writers are not employed by the Ministry of Tourism. Expressing the authentic soul of Africa is not their mission. Let's understand

once and for all that we do not have a collective voice. We have not sworn allegiance to anyone! Let's not tense up around issues of identity. They constitute the reservoir globalization drinks from! The best thing that can happen to African literature is that she is not perpetually reminded of Africa."[58] Similarly, Tanella Boni cannot be said to be but a committed novelist and poet because she has been very vocal on a number of political issues.[59] Her literary production should not be collapsed into one precise category, that of *littérature engagée*, nor understood essentially in terms of previous works in francophone African literature that are deemed *engagés*. In short, various forms of contemporary African poetics can no longer be constructed as stringent exclusives.

For the longest time, commitment was the measure by which the canon of francophone African literature was established.[60] What strengthened this false impression was first the historical context, second the perception of a necessity of engagement by critics, and third the writers themselves. In times of intense social transformation, political and social forces exert considerable influence on the artists (Jothiprakash, *Commitment as a Theme in African American Literature: A Study of James Baldwin and Ralph Ellison*). The general rallying to participate in the construction of a new and independent Africa led to an idealistic convergence that logically privileged the collective. This, however, resulted in an understanding of African literature that was often limiting.

Just as there is a legacy to the "enduring militants," there is also a legacy to those who refute that view and see literature in individual terms. One could say that Mabanckou's stance on engagement and the function of literature in *Lettre à Jimmy* echoes that of Lopès in *Dossier classé*, for instance.

> One would object to me that there is a duty of commitment, that it is necessary to put on notice those who are taking the continent down. . . . But what is the meaning of Engagement if it leads to the erasure of individual traits? Many hide behind this mask to lecture us, to impose on us a vision of the world whereby there are on one side the true sons of Africa, and on the other, the ungrateful—assuming that the latter are also considered as the servants of Europe. I am naturally distrustful of those who brandish banners. They are the same people who clamor for "authenticity," the very idea that has thrust the African continent into tragedy. (77)

Yet, following his participation in a colloquium on memory in Kigali,

Rwanda, July 24–27, 2008, Mabanckou interrogates the necessity of engagement anew in his blog, saying:

> A work of fiction conveys a discourse, and this discourse is the image that the writer holds of the world, the image he would like to impress upon the reader. No literature is neutral. . . . Each writer is thus *engagé*—not to say, *enragé* [enraged]. By celebrating life, he commits to a certain era. Stirring up the past, he commits to his era. Listening to the murmurs of the other world, he commits to his era.
>
> It is up to scholars to untangle this discourse, to deconstruct it, to gauge the extent to which we provide—sometimes unconsciously—grist to the mill of negationists, to those who favor a re-writing of History. They expect such fictions. And they will applaud loudly if the negationist writer is from Rwanda. ("Rwanda, ce génocide qui nous mine la conscience").[61]

The notion of engagement is still operative today, but it has undergone a semantic explosion and taken on many new connotations. The nucleus of literary themes in francophone African literature may not have necessarily changed, but it has gained a wider scope. As will be shown in Chapter 2, "The Practice of Memory," and Chapter 3, "Lifting the Burden? Francophone African Writers Engaging in New Aesthetics," writers are letting the power of the imaginary play a more prominent role. Thus the manner, the style, and the techniques used to create verisimilitude, as well as the writer's perception of her/his implied reader, have shifted. Since 2000, however, African writers have become more vocal, individually and collectively. A visible instance of the endurance of engagement was demonstrated by the many responses from African intellectuals/writers to French president Nicolas Sarkozy's speech at the Université Cheikh Anta Diop in Dakar, Senegal (July 26, 2007).

CHAPTER TWO

The Practice of Memory

The poet appropriates the voice of the people and the full burden of their memory.

WOLE SOYINKA, *The Burden of Memory: The Muse of Forgiveness*

Remembering is an act of lending coherence and integrity to a history interrupted, divided, or compromised by instance of loss. We engage in history not only as agents and actors but also as narrators and storytellers. In narrative, we may be able to redress forcibly forgotten experiences, allow the silences of history to come to word, and imagine alternative scripts of the past. Our understanding of the present is invariably predicated on actual or imagined links to, or ruptures from, a recalled past.

AZADE SEYHAN, *Writing Outside the Nation*

Memory and the "duty of memory" are themes that have become prevalent in contemporary discussions of history and literature. Following World War II, with the articulation of the notions of "crimes against humanity" and "genocide" through the United Nations Charter, the prosecution of responsible parties, and the emergence of testimonial narratives related to the Holocaust, Western societies have been reconceptualizing their relationship to the past. In the latter half of the twentieth century and the beginning of the twenty-first century, demands for former imperial powers to recognize and admit crimes committed during their colonization of Africa and the neocolonial period have steadily been brought to bear. However, this questioning has taken place in an international context whereby memory has often been exploited politically and culturally. As Tzvetan Todorov observed in *Les abus de la mémoire* (The abuses of memory, 1995): "The cult of memory is not always useful to the cause of justice; nor is it useful to memory itself" (58). Memory is not just about righting wrongs or restoring meaning, and the relationship between past and present is not solely based on cause and effect. What is memory after all? Is it individual, collective, or both? How is "collective" memory to be transmitted, and can this transmission be devoid of ideology? What is the basis on which to rebuild or construct a meaningful and encompassing history after war, genocide, and the mass murder of civilians? What kind of understanding of the notions of "origin" and "authenticity" do such traumatic events call for or rebuke? Is memory fixed and immutable, or is it stratified? Is it limited to the use we make of our past? How is it constructed, and to what extent is it part of a cultural architecture and linked to the political construction of the nation?

In "Une relecture des *Lieux de mémoire* au regard du vécu africain"[1] (A rereading of *Lieux de mémoire* from the standpoint of African experience, 2006), the historian Doulaye Konaté signals that the contemporary understanding of the relationship between history and memory has changed and been conceptualized differently, notably through *Les lieux de mémoire* (1984–1993; *Realms of Memory: Rethinking the French Past*, 1996), the three-volume collection of essays under the direction of Pierre Nora and Charles-Robert Ageron: "An ambitious endeavor aiming to provide a rereading of French history, *Les lieux de mémoire* . . . carries out the deconstruction of the official history symbolized by 'Le Petit Lavisse'[2] to address the silences in contemporary France's history and memory" (9). Although Nora's work was limited to metropolitan France and failed to extend to an analysis of its colonial past, it marked "the end of history-memory . . . that linked republic, nation and France" (11). Because the national past is no longer viewed as a key to the future, history and memory are no longer conceived of correlatively, and memory has become the sole "promise of continuity."

Christiane Taubira, the deputy from French Guiana who gave her name to the May 21, 2001, law declaring the Atlantic slave trade and slavery to be crimes against humanity,[3] comes back to Nora's failing in a chapter in the book *Rwanda: Pour un dialogue des mémoires* (Rwanda: for a dialogue between memories) provocatively titled "Mémoires universelles" (2007, 147–64). In that chapter, she devotes a separate section to Nora's treatment of colonization in his volumes. Stressing that out of five thousand pages, none are concerned with the monuments, the territories, or the landscapes that are part of the colonial legacy, she shows that even an allusive title such as "Contre-mémoire" (in Nora's chapter on Vendée's loyalty to the king during the

1789 French Revolution) does not encompass other resistance movements, such as the 1950s anticolonial resistance movements. She then notes that in the chapter on North America, there is a comparable blank regarding slavery. Taking Camp Joffre in Rivesaltes, France, as an example, Taubira further demonstrates that all memories do not hold the same value. Today, although Camp Joffre is a site emblematic of World War II, known as a place where Jewish prisoners were in transit before being deported to Auschwitz, the memories have gone blank about its other historic functions.[4] Noting this, Taubira reflects on and questions the concept and implications of a singular memory that claims to be universal.

Quoting Eduardo Galeano in *Memoria del fuego* (1982–1986; *Memory of Fire*, 1998), Taubira also reminds us that "there is no neutral History. Even after it has been burnt, torn apart, cheated on, human memory refuses to be silenced. The pulse of the past continues to beat, alive, in the veins of the present times, even if present times do not want it or do not know it" (148–49). Linking universal memory and power, in the context of the October 2005 suburban "riots" in France, Taubira explains that memory can be universal only if social justice is one of its core tenets, that is, if it concerns itself with the representation of a national history based on the representation of the full experiences of the national collective. Like Konaté, she believes that the relationship between history and memory is being queried anew today because the question of citizenship begs to be answered. Indeed, pressure had been mounting on the French government with the 150th anniversary of Schoelcher's abolition of slavery (1848). On May 23, 1998, a demonstration in Paris had gathered 40,000 people, mostly of African descent, publicly reclaiming their ancestry and voicing their collective desire to break with historical anonymity. Today, this event is regarded by many as the beginning of "la quête identitaire" of French citizens of African and Caribbean descents. Taubira's address before the French Assembly on February 18, 1999, on the "reconnaissance de la traite et de l'esclavage comme crimes contre l'humanité," and the adoption of the law in 2001, were sustained by that popular movement.

Inasmuch as "the right to memory precedes the duty of memory," a failure to take stock of this reality poses a threat to society's stability and growth. Hence, for Taubira, "while an assumed memory may strengthen social structures, an obfuscated memory may contribute to their disintegration. While an articulated memory has soothing powers, a memory denied is cause for frustration" (150). Finally, Taubira drives her point home by saying that

> Universal memory is not necessarily one that spreads across the entire surface of the earth. It is not primarily spatial. . . . In order to be believable and strong in its lack of differentiation between time and space, universal memory presupposes a fluid circulation between the knowledge of facts and their agreed upon importance, a restrained reverence, and commemoration, all of these stemming from a shared understanding of the Nation.
>
> . . . A common destiny can only be erected upon the foundations of equal rights that are truly respected, and on the sharing of symbolic resources at least as equitably as the sharing of economic, social and cultural resources. . . . The question of memory is related to that of our living together with awareness and in a spirit of existential, not to say ontological, empathy. Power and the powerful public institutions that guarantee the relevance of its solemnity must be accountable for it. (150–51)

The historians Catherine Coquery-Vidrovitch, Gilles Manceron, and Benjamin Stora agree with Taubira's central argument and see it as a systematic pattern of France's contemporary politics. In "La mémoire partisane du Président"[5] (The partial memory of the president, 2007), they highlight a trend in recent French political discourse, especially in Nicolas Sarkozy's 2007 presidential campaign, and now under his presidency, that reflects a deliberate refusal to confront France's responsibilities in regard to historical events. This includes "refusing to take any critical look at colonization. In order to win over the fraction of the electorate most nostalgic for the Empire, and often associated with the Far Right, the future president of the republic has allowed for a re-launching of the idea of a positive colonization" (19). Coquery-Vidrovitch, Manceron, and Stora read this approach/trend as a form counter to collective responsibility. According to them, this approach "makes it possible to describe a historical process such as colonization leniently so that historians do not have to pass a moral judgment on it. It is the examination of the facts that leads them to notice (and to explain) a clear contradiction with the principles of liberty, equality and a people's right to independence, principles to which nineteenth century Europe has otherwise had a tendency to adhere" (19).

Both Sarkozy's political campaign and his current presidency articulate a discourse of "anti-repentance" that fuels a war of memories. Sarkozy "answers to political objectives, not only to unite the Right, but also to hinder France's Left which, since its break-up during the Algerian war, has never clarified its discourse on the colonial question" (19). Thus we see that there is still a need to clarify and confront this relationship to the colonial past both in terms of repentance and knowledge.

As alluded to in Chapter 1, Sarkozy's July 26, 2007, speech, delivered at the University Cheikh Anta Diop in Dakar, Senegal, demonstrates the perpetuation of France's long-standing habit of telling Africa and Africans "what they must think" (Tadjo, "Sous nos yeux, l'histoire se répète!" [History repeats itself under our very eyes], 20).[6] In that regard, Robert Young's chapter on history in *White Mythologies* (1990) further specifies the role and space of history in a postcolonial and poststructuralist take. Young makes the point that history is the most important issue for postcolonial writers. Likewise, Glissant, Gilroy, Spivak, and Bhabha's works encourage us to rethink history, especially in its Western epistemologies.

Concurring with Taubira, Coquery-Vidrovitch, Manceron, and Stora, Konaté notes that a stronger demand is being voiced for history to be understood in multidisciplinary terms and for historians to stop "monopolizing" the discourse on history and widen the scope of their investigations. In addition, he raises the issue of the relevance and applicability of Western historical discourse in both making sense of and giving meaning to different histories: "Is western historical discourse the only meaningful discourse to account for the relationship between a society and its past?" (11). Finally, even if the full extent of France's colonial and postcolonial pasts, particularly in Africa, were examined, and the lives of the generations of Africans who have lived in France acknowledged as integral to that country's past, how would history account for the fact that oral traditions serve as the basis of African collective memory?

Memory is an idea frequently referred to today in the field of African literature, but it is hardly a new issue. With the exception of Diop in *Le temps de Tamango* (1981), Yambo Ouologuem in *Le devoir de violence* (1968), and Etienne Goyemidé in *Le dernier survivant de la caravane* (The caravan's last survivor, 1985), comparatively few African writers have explored the times of the slave trade. Kangni Alem's 2006 article "La mémoire des traites et de l'esclavage au regard des littératures africaines" (The memory of the slave trades and slavery through African literatures) decries the silence surrounding the question of slavery in France and in African literatures, and urgently calls for more literary/fictional explorations of this topic—which he addressed with the publication of his his 2009 novel, *Esclaves*.

> Whereas in North American and Caribbean literatures, slavery and its immediate corollary, the slave trade, provide the implicit or explicit framework for many novels and narratives, the reluctance of African literatures to broach this question betrays the extent to which it is both forbidden and trivialized through silence. . . . How indeed does one explain the faltering of fiction and its eloquent silences when one knows that the ingrained attitudes that made Africa complicit with the slave trade call for a reinterpretation through a variety of inquiries, and that only this process can generate an objective rapport with history? (17)

Many francophone African writers have worked extensively on representing the colonial and postcolonial periods. Furthermore, authors such as Ahmadou Hampâté Bâ, Ouologuem, Kourouma, Kane, Diop, and Essomba with *Le dernier gardien de l'arbre* (The last keeper of the tree, 1998), Effa with *Le cri que tu pousses ne réveillera personne* (Your scream will wake up no one, 2000), and Monénembo with *Peuls* (2004), have explored the ramifications of precolonial African history using epic, foundational myths, and great genealogies.[7] Other writers, such as Mongo Beti, Liking, and Nganang have worked at filling some of African history's silences and reconfiguring the memory of nationalist struggles.

Since 2000, however, the issue of memory has become a focus in francophone African literary production. As the following list indicates, more than a dozen novels are centered explicitly on the interweaving of memory and history. Other narratives, such as Mariama Barry's *La petite peule* (2000; *The Little Peul*, 2010), Kossi Efoui's *La fabrique des cérémonies* (The crafting of ceremonies, 2001), Nimrod's *Les jambes d'Alice* (Alice's legs, 2001), and Diome's *Le ventre de l'Atlantique* (2003; *The Belly of the Atlantic*, 2006) are indirectly related to this corpus.

Table 1 highlights the following points: First, authors writing both on and outside the continent work on the issue of memory. Second, the place of writing does not elicit a specific treatment of memory. The narrative configurations of memory are multiple and point to an overall recrafting of history and myth. Third, five of the writers, Diop, Monénembo, Boni, Ken Bugul, and Tadjo have produced two or more books on the subject, without necessarily displaying a formal continuity. Fourth, the Duty of Memory Project on Rwanda forced the participating writers to engage in a cultural and histori-

TABLE I

Memory as Focus in Francophone African Literature
at the Turn of the Twenty-First Century

Author	Title	Date of Publication	Place of writing	Place of narration
Tanella Boni	Les baigneurs du lac rose	1995	Ivory Coast	Ivory Coast, Senegal, and France
Boubacar Boris Diop	Le cavalier et son ombre	1997	Senegal	Senegal
Tierno Monémbo	Cinéma	1997	France	Guinea
J. R. Essomba	Le dernier gardien de l'arbre	1998	France	Cameroon
Ken Bugul	Riwan ou le chemin de sable	1999	Benin	Senegal
Bessora	53 cm	1999	France	France
Ken Bugul	La folie et la mort	2000	Benin	somewhere in Africa
Boubacar Boris Diop	Murambi, le livre des ossements	2000	Senegal and Switzerland	Rwanda
Monique Ilboudo	Murekatete	2000	Burkina Faso	Rwanda
Monénembo	L'aîné des orphelins	2000	France	Rwanda
Véronique Tadjo	L'ombre d'Imana	2000	England	South Africa and Rwanda
Aimée Gnali	Beto Na Beto	2001	Republic of Congo	France and Republic of Congo
Raharimanana	Nour, 1947	2001	France	Madagascar
Alain Mabanckou	Les petits-fils nègres de Vercingétorix	2002	United States	Republic of Congo
Patrice Nganang	Temps de chien	2001	United States	Cameroon
Henri Lopès	Dossier classé	2002	France	United States and Republic of Congo
Ken Bugul	De l'autre côté du regard	2003	Benin	Benin, Senegal, and Ivory Coast

TABLE I (CONTINUED)

Author	Title	Date of Publication	Place of writing	Place of narration
Michèle Rakotoson	*Lalana*	2002	France	Madagascar
Natacha Appanah Mouriquand	*Les rochers de poudre d'or*	2003	France	Mauritius
Werewere Liking	*La mémoire amputée*	2004	Ivory Coast	Cameroon
Monénembo	*Peuls*	2004	France	West Africa
Véronique Tadjo	*Reine Pokou*	2004	South Africa	Baoulé Kingdom, Ivory Coast
Kangni Alem	*Esclaves*	2009	France and Togo	Brazil

cal context mostly foreign to them. It pushed them to concentrate on a given event, time, and space, and to interrogate their universal implications. This bore consequences for their perceptions of themselves as African intellectuals as well as for their aesthetics. Last, Ken Bugul has moved from the autobiographical vein to fictional memory whereas Lopès has used the detective novel as a vehicle to investigate the past.

In some respects, memory epitomizes francophone African literature at the turn of the twenty-first century just as "denunciation" epitomized that of earlier generations. But, as we have seen in Chapter 1 regarding the "enduring militants" debate, what matters is not so much the preeminence of the theme of memory but the ways in which memory has been represented by the writers and in turn framed by critics. In a 1999 interview in *Le Lynx*, Monénembo is described as having moved from "the novel of denunciation to the mythological [novel] (3) with *Cinéma* (1997)."[8] Following this line of argument, are we to infer that *L'aîné des orphelins* (2000) is necessarily a novel about memory because it belongs to the Duty of Memory Project? Are the categories of "denunciation," the "myth," and "memory" mutually exclusive? Ricoeur's concept of the "thwarted memory,"[9] an obsessive and totalitarian memory reconstructed by dictatorship, helps us understand the "novels of denunciation" as another facet, albeit indirect, of the representation of memory. Indeed, is there such a sharp ideological difference between a literary "duty of commitment" and a "duty of memory"? Is engagement more readily perceptible in the "novels of denunciation" because they are mostly textualized in realistic terms as opposed to the "novels of memory," the crafting of which is more modernist? A writer as clearly identified as committed as Diop seems to fit the "denunciation" category better than someone like Monénembo. However, all of Diop's novels belie this assumption because they are related to the issue of memory. What we are facing then is not only the issue of how critics label a given book but also how that label becomes operative in the historiography of African literature and how certain writers are assigned to certain positions.

One could consider that the current prevalence of the theme of memory is a new stage in the redefinition of the role of the African writer as the historian of her/his continent. Denunciation, myth, and memory thus come to manifest three different relationships to the writer's historical context.

In this chapter we examine the literary commitment to memory and its processes according to three themes: First, confronting and reconstructing the past: the figure of the national hero in Diop's *Le cavalier et son ombre*, Monénembo's *Cinéma*, Nganang's *La joie de vivre*, and Liking's *La mémoire amputée;* second, revamping and subverting the myth: Effa's *Le cri que tu pousses ne réveillera personne*, Boni's *Les baigneurs du lac rose*, Tadjo's *Reine Pokou*, and Raharimanana's *Nour, 1947;* and third, Rwanda: Ecrire par devoir de mémoire, the Duty of Memory Project on the 1994 genocide in Rwanda.

CONFRONTING AND RECONSTRUCTING THE PAST: THE FIGURE OF THE NATIONAL HERO

Taken as a whole, Diop's oeuvre demonstrates a long practice of writing about memory, whereby the narrator or the protagonist embarks on a quest to recover someone who, or something that, disappeared. From *Le temps de Tamango* (1981) to *Les tambours de la mémoire* (The drums of memory, 1990) to *Les traces de la meute* (The traces of the pack, 1993) to *Le cavalier et son ombre* (1997), the author typically uses a combination of narrative voices and protagonists trying to find the lost link. *Le cavalier et son ombre* raises the question of searching for and confronting the past by looking at African heroes, to reflect on who best embodied African values in precolonial Africa. The narrator, Lat-Sukabe, searches for Khadidja, his former lover. Going south, he embarks on a journey that tests both his personal values and those of his people. *Le cavalier et son ombre* is a beautiful demonstration of the art of storytelling in which the magical and the real cohabit, intertwine, coincide, and intersect at several points. The shift in narrative viewpoints invites readers to constantly reassess their interpretation and understanding of the unfolding of plot. A series of tales within the tale, the novel is a memorial opus, raising philosophical questions about the African past (the mistakes of history, what defines a hero or heroine, who the African heroes are), the present (civil wars and genocide), and the future (looking for Tunda, the child who will bring hope).

Textually, the encounter between facts and fiction raises not only the question of the choice of representational modes but also, to use Jacques Rancière's terminology, the questions of the "ethical system of images," the "sharing out of what can, and cannot, be represented," and the "unutterable/unredeemable" (*Le partage du sensible,* 29). Indeed, if these are characteristics of postmodern art, what are the implications with regard to its visibility?

Taking as a point of departure the fact that "the aesthetic revolution redraws the map as it brings together two elements: it blurs the distinction between the reason for facts and fictions, and historical science's new models for rationality" (56), Rancière remarks that "the fiction of the aesthetic age has defined the relational models between the presentation of facts and the forms of intelligibility that blur the boundary between factual and fictional reason" (61). As such, he sees a parallel between the writing of history and the writing of stories as they both refer to the "same protocol of truth" (61). In that sense, *Le cavalier et son ombre* can be said to be searching both for history and new aesthetics about storytelling.

In her chapter, "Shadowing the Story-teller,"[10] Nasrin Qader analyzes quite finely the particular spatio-temporal configuration of the story's time in *Le cavalier et son ombre*. Characterized by a double directionality, it is turned simultaneously toward the past and the future, the present being that of the time and space of storytelling. To Qader, the "imaginary dialogue focalizes on two problems: that of beginning a story and that of the story's connection with a truth that cannot be verified, in the present as present" (91–92). Storytelling causes the readers to feel contemporary with both Lat-Sukabe's and Khadidja's experiences, particularly their "continuous suffering of discontinuity" (94). Through her tales, Khadidja also comes to evoke the 1994 genocide in Rwanda: the violence in the kingdom of Dapienga and the division between the Mwa and the Twi, where one has to be exterminated, are clear reminders of that tragedy.

In his chapter "Génocide et devoir d'imaginaire" (Genocide and the duty of imagination), Diop, commenting on the approaches to the genocide in both *Le Cavalier et son ombre* and *Murambi*, offers a very critical outlook of his former approach in the first work: "For Khadidja to say that 'Rwanda is causing her pain' is in fact ludicrous. The real suffering was endured by others. Very removed from their pain, the writer whose intention is simply to 'make believe' through a thousand stylistic gimmicks, has actually only experienced pathetic aesthetic anxieties . . . it was nothing but a literary experience" (26–27).

Beyond its elaborate crafting of storytelling and its subtle rendering of the relationships between narrator and narratee, between author and readers, the novel addresses key questions regarding postcolonial societies, particularly with regard to history and heroic figures. An unexpected figure of change, the Cavalier is emblematic of the dilemmas surrounding the notion of heroism and the failure of revolutionary ideology: "Instead of heralding an era of peace and hope, sovereignty becomes the place of another kind of violence to which le Cavalier himself falls victim; Revolution thus ends in terror" (Qader, 115).

Interestingly, this scenario of a failed revolution can already be found in Diop's first novel, *Le temps de Tamango* (1981), a rewriting of Prosper Mérimée's short story, *Tamango* (1829), where revolution, albeit projected in 2025, comes to naught and justice remains a utopic idea.[11] Here too, as in *Les tambours de la mémoire*, *Murambi*, and *Kaveena*, Diop addresses the question of moral responsibility, ethics, and justice, by crafting a complex narrative that conflates times and space, story and storytelling. As a result, the reader is given a sense of contemporaneity, of a past brought into the present, and a present coinciding with the reader's experience.

A text such as *Murambi* not only participates in the reconstruction of collective memory but also contributes to redefining simultaneously the nature of "the unreal and edited quality of words" and that of "the literary illusion of reality" (Rancière, *The Politics of Aesthetics*, 65). This also means pushing the limits of the unbearable, the unfathomable, and the unspeakable, while at the same time reconfiguring "the territory of the visible, the thinkable and the possible" (Rancière, 65). Thus, Diop, with the writers engaged in the Duty of Memory Project, pushes the limits of African literature and redefines the meaning of the *engagé* writer.

Diop's participation in the Duty of Memory Project has had long-term consequences for his writing. If, in the short term, it meant a need to return to his mother tongue and resulted in the publication of a novel in Wolof, *Doomi Golo*,[12] as well as a collection of poems, his exploration of the history of Rwanda has also had a more enduring consequence. Published in 2006, *Kaveena* represents a turning point, both in terms of his looking at Africa's recent past, especially Senegal's, and the way that Diop renews his writing: the quest has become an investigation.

In his digging out a silenced history as in his evocation of political conniving between African states and France, and of news items such as the young Kaveena's horrible murder, Diop's writing of violence and suffering raises the question of new modes of representation of history, and of new aesthetic forms—a topic we will come back to in Chapter 3.

Similar questions about history and representation are posed by Monénembo in *Cinéma*, but through a different approach. By adopting an autobiographical or semiautobiographical narrative, Monénembo takes his readers back to the Guinea of his childhood and looks at the past through the eyes of a child. He contemplates what made the Guinean youth of his generation dream, what roles Western films and Western heroes played, and how Sekou Touré finally proved to be a pale reflection of the virtual heroes on the screen. Although depicting the world through the eyes of a child is a classic literary device, it should be noted that this was the first time Monénembo used that narrative technique combined with autobiographical references. He would use the figure of the child again in *L'aîné des orphelins*, where the representation of the child as hero and bearer of his community's traditions is, however, much more ambivalent.

Essomba's *Le dernier gardien de l'arbre* (1998) and Liking's *La mémoire amputée* (2004) also make use of the child/teenager motif, but each writer subverts that model in an original way. *La mémoire amputée* is particularly noteworthy because a female child/teenager, Halla Njoké, is the heroine, the one to lead her community forward, and the initiated transmitter of both her grandfather and her grandmother's wisdom.

Liking's training and creative works are grounded in a vision that posits the understanding of memory and the past as a condition to apprehending the present and the future. Both the organization of her Kiyi Mbock village and her fictional writing articulate her belief in the interconnectedness of ethics and aesthetics. Combining ethics and aesthetics is her way of responding to crises and dealing with reality. *La mémoire amputée* differs from Liking's previous novels, especially *Elle sera de jaspe et de corail* (1983; *It Shall Be of Jasper and Coral*, 2000) and *L'amour-cent-vies* (1988; *Love-across-a-Hundred-Lives*, 2000). Although Liking keeps the "chant roman" (song-novel) as a genre, she opts for a more immediately accessible narration. Her exploration of memory remains intrinsic to her creative vision of the artist as cultural activist; however, it becomes firmly grounded in a realistic rendition of daily life in Africa. As the character of Tante Roz stresses: "Our only truth is the memory of our memory. . . . If you really want to honor me, you should first unearth what your own memory holds. Track down its transformations and its metamorphoses" (2007, *The Amputated Memory: A Song-Novel*, 6).

Initially presented as a tribute to the pivotal women in the narrator's life, Mère Naja and Tante Roz, *La mémoire amputée* can at first glance be interpreted as a text about individual memory. Yet, beyond Halla Njoké's singular memories, Cameroonian history—particularly that of the Bassa people—emerges. The narrative structure operates with two textual devices and goals: the recognition of the importance of older women's legacy and a reinscription of the Bassa culture in Cameroonian history, particularly the anticolonial struggle and the Bassa resistance embodied by Ruben Um Nyobé.

Liking gives an interesting twist to the autobiographical vein. On the one hand, the author seems to perfectly follow Philippe Lejeune's "autobiographical pact"; on the other, the narrator simultaneously abides by traditional Bassa teachings requiring that individuals be responsible for the well-being of their community in the best way they can.

Looking at the past starts with looking inward. *La mémoire amputée* also reflects on the blank spaces of history, on the silences of Africa, its lack of reliable material, and the general absence of archives. In this way Liking underscores the artificial nature of history itself, especially in a postcolonial context: "Pull but some snatches of our Unwritten History. You know that we've been living in a context that made us choose oblivion as a survival method, a secret of life, an art of living" (6–7).

The manipulation of official archives and historical documents, on the one hand, and the silences left in the history of Cameroon, on the other, are central to Liking's narrative. In that respect, Fanny

Pigeaud's article "La guerre cachée de la France"[13] (France's hidden war) is most compelling. Addressing the lacunae and silences of the French colonial past, especially with regard to Cameroon and the fierce repression of the anticolonial movement and its leaders, Pigeaud shows that whereas France's role in Algeria during colonization is fairly well known by the French, a form of illiteracy exists when it comes to sub-Saharan countries such as Cameroon. Furthermore, as shown by Liking and Nganang's *La joie de vivre*, independence did not change the status quo. A similar silence has been perpetuated since independence by the Cameroonian government about the end of the fifties and the repression of anticolonial movements, including the extermination of Bassas and Bamilekes.[14]

Metaphorically, Halla Njoké's father's deep transformations mimic those of the country. Photographs keep track of the successive changes he undergoes: pictures show him as a maître d', a nurse, a soldier, and a civil servant. As he climbs the social ladder, he dissociates himself from his village and his family. Won over by the colonial system, he collaborates with the State, both during and after the colonial period: "There was nothing but alarming news about my father: he had become a consultant to the Whites, a 'collaborator,' as this new class of people was known from that time on" (66). His collaboration includes helping the authorities hunt down the legendary Mpôdôl and his followers hiding out in the bush. "Mpôdôl," in the language of the Bassa, means "the one who carries the demands of the people," hence the prophet, the spokesperson. It is a direct reference to Um Nyobé who was Bassa and emblematic of the anticolonial struggle.

Through the eyes of a girl and her recollections of certain events, Liking uncovers the parts of Cameroonian history left in the shadow and the deeply rooted culture of political resistance against the centralized State among Bassa and Bamileke peoples. Both Liking and Nganang represent the fierce repression that took place against the Bassas and the Bamilekes in the late 1950s. Tante Roz is especially interesting as a character because of her involvement in grassroots resistance: "She was the main resistance organizer in the region. . . . She had made the food supply and rationing completely subservient to her by becoming its director's mistress. She could therefore collect all the leftovers from the officers' mess and have the women make them into meals again before she deposited them outside the camp, for the resistance fighters to pick up. Indeed, for three years, the Bondjock battalion unwittingly provided the resistance with sugar, milk, smoked fish. . . . She also organized small teams to sabotage the machinery intended for opening the road to the Elephant Forest" (65). Contrasted with her collaborationist brother, her character invites the reader to rethink women's role in the Cameroonian nationalist struggle and indirectly sheds new light on the meaning of tradition and traditional values.

Liking approaches the issue of power and corruption, and that of the heroic figure and its death, through "the meanders of memory."[15] The changes undergone by Cameroonian society, namely the deconstruction of the family and of rural life, the consequences of urbanization on the youth, and the father's loss of a culturally relevant "groundedness" become metaphors for the changes undergone by the nation, and its failures. Through her own recollections, the narrator also braces herself to speak out about her personal silences and traumas. The title, *La mémoire amputée*, is, in that respect, indicative of a symbolic violence to be juxtaposed with the sexual abuse Halla Njoké has been subjected to by her father. The representation of this traumatic experience enables Liking to "break the emptiness of silence"[16] that primarily affects women and to broach issues that are taboo, such as incest.

By extending to her entire community and beyond, Liking becomes a kind of *griotte*, the storyteller, the *Hilun*[17] of the Bassa people, and by extension, of the Cameroonian community. Liking thus expands on the legacy of the previous generation of writers, such as Mongo Beti, Kourouma, and Tchicaya U Tam'si, and their explorations of collective history at the time of anticolonial struggle. However, unlike her predecessors, who "relegated legends, myths, and the personal to the background, privileging historical facts over memories" (Mongo-Mboussa, "Les méandres de la mémoire" [The meanders of memory], 68), Liking adopts an approach whereby she starts from memory to guide her readers toward history. She does this through personal recollections engaging her readers in an interactive process of reconstruction and of piecing events and memories together.

Although the central preoccupation of Nganang's *La joie de vivre* (2003) is likewise to represent the nationalist struggle, in this case the struggle of the Bamilekes of western Cameroon from the mid-1950s to the mid-1970s, he adopts a different narrative technique, particularly in regard to character delineation and buildup. Liking conveys history through an elaborate portrayal of characters; Nganang, in contrast, and in this novel in particular, chooses to ground his story in specific facts and dates and offers a more stylized characterization. In *La joie de vivre*, the sociohistorical and political context is intrinsically part of the narration, and the protagonists become mere embodiments of the rival forces that are part of the dynamic of the country's history.

In *Le principe dissident* (The principle of dissidence, 2005), Nganang highlights two seemingly contradictory aspects of Cameroonian society. On the one hand, newspapers and news reports seem to indicate that absolutely nothing is happening: the facts related in the press reflect banal current events. On the other hand, one has the persistent feeling that that state of relative "peace" is fragile and that, in fact, the superficial banality of daily life covers up deep-seated silences and fears: "This fear of war, every Bamileke recognizes it in the eyes of his parents, who experienced the unrest of the 1950s, when they say: '*ntchou ke' baa'sa—war is not a game.*' And I am a Bamileke." Nganang underscores the idea that "things can fall apart at any moment" (18), as happened in Ivory Coast, for example: "Yes, we are all aware of it, even if we do not say it clearly enough, even if our streets are quiet and our newspapers deadly boring, we live on the verge of the nightmare. Each of our parents trying to send his child abroad does so with the certainty that misfortune is already near" (19).

Drawing a parallel between a hardware store owner, his parents' neighbor, who used to frantically sell machetes without necessarily understanding the implications of his action, and the situation in Rwanda in 1994, Nganang reintroduced this scene in *La joie de vivre*, in the context of the 1950s, "to commemorate another genocide, perpetrated from 1956 to 1970 in the high plains of Cameroon's western region, in Bamiléké country, in the *grassfield*, and for which no one has yet been punished. I used it to describe my elders' despair and their entry into the tunnel of a fear that they have not yet shed, the fear of our dispossession, first by Ahmadou Ahidjo's regime and then by Biya's, with the well-known support of France which, as in Rwanda, will have had a hand in mass murder" (20).

However, if *La joie de vivre* uses the 1950s and some episodes of the anticolonial struggle, notably the ruthless repression of the Bamilekes, and if the historical and sociopolitical context is an intrinsic part of the narrative and the protagonists are symbolic representations of the different rival forces that make for the dynamics of the country's history, the novel is also concerned with contemporary, and popular, Cameroon. In fact, as was the case with *Temps de chien* (2001), this book attempts to take the pulse of the country.

Nganang uses the same point of departure as Liking, the mid-1950s, and guides his readers through a changing "homeland." Moving from yesterday to today, he depicts the ethnic tensions and the Bamilekes' genocide, and alludes to the different phases in the U.P.C. (Union des Populations du Cameroun) resistance, Ahmadou Ahidjo's becoming Cameroon's first president, the 1970s and the *Ahidjoïsation* of the country, the urban centers of Douala and Yaoundé, the uprising against Paul Biya, Ahidjo's successor, and finally, the consequences of these transformations on the common people.

If, by respecting the chronology of events and inscribing his narrative in specific dates and events, Nganang strengthens "l'effet de réel" in his book, he also cloaks his protagonists, Mambo, Mboma, and Kemi, in the myth. His treatment of the myth, however, departs from that of Liking and Boni because of its jovial and sharp, cinematic and sketch-like qualities. Mambo, Mboma, and Kemi are at the roots of a bittersweet reflection on today's Cameroon. Monstrous and innocent, wicked and resilient, they are marked by the exceptional circumstances of their birth and by the adverse determinism of their ghetto-like surroundings.

Mambo and Mboma are twins locked in a fiercely hostile opposition regarding who was born first and who will assume authority over the other. The figure of twins in literature is nothing new. Yet, from Bolya Baenga's *Cannibale* (1986) to Mongo Beti's *L'histoire du fou* (1994) to Dongala's *Les petits garçons naissent aussi des étoiles* (1998; *Little Boys Also Come from the Stars*, 2001), the theme has developed fruitfully in francophone African literature.[18] Kemi, Mbambo's and Mboma's sister, transforms the script associated with twins: born within a few months after their birth, she is often mistaken by others as their triplet. Mambo and Mboma's length of gestation, the time between their deliveries and that of their sister, all contribute to creating an ambiguous atmosphere in which the myth is repeatedly subverted or tested. The entire family plays on that confusion, using it to its advantage when necessary, for instance when they try to escape the cleansing of Bamilekes and flee to Douala.

As noted in Chapter 1, Nganang can be placed in Mongo Beti's literary lineage, especially in his fictional inscription of Cameroonian resistance movements and traditions. Mongo Beti, however, relied heavily on history, on a classic use of the French language and Greco-

Roman myths, and on literary realism, whereas Nganang depends on a subverted interpretation of the myth and infuses his writing with the vernacular. Both writers converge in grounding their texts in the *principe dissident*, in their self-avowed allegiance to the common people of Cameroon, and in their construction of fallible heroic figures. Nganang emphasizes the many weaknesses of his protagonists, underlining their lack of awareness, their failure to read their social and political environment, and their unquestioned sense of doom. He shows the general effects of economic poverty on the choices people make or feel they can make, and on their view of themselves and what they feel they can do with their lives—not just in economic terms. In that respect, *La joie de vivre*'s narrative communicates an idea coined by Mongo Beti, that of *la politique de l'édredon* (the politics of the down comforter) because it describes Biya's regime's stifling of its citizens' political will and hopes.

Finally, Liking and Nganang both perpetuate and dismantle a number of familiar representations of colonial and postcolonial life in Africa. They make it clear that internecine rivalries and the political persecution of the Bassas and Bamilekes can no longer be attributed to the colonizers only. In doing so, they revisit the Fanonian understanding of colonial and postcolonial violence.

With *Cinéma*, Monénembo continues to put pressure on the contradictions in African history. He demonstrates that the cinematic genre of the western is a locus of Western mythmaking and raises the following questions: First, how does the Western mythmaking model inform the figure of the African national hero, in this case, the type of hero, or political leader, promoted in Guinea during that period? Second, how was this kind of fascination for the white man, and this model of masculinity and power, not readily perceived as a total contradiction of the values of self-sufficiency, cultural self-reliance, and political enfranchisement that were heralded by official discourse? Third, to what extent did the western contribute to the long-term identification of generations of Africans (and people all over the world) with the American west, and determine their dreams of immigration?

What the different novels in this section highlight is the renewed interest in history. Unlike their predecessors and the Négritude voices, these writers do not aim to evoke the beauty and cultural riches of their respective countries but to confront the errors, weaknesses, and silences of their history. *Cinéma* (1997), *Le cavalier et son om-*

bre (1997), *La joie de vivre* (2003), *La mémoire amputée* (2004)—all proceed from that perspective. Departing from a necessarily realist representational mode of history, they create aesthetics offering a new inscription of the political (unconscious).[19]

REVAMPING AND SUBVERTING THE MYTH

Generally understood, a myth is a "traditional story concerning the early history of a people and typically involving supernatural beings or phenomena."[20] The myth is not truth and can be a misrepresentation of it.

In *Myth, Literature, and the African World* (1990), Soyinka points to the connection between myth, ritual, and "the self-apprehension of the African world" (ix). He explains, "[I]n Asian and European antiquity. . . . Man did, like the African, exist within a cosmic totality, did possess a consciousness in which his own earth being, his gravity-bound apprehension of self, was inseparable from the entire cosmic phenomenon. (For let it always be recalled that myths arise from man's attempt to externalize and communicate his inner intuitions)" (3). Kane's *L'aventure ambiguë* (1961) already pointed to this idea, showing that the colonial experience had shattered the traditional sense of cosmic totality and challenged African people's sense of their cultural centeredness. The Négritude movement tried to remedy this problem by exalting the values and beauty of African historical and cultural productions. The myth was central to this attempt at reanchoring the African psyche in a proud sense of heritage. Négritude, however, modified the function of myth. It evolved from an instrument for social conformity, adherence to and perpetuation of cultural values, to a romantic rallying, which in turn affected what Soyinka calls the Africans' "self-apprehension."

The "enduring militant" writers we referred to in our first chapter renegotiated Négritude's tenets by exposing the fractures of the colonial world, especially in subverting the myth. Most of them used derision to that effect. Mongo Beti did so by appropriating the Greco-Roman mythology and using it as a lever to both denounce Eurocentrism and expose the imperialism inherent in its heroic figures. Sony Labou Tansi went a different way. Combining magic realism with the baroque and derision, he featured a tragically jubilant subversion of the myth. Monénembo's engagement with the myth is subtle but recurrent. The mythological elements he intersperses in his works function as clues (*clefs*). They provide an additional textual layering that the reader may decode. Among the new generations of writers, Bessora gives us a farcical writing of history and its myths, for instance in *53 cm* through the character of Saartje Boorman. The myth is divorced from its traditional interpretation and is derisively rendered as both a mystification of history and a historical mystification.

There is an oxymoronic quality to the enduring militants' subversion of the myth. Although they mock the traditional definition of the myth and underline its oppressive and blinding nature, they concomitantly expand on its literary representations. Thus, interestingly, these writers have contributed to a richer dramatization of the myth and to a critical examination of its relation to the concepts of origin and authenticity.

That relation was probed further by African critics of younger generations, such as Mbembe, who, in *On the Postcolony* (2001), links the myth to the West's difficulty in recognizing the African Subject: "But it must not be forgotten that, almost universally, the simplistic and narrow prejudice persists that African social formations belong to a specific category, that of simple societies or of traditional societies. That such a prejudice has been emptied of all substance by recent criticism seems to make absolutely no difference." Mbembe emphasizes that not only does the understanding of the myth remain eurocentric, but it is also emptied of substance: "[N]arrative about Africa is always pretext for a comment about something else, some other place, some other people. More precisely, Africa is the mediation that enables the West to accede to its own subconscious and give a public account of its subjectivity" (3).

Today, the myth is crafted in a variety of ways in francophone African literatures.[21] Regarding African literature in French, three main approaches can be identified: First, Effa reconnects with Soyinka's definition of the myth as a basis for self-apprehension. Second, authors such as Boni and Tadjo revisit foundational myths to understand mechanisms ruling modern African societies and gauge their potential for change. Third, Raharimanana and Rakotoson use myths of precolonial and colonial resistance to represent the continuing struggles in postcolonial Madagascar and do justice to Malagasy history.

GASTON-PAUL EFFA

For Effa, myth is not truth; it is the means to search for it, to ground his quest for "self-apprehension" in the cultural ferment of his coun-

try of origin. Although the conjuring of the mythic Cameroon is the
main impetus behind his writing, it no longer exists outside his imagination. Effa's approach to the myth has an essentialist quality because
it is ontological and concerned with the intimate nature of Being.
Tout ce bleu and *Mâ*, for instance, do not tell a story. Rather, they
describe the tremors of the soul. In Effa's novels what matters are not
the relationships between characters, or what happens to them, but
the extent to which their suffering has a transformative and redemp-
tive value, and the ways it puts the protagonist in touch with his or
her sense of self. Effa's chiseled use of the French language reveals an
existential rapport with writing and the narrative process. The word
is the tool with which to carry out the necessary quest. It ultimately allows for the trauma of origin to be told so as to be reinvented
and transcended: "Every day, the writer invents both the son and the
mother" (2002, *All That Blue*, 39). The old myth of the mother's sacrifice is revisited as the emphasis shifts to the tearing apart of child
from mother (*Tout ce bleu*) and mother from child (*Mâ*). From then
on, the narrative is subsumed by the idea of separation, on which it
rhapsodizes.

With *Le cri que tu pousses ne réveillera personne*, Cameroon disappears from the narrative. The mythic country is no longer culturally identifiable and becomes more generically African. The aesthetic
of the scream that was already operative in *Tout ce bleu* and *Mâ* is ac-
centuated. We will examine more specifically what we mean by "aesthetic of the scream" in our next chapter, but let it be said for now
that we link this notion to Soyinka's conception of "stridency." Soyinka applied that concept to the 1970s generation of African writers
and saw it as a reaction to "threats to [their] self-apprehension" (xi).
He opposed it to the romanticization of the myth by Négritude writers. Regarding Effa's production, three things are at work: First, the
notion of stridency is still applicable, although outside the context of
Négritude. Second, the lyrical and essentialist nature of Effa's writing
and the strong emotions at the core of his narratives lend a romantic quality to his oeuvre. Third, the "scream" counteracts a romantic
interpretation of Effa's work by renewing the function of the myth.
Here, the myth operates as a means to anchor oneself in African/
Cameroonian culture. It also helps the writer come to terms with the
fact that he is Cameroonian by birth but was cut off from his familial
roots early on to be educated by French Jesuits, and then to live and
write in France.

TANELLA BONI AND VÉRONIQUE TADJO

Boni's *Les baigneurs du lac rose* proposes a stratified approach to memory. The story is constructed around a series of juxtapositions. The fictional characters double up with heroic and mythic Western and African figures: Yêté/Samori, Yêté/César, César/Fred Ogun, Yêté/Lénie, Lénie/Diane. This thematic interweaving operates in relation to the "imaginary pantheon" referred to in the title of the first chapter and sets the tone for the general demystification of the myth at the core of this book. An additional dimension is created through a blurring of geographical borders, the merging of certain places into one (for example, Abidjan and Paris, Africa and Europe), and the erasure of the distinctions between past and present.

A meditative reflection, *Les baigneurs du lac rose* hinges on three concepts: history, (story)telling, and gender. The intellectual and literary intent of the book is to inscribe daily life in the myth. Through a reworking of the myth of Samori, the legendary nineteenth-century warrior who founded the Mandinka Empire and resisted French rule, it aims at reassessing the link between official and popular history. In her quest for the truth about Samori, Lénie tries to dissociate history from the idea of conquest and asks who the "real" heroes in African history are.

In *Les baigneurs du lac rose*, Boni ponders the history of her generation. The themes of history and memory blend as the book fictionally conjures up the memory of the struggles Africans of this specific age group faced. Yêté, Lénie's lover—who is said to have taken his baccalaureate exam during the Vietnam War—is at the center of this reconsideration.

Each character in the novel has a specific relationship to the act of enunciation—and hence, to the rhetorics of personal and political engagement. Caught in the flow of his words, Yêté is a compulsive storyteller, and his stories make sense only to those who engage in what he is saying. There is an uncompromising sincerity about Yêté's attitude and choices. At the end of the book, when Lénie and he meet again after a long period of separation during which she has searched for him, Yêté has become a painter. His discourse has moved from the written to the figurative, thereby opening new avenues for communication and interpretation. Silence is no longer an absence of words, but an accepted fact of communication.

Lénie's relationship to elocution is also transformed in the course of the book. At the beginning, she feels that she is able to communicate only by reporting events as a journalist and that, unlike Yêté, she is unable to become a *griot(te)*. As the narration proceeds, though, and her investigation into Samori's life and deeds gains focus, she learns how to weave a tale. She acquires the status of storyteller as well as that of historian through her deconstruction of the myth of Samori as a masculinist model of conquest.[22] In contrast, César, who, in their younger days, was Yêté's principled, if cocky, comrade-in-struggle, has become a smooth talker. His speech and manner are expected, scripted, and vain. He no longer cares whether he engages his interlocutor or not; his discourse has closed in on itself.

Thus, the narrative dynamic of *Les baigneurs du lac rose* represents the multifaceted relationship between speech and power, and between speech and (political/emotional/artistic) commitment. The ways in which Yêté and Lénie wrestle with their ideals, and their long and winding road toward themselves and each other, feature a vision of human existence in which engagement endeavors to be free of dogma. The following passage evoking Lénie and Yêté's reunion shows that Boni also built her narrative on the relation between speech, commitment, and desire: "He had taken back these words that circulated like old women's tales, authorless, carried by the wind. And suddenly, he felt an immeasurable pleasure at appropriating these words, neither true nor false, which allowed him to welcome a woman passing by, unannounced like the rain" (27). Through her characters, and more particularly Yêté and Lénie, Boni proposes that historical configurations may possibly be reinterpreted and new male and female heroic figures constructed. She also calls for a new relational model between women and men whereby commitment makes room for the fluctuations of time and desire.

Boni's work on gender in this book may, however, seem paradoxical. On the one hand, the writer takes her characters away from sexual determinism by inscribing them in a passionate relationship based on change and respect. On the other hand, her construction of a feminine/gendered memory causes her narrative to lean on a problematic mix of feminism and essentialism. *Les baigneurs du lac rose* contains a number of assertions that take away from the otherwise thought-provoking gender analysis crafted within the narrative. While a "woman's memory" (93) is a notion worth debating, if only for the prevalence of the idea in other women's texts, notably Liking's and Tadjo's for francophone African literature, and for its centrality in the theoretical debate on the inscription of women in collective memory, Lénie's assertion that "all men are wandering conquerors" (85) seems tautological. It falls short of the complex reworking of history proposed by the novel and trivializes the book's poetic appeal for more political representation for (African) women (121).

Why did Yêtê disappear for so long when he loved Lénie? Why could he not fight with/for her? Will they *find* each other? What is the historically operating value of Samori as a heroic African figure?[23] What did he stand for in the imagination of African peoples, particularly those in their twenties when their countries gained independence? What does he represent to their counterparts today? Does he embody the same hopes and projections? Has history shown that the idea of a hero must be done away with? Or will the recognition and creation of heroines reshape our collective myths for the best? *Les baigneurs du lac rose* does not give any answers, and thankfully so. It leaves these questions for each reader to ponder.

Other factors contribute to the specific elaboration of memory in *Les baigneurs du lac rose*: First, the book was written in the mid-1990s, as intolerance, racism, and violence were growing in Ivory Coast, and Boni engaged in a process of making sense of the situation through the means of literary fiction. Second, references to Oradour-sur-Glane as well as the struggles of different generations of African students in France show that Boni's understanding of memory in *Les baigneurs du lac rose* is informed by, and pushes against, the process of re-memorialization that started in France in the 1980s and picked up steam in the 1990s. In that respect, the book's reiterated injunction to "dream history" extends to both Africa and France (87). It points to the need to see through history books and official commemorations and makes laughter (read: a humorous critical sense) the necessary condition for understanding our societies' evo/convo/lutions. Third, *Les baigneurs* challenges ideological definitions of history and African literature as (stereotypically) *engagée*. Cloaking the theme of memory in the myth, Boni runs the risk of writing a demanding book, one not readily accessible to most readers.

L'ombre d'Imana: voyages jusqu'au bout du Rwanda (2000) marked a departure from Tadjo's previous work. Writing about the 1994 genocide in Rwanda pushed her to examine the context of Ivory Coast, this time through the foundational myth of Queen Pokou's sacrifice and the advent of the Baoule kingdom.

Reine Pokou is divided into three parts: "Le temps de la légende"

(Telling the legend), "Le temps du questionnement" (Questioning the legend), and "Le temps de l'enfant-oiseau" (The bird-child). The first part presents a fairly faithful account of Reine Pokou's legend, as it is generally known and taught at school. Part 2, which is more developed and subdivided into five sections, questions the legend and the veracity of history: "But is the legend true? Did the waters really part to let the fugitive people go?" (42).

The recurrence of this central question signals Tadjo's need to query the meaning of Queen Pokou's sacrifice. Inasmuch as the idea of sacrifice was central to the "enduring militants" generation and to the politics of nation building, one could consider that Tadjo is asking if there are returns for such sacrifice, and if notions of a collective subject and a common struggle are still valid. Taking the question one step further, she wonders how a mother could sacrifice her child and asks why it is that women are always the ones asked to sacrifice themselves: "Why is it always that women see their sons leave? Why is it that love is not strong enough to stop the war, to protect them from death?" (42). The essentialist assumption that mothers are more peaceful and more likely to speak out against war is not what is at stake here. Although Tadjo never really questions the prescription of motherhood as the epitome of woman's plenitude, she does rebel against a prescriptive notion of power, specifically when it comes to women. Reflecting on the meaning of rituals, legends, and myth, she proceeds to think of five other possible scenarios and ways to rewrite the legend.

The first reinterpretation imagines Queen Pokou unable to survive her loss and throwing herself into the river to join her son. A figure of Mamy Watta, she destructively seduces both men and women, while her "ocean-child" remains pure of any wickedness, untouched by man's greed.[24] In this version, Tadjo weaves through the metaphor of original purity and develops the myth of the child as the bearer of supernatural forces and wisdom. The use of the conditional mode insists on possibility rather than on dogma.

In the second reinterpretation, the author imagines a scenario whereby Pokou refuses to sacrifice her child and instead exhorts her people to fight. The narrative unfolds as follows: after initially being given protection in a village, mother and child are found out and sold as slaves to the white man. Here, Tadjo ties Pokou's legend to the history of slavery. In doing so, she questions Africa's responsibility in the trade, in "la grande trahison" (60) (the great treason). The dehumanizing experience of enslavement and of the forced passage is conveyed by the metonymic use of body parts to speak of men and women: "In the holds, body against body, tossed about by the waves, they crashed into the damp walls. The salt deepened their wounds. The excrements rotted their flesh. The stifling stench. The vomit. Only the rats celebrated the feast" (58).

Tadjo creates a sequence of narration and experiences combining myth and history, tying together the origins, the ancestral land, exile, and slavery. Evoking the "Maroon slaves' revolt," Tadjo imagines a new scenario whereby Pokou's son and his brother (born on the forced passage) are among the leaders of the rebellion, later to be caught and hanged. Pokou survives them and finds a new freedom, but remains alone following these events. As in Tadjo's previous works of prose and poetry, the narration is articulated around a number of fundamental questions such as "What was the point of suffering?" (61). In this picture of the great exile, memory serves as anchoring, the last mooring in the ancestral land and the last hope to return. Forgetting is one more step to one's estrangement, while "new beliefs [are] making headway" (61).

In the third reinterpretation of Pokou's sacrifice, Pokou follows the diviners' order, sacrifices her son, and lets herself fulfill her political destiny as queen of the Baoulé people. However, in journeying with them to find a place to settle, the remembrance of her child comes back to haunt and torment her. This section can be likened to "la colère des morts" ("The Anger of the Dead") in *L'ombre d'Imana* in that it insists on the need to remember the dead and honor them properly. The narrative conveys that a sense of completion and normalcy can return only once the funerary rites have been performed and the living are at peace with the dead. In order to cure Pokou of her obsession with her son, it is recommended that a statue of the child be carved. This statuette operates as a substitute (or fetish) for the child and as a phallic symbol. There are two different ways of looking at this representation. One is to consider that art takes on its full potential as a form of healing and salvation. Because of the substitution and the respect of rituals, a natural balance is reestablished, and Queen Pokou and the Baoulé are able to find a new beginning: "Then, in that very place, the people erected a new city, they built a new life, found hope" (73). Another possible interpretation is that Pokou caressing the statuette manifests her desire for the phallus and her lack ("manque") thereof—which obliquely poses the question of women and power in psychoanalytic terms.

In the next rewrite, Tadjo approaches the legend from yet another angle whereby the child's father is given a voice. He is no longer a warrior as in the original legend, but a Muslim merchant traveling north, who brings Pokou presents from faraway places. Tadjo picks up the narration as Pokou's reputation suffers from her prolonged celibacy and barrenness. The writer thus creates a stark, albeit fairly conventional, contrast between Karim's amorous discourse, awakening Pokou to love anew, and their confrontation when she contemplates sacrificing their child and he tries to convince her otherwise. From that moment on, Pokou makes it clear that the child is hers and her people's, but the father's beliefs (including religious ones) are not hers. She carries out her decision and throws the child into the tumultuous waters while she has Karim executed. Blinded by her thirst for power, Pokou cuts herself from the ties that made her human. The section returns to the initial question about motherhood, maternal feelings, and power, and points to their possible incompatibility: "It is said that a woman can experience the highest forms of power only by refusing motherhood. Did Pokou sacrifice her son for that reason?" (80).

The last section, "Les paroles du poète" (The poet's words), tries to imagine yet another possible scenario: that Pokou's son might have been replaced by a nephew or the son of a slave, or might not have been a child but a young man who stepped forward and offered to be sacrificed. As in Tadjo's previous works, the third and final part of *Reine Pokou* leaves us on a hopeful note, the spirit of the child protecting the community from high above.

MICHÈLE RAKOTOSON'S *LALANA* AND JEAN-LUC RAHARIMANANA'S *NOUR, 1947*

Several of Rakotoson's novels explore Malagasy roots. In *Le bain des reliques* (The bath of relics, 1988), the author looks at traditional rituals and brings her readers to reflect on the sociopolitical structures of the country. In *Henoÿ—fragments en écorce* (Henoÿ—bark fragments, 1998), Rakotoson renews one of the Western myths par excellence, the Orpheic myth, and the way love and death are intertwined. As in the Orpheic myth, Tiana, searching for Bodo, crosses the River of Death. Through her choice of a male protagonist, her evocation of a man searching for the woman he loves in hell, Rakotoson finds a way to connect her readers to the infernal quality of Malagasy colonial history. In doing so, the author debunks the traditionally exotic image of the "Mascareigne islands," of the Baudelairian "Aimer et Mourir" invitation, rejecting thereby the woman-as-island metaphor, of women circumscribed within a certain frame.[25] Rakotoson transforms the myth of love and death, taking the reader down the path of the Malagasy past and memory, eventually to raise the fundamental question: Should we, and can we, resist our past? Like Raharimanana in *Nour, 1947*, Rakotoson invites her readers to confront history.

With *Lalana* (2002), Rakotoson carries on her exploration of Malagasy history, where individual and collective memories, the distant past and the present now intersect. Through the story of two young male students, Rivo, terminally ill, and his companion, Naivo, who accompanies him on his last trip to the seashore—Rivo's last wish—Rakotoson addresses the issue of AIDS and touches on the stigmas attached to homosexuality in Africa. It should be noted that few francophone African writers—Ken Bugul, Angèle Rawiri, Sami Tchak, Frieda Ekotto, and Leonora Miano—have addressed the topic of homosexuality, albeit sometimes only in passing. Here, Rakotoson denounces the social rejection frequently associated with AIDS in a country where people are deprived of the most basic necessities and denied access to medication.

Like Boni's *Les baigneurs du lac rose*, *Lalana* is articulated on a series of juxtapositions. Rivo and Naivo's journey to the seaside runs parallel to another journey, that of Queen Rasoaherina, and before her, her ancestors, King Radama Ier and his aunt Ranavalona.[26] The metaphors for illness and suffering are combined with images of decay, erring spirits, and mortuary rituals. The reader is taken along on this trip to an in-between land of dream and folly, where the daily tragic drama of Rivo's suffering cohabits with Naivo's feelings of anger, fear, and repulsion about this trip, where modern Madagascar cohabits with the immemorial times of Malagasy dynasties. The evocation of mortuary rituals, of Christian religious practice and rituals in daily gestures and behavior, contributes to an intimate blending of yesterday and today.

Rivo's meeting with death coincides with the readers' meeting with history. Individual memory intersects with the Malagasy people's collective memory of the dead. The final scene of Rivo's drowning as he walks into the waves and Naivo collapses on the shore, unable to save him, acts as a catalyst for the surge of both memory and history. Naivo laying Rivo to rest in the sea can also be read as his giving Rivo back to "la mère" as *côtiers'* (coastal) traditions call for. By paralleling the two journeys, that of Rivo and that of the queen, and fusing yesterday and today, Rakotoson seeks to enable Malagasy people, at least those literate in French, to reconnect with and reappropriate their history in a very personal, intimate way. Thus she brings history back into the present moment, adding to its meaning and life. In this context, the seashore and the coast become *lieux de mémoire*, "the ultimate embodiments of a memorial consciousness that has barely survived in a historical age that calls out for memory because it has abandoned it" (Nora, *Realms of Memory*, 12).

Nour, 1947 marks a turning point in Raharimanana's career. This first novel represents a more complex literary endeavor, particularly with regard to composition, to the weaving in of history, and to the elaboration of characters that, in the author's preceding texts, had remained mere sketches. However, one finds in *Nour, 1947* the familiar and recurrent figures of Raharimanana's narrative world: women with torn bellies, children throwing themselves off a cliff and crashing on the rocks below (12–13), Dziny, the mythical female ancestor.

The composition of *Nour, 1947* is extremely elaborate, and it does not fit a classic conception of the novel. The book is structured in seven "nights" spanning from November 5 to 11, 1947, and duly dated. Each chapter (or "night") has subparts with titles of landmarks in Malagasy and French colonial history: "Ambahy," "La grande île," "La Jonquière," "Tsimiamboho, le camp de ceux-qui-ne-tournent-pas-le-dos." These subparts also include references to specific historical periods,[27] excerpts from diaries written by different Catholic missionaries in dire straits in Madagascar, and mythical passages cryptically recounting the stories of the main characters, four political militants. These characters are evoked for the first time only during the "Third Night," and the character of Nour comes up only on page 71 of this 212-page book. Benja, Nour's long-lost brother, and the other nationalists, Jao and Siva, appear in the next chapter.

Nour, 1947 is also an in-depth intellectual inquiry into the thousand and one layers of Malagasy history. This novel is demanding of its reader, who needs to be aware of the historical references to fully understand the writer's approach. This does not mean, however, that *Nour, 1947* is strictly a historical analysis; it is among other things a magnificent literary opera. And the discontinuous logic that weaves and unweaves the narrative allows for the question of memory to stay at its center and to generate new spaces of interpretation.

The historical events that ground the narrative range from Madagascar's first colonization by the Maltese and the Polynesians to the great nationalist movement of 1947 and its ferocious repression by the French colonial power.[28] Between these two poles, Raharimanana alludes to many events and periods: the arrival of the first Europeans in the sixteenth century, the long struggle for influence between Protestant and Catholic missionaries, the battles between the ancestral kingdoms and the assertion of the Merina dynasty at the end of the eighteenth century, the reigns of Ranavalona I and II in the nineteenth century, French colonization from 1896 on, Galliéni's "politique des races," Ranavalona III's exile, World War I and the (often forced) drafting of Malagasy men to defend the "motherland," the birth of nationalist sentiment, World War II, the defeat and occupation of France, the Pétain government and the Holocaust, the rise of political consciousness among Malagasy students and demobilized Malagasy soldiers in France and on the island, the occupation of Madagascar by the English, the "Libération," and the return of the French order. As the following excerpt shows, the writer is the one who, by reconceiving History, gathers the multiple "thread[s] of time," fights against collective amnesia, and conjures up the possibility of national togetherness: "Forgotten. Everything forgotten. We have closed our eyes so tight on our origins that the thread of time broke and made us blind. Who can now boast about knowing where we really come from? We have lost our past and our time is thus scratched. Our present limps, our future fades away. . . . Will we know one day that we used to be one nation?" (21).

This literary reconstruction of Madagascar's history is interesting in several ways: First, *Nour, 1947* encapsulates Malagasy history until the end of 1947. It does not mention another, more recent, emblematic moment of Malagasy nationalism, the 1972 student demonstrations that led to President Philibert Tsiranana's departure. The 1972 demonstrations are broached elsewhere in Raharimanana's fiction, in his short story "Anja." Second, the character of Nour does not appear for the first time in the novel by the same name, but in "Les Conquérants" (The conquerors), a short story in *Rêves sous le linceul* (Shrouded dreams, 1998). In "Les Conquérants," Nour represents the founding maternal figure, mythical and mystifying. Third, the date of November 1947 appeared first in another of *Rêves*'s short stories, "Fahavalo," in which the writer took pains to indicate in a footnote that "fahavalo" meant "enemy" and was a "term used by the French colonialists to refer to the Malagasy insurgents between 1896 and 1946" (71).

In this context, then, *Nour, 1947* is also an attempt to synthesize what Malagasy identity might mean today as well as the island's current potential for subversion. Working on memory, Raharimanana aims at going beyond ethnicism. It is noteworthy that the endogenous myths evoked in his work do not exclusively belong to the author's ethnic origin. This is an important element in Raharimanana's positioning regarding his country of origin and his Malagasy readership.

Nour, 1947 is not an ill-assorted collection of fragments; it is a puzzle, an exercise in making disparate elements converge. It is a renegotiation of historical and linguistic fractures and polarized identities. *Nour, 1947*'s polyphonic quality aims at raising the following questions: Who speaks for the various voices in Madagascar? Which of these voices are heard? Which voices produce significant echoes? These questions are essential to the island's political life and particularly interesting when one considers the importance of consensus in the traditional Malagasy understanding of the decision-making process.

The oppressor/oppressed paradigm is neither a unifying principle of Madagascar's history nor a narrative principle in *Nour, 1947*. If this novel brings back to memory the horrors of French colonization as well as the symbolic moments in the nationalist protest movement, it does not articulate nationalism as the manifestation of a primordial collective claim. As it is depicted in the novel, anticolonial nationalism opens up possibilities of unification but also highlights historical fault lines. The passage below clearly communicates that all aspects of colonization need to be reexamined.

> Then other men came. . . . They talked to us of other gods—of a single, other, god. . . . Did we become aware of our profound unity through the prism of the "other"—the unity of our languages, the unity of our gods? Did we let go of our narrow vision of the world? . . . We sold them our brothers and companions as slaves. . . . We were unable or unwilling to believe that they were coming to us not as a man meeting another man, but as a master to his slave. . . . We did not know that they negated our very humanity. But were we ready for that—we who once believed we were the only men on earth? (21–22)

To summarize, a number of novels show a definite attempt to reconcile with traditional values: whether with the "Earth"—Effa and Tadjo—or with the therapeutic value of the myth—as in Lamko's *La phalène des collines* (2000), Liking's *L'amour-cent-vies* (1988),

Tadjo's *Le royaume aveugle* (1990; *The Blind Kingdom*, 2008) and *L'ombre d'Imana* (2000), Boni's *L'atelier des génies* (The genies' workshop, 2001) and Sow Fall's *Le jujubier du patriarche* (1993). At the same time, the pressure that Tadjo applies to the Reine Pokou foundational myth invites readers to challenge the metaphorical process of cognition constructing the myth as the social binding of the nation. Here, unlike in Effa's work, the myth is disconnected from the notion of origin. Similarly, in interrogating history further, Boni, Raharimanana, Rakotoson, and Tadjo participate in the reconfiguration of the hero traditional to official history and to history itself.

"RWANDA: ECRIRE PAR DEVOIR DE MÉMOIRE" / THE DUTY OF MEMORY PROJECT

In 1998, ten writers were invited by Fest'Africa, an annual African festival of literature and cinema taking place in Lille, France, to participate in a writing-in-residence program. This project was called "Rwanda: Ecrire par devoir de mémoire" (The Duty of Memory Project), and mostly included authors who had been guests at the festival since its inception in 1993. The premise of the project was that there was a critical need to break the general silence in Africa regarding the 1994 genocide in Rwanda and allow Africans to speak out on this dramatic issue, especially given the fact that most of what had been written on the subject had been produced by Western journalists or scholars.

The project was funded through two main sources: the Fondation de France contributed 700,000 French francs in 1998 to enable the writers to spend two months in residence in Rwanda. Three million French francs were also allocated by the European Union in 2000. This made it possible for Fest'Africa to organize a large-scale festival in Kigali in June 2000, during which the authors' works were presented to Rwandans, and to which French and francophone journalists and writers not writing for the project were also invited (for instance, Raharimanana, Yves Simon, Colette Braeckman). The now late Senegalese filmmaker Félix N'diaye's *Rwanda-Mémoire* used the festival and the project as a point of departure to reflect on postgenocide Rwanda. *Rhizome,* a play by Lamko, created from excerpts of the books produced by the different authors in the Duty of Memory Project, was performed on stage during the festival and thereafter toured in Africa and Europe. It should be noted that the actors and extras originated from many different African countries.

The ten authors involved in this project were Diop, Monénembo, Waberi, Tadjo, Lamko, Ilboudo, Vénuste Kayimahe, Jean-Marie Rurangwa, Djedanoum, and the Kenyan Meja Mwangi. Among these writers only two are Rwandans: Kayimahe and Rurangwa, also first-time authors. Kayimahe produced a testimony, *France–Rwanda: les coulisses d'un génocide* (France–Rwanda: behind the scene of a genocide, 2001), and Rurangwa wrote an expository essay, *Le génocide des Tutsi expliqué à un étranger* (The Tutsi genocide explained to a foreigner, 2000). In contrast to Holocaust literature, "Rwanda: Ecrire par devoir de mémoire" was an artistic response essentially by non-Rwandans. This is not to say that there was no testimonial literature on the 1994 genocide in Rwanda. In fact, such works as Yolande Mukagasana's *La mort ne veut pas de moi* (Death does not want me, 1997) came out first, and Mukagasana herself has since been a regular guest and participant in Fest'Africa. Since 2000, many more testimonial narratives have appeared. As noted by Catherine Coquio in *Rwanda: le réel et les récits* (2004), the presence of these initial testimonies prompted writers of the project to reflect on aesthetic choices, notably on the distinction between testimonial literature and fiction: "The emergence of a corpus of testimonial narratives by survivors forced the African writer to rethink the limits and constraints of her or his own literary 'testimony,' that is, to reformulate the traditional idea of engagement that decades of Afro-pessimism had caused her/him to shelve" (138).

In Souâd Belhaddad and Esther Mujawayo's *SurVivantes* (2004), Belhaddad reflects on the form of the narrative, how to best convey the direct testimonial tone and value of the narrative. The first sequence of the book thus channels Esther's words as they come: "This sequence is based on reworked interviews, the oral quality of which I left intact, not to create specific stylistic effects, but rather to translate as closely as possible the trembling, the hesitations, the knots and the staggering of this discourse" (10). Certain choices, such as the use of the present tense versus the imperfect, for instance, have particular implications. As Belhaddad notices: "Almost every time the genocide is recalled, under the pressure of the memory and especially, that of the trauma, Esther unconsciously switches from using the imperfect at the beginning of the sentence to using the present" (12). Belhaddad further explains that having chosen to privilege the testimonial form, she decided to keep the repetitions and redundancies that she would have otherwise deleted in another form of journalistic work: "[J]ournalistic reflexes should have pushed me to condense and polish what

Esther was saying. But doing so would have been a trap, something conflicting with the very purpose of our work: to restore the words of the survivors, which have so little space to be expressed, especially when Esther speaks of and questions the non-intelligible. Very little space because these words are cause of upset, and can be brutal, relentless, heavy to bear, not to say redundant" (10).

The fact that ten authors, men and women, would collectively agree to commit their personal time and artistic expression to produce a piece of fiction on a given issue, within a certain deadline, was an unprecedented phenomenon in African literature. The different texts were presented in June 2000 in Rwanda at the first Fest'Africa festival to occur on the African continent, as well as at the regularly scheduled Fest'Africa gathering in Lille in November.

A noticeable feature of this project is that it does not exhibit the usual compartmentalization of African literature. For the first time, anglophone writers such as the Kenyan Mwangi and the Ugandan Goretti Kyomuhendo, joined their francophone peers in a collective literary endeavor. Additionally, unlike most collective literary productions usually gathered in a single volume or under the same publishing label, these books appeared under what was then each author's publishing label: Diop at Editions Stock, Monénembo at Editions Seuil, Tadjo at Actes Sud, and Waberi at Serpent à Plumes. The writings of Ilboudo, Lamko, Djedanoum, and Rurangwa were published by Les Editions du Figuier in collaboration with Fest'Africa.[29]

The context of the production of these works is also noteworthy. Most of the writers spent their two-month residency together, at one time, in Kigali. During those two months, they visited the main sites of the 1994 genocide, spoke with survivors, and went to places of detention where they met people waiting to be brought to trial for genocidal crimes. This collective experience had rippling effects on the books and produced recurrent motifs and characters. Yet writers dealt individually with this experience, and their fiction reflects their personal sensitivity as well as their intellectual and political grasp of the genocide and its aftermath. Each of the writers had to address the same question: How does one write about the unspeakable, fictionally?

The philosophical questions pertaining to loss, memory, testimony, and history have been broached, notably by literature on the Holocaust. The relationship between the present and memory, the role of the witness and that of the survivor, the social stake of memory, remembering and forgetting, commemoration and reconciliation, the construction of a new collective history, and the reliability of memory as narrative discourse are part of a universal body of literary works.[30]

The Duty of Memory writers were confronted with issues similar to those faced by authors who had written about the Holocaust. In *L'écriture ou la vie* (1994; *Literature or Life*, 1997), Jorge Semprun sees fiction and fictionalized testimonials as the only possible modes to represent the complex magnitude of a genocide. He also emphasizes that such a representation is always tentative compared with the actual events: "Only those able to turn their accounts into an artistic artifact, a creative or re-creative space, will reach this substance, this apparent density. Only the controlled mastery of artifice will partially transmit the truth of testimony" (273). However, for Semprun, the fictionalization of genocide should not rely on the invention of events to reinforce narrative veracity. This is particularly important to avoid negationist undercurrents. In *La mémoire saturée* (The saturated memory, 2003), Régine Robin points out contrapuntally that an aesthetic layering is needed to uncover the naked truth: "One needs artifice to make reality believable and understandable" (274). Yet Robin also remarks that Berel Lang insists on the morally problematic recourse to fiction in order to represent the Holocaust. For Lang, the moral quandary is that the anonymous and impersonal death of Holocaust victims is individualized through storytelling and that their collective suffering is erased.

This raises questions of verisimilitude as realist fiction strives for the illusion of transparency and immediacy. Does this imply that postmodernist writing is more pertinent to the aesthetic inscription of horror, chaos, and violence? Does one need to strike a balance and, in that respect, did the Duty of Memory writers try to adjust their aesthetics so as to "speak truth to fiction"?

An important parameter regarding the project is that it took place only four years after the 1994 genocide in Rwanda and that the books started to be published six years after the fact. This marks a significant difference from Holocaust literature. It should be noted that although Primo Levi's *Se questo è un uomo* (*Survival in Auschwitz*, 1961) came out in 1947, it was largely ignored then and only became a best seller after the 1961 Eichmann trial. Memory took a longer time to decant and be confronted before Holocaust literature emerged. In the case of the Rwanda Project, these works came out before the trials and to this day national reconciliation is still in progress, further complicated as it is by the situation in the Congo (RDC).

The notion of a *duty* of memory is explicit in the Duty of Memory Project, and its prescriptive aspect was one of the elements that attracted criticism. Coquio has remarked that "the concept of 'travail de mémoire' [reworking of memory] was inspired by that of 'travail de deuil' [coming to terms with loss] and came to replace that of 'devoir de mémoire' [duty of memory]" (216).[31] In turn, the idea of a duty conjures up that of engagement and points to a literature that is instrumentalized and morally bound, which many African writers reject today. It is noteworthy that the issue of engagement also comes out in personal narratives. Mujawayo, for instance, underlines early on in her narrative that "apart from my Rwandan friends who are widows like me, there are only two people with whom I can really let it out and tell what happened, just like that, for no reason. . . . With each of them, I can really let go and at times, when I am tired, I tell myself, without any scruples: 'I am going to call them up, just to recount what happened, and this time, I will do this for myself, not for commitment's sake'" (17). However, the polemics generated by the project were catalysts for fruitful discussions and reconsiderations, including those about the role and responsibility of the contemporary African intellectual. It gave that issue a new visibility.[32]

The body of Holocaust literature was built one book at a time, over several decades, and it is still being constituted. The project Rwanda: écrire par devoir de mémoire is more circumscribed in nature, although it has inspired many satellite artistic responses.[33] The idea of a moral imperative, of a *pacte de vérité*, operates differently in each case: in Holocaust literature, it is de facto, and it came from within the Jewish community; in Rwanda: Ecrire par devoir de mémoire, the *never again* was articulated by people from different African nations, living on the continent or not, most of whom were discovering Rwanda for the first time. The old idea of Pan-Africanism, of an overarching African identity, played a role in the writers' motivation to participate in the project, even if it did not necessarily convince critics.

This brings up the issue of the objectives of the project as well as that of its readership. What are the different systems of identification and dissociation at work in these narratives? What responses is the writer trying to elicit in the reader? To what extent do these books reinforce or undercut the perception of African literature as a metanarrative on oppression? Does a dramatization of victimization bestow a deceptively heroic quality on the writer, the reader, and the act of reading?[34]

To write about a genocide and to talk about a *duty* of memory obviously raise a number of questions, questions of form and aesthetics but also of politics: What does it mean today to be committed to a sociopolitical reality? How do the works of the writers of the Rwanda: Ecrire par devoir de mémoire project reflect their engagement vis-à-vis the Rwandan question? How did their participation in this project affect their writing and their view of themselves as writers? Did they, consciously or unconsciously, see their narratives as mechanisms compensating for the suffering endured by that country? How did women approach the question compared with their male colleagues, and is gender a pertinent analytical category here? Finally, did the writers lay down bases for a rethinking of the stereotypical perceptions and representations of Africa as a continent of catastrophic disasters, famines, AIDS, and barbarism, and of Africans as the eternal "wretched of the earth"?

Memory grows old, and these fictional representations of the 1994 genocide will be contextualized differently as time goes by. Memory is also about forgetting,[35] and history is made of events that are memorialized and of others that are silenced. There is a form of silence that is useful in getting beyond the experience of trauma and in putting an end to its obsessive replay. What Freud called *durcharbeit* is the condition of the mourning process, a necessary step both individually and collectively. Since all discussions about genocide inevitably lead to a reflection on the ways it is supposed to be or not to be represented, spoken about, and inscribed in a given society's collective past, we need to come to an understanding of how the project's narratives operate within or outside the normative frameworks of storytelling. For instance, do they make room for chaos and silence? Do they move the reader toward a normative type of closure (reconciliation, salvation, reuniting, returning, going back to one's "old" life), that is, are these narratives predicated on a consensual understanding of literature? The reception of the project, its financing, publishing, and distribution structures, have been addressed at length by Coquio in *Rwanda: le réel et les récits*.

As previously mentioned, a nexus of common images emerges from these different texts. One image in particular has struck the writers' memories and haunts their readers: the horrific vision of a young woman named Thérèse Mukandori, whose body was found on the Nyamata site impaled on a wooden post.

A number of the novels take place during the genocide itself, or as an expatriate returns, visiting people and places in an attempt to understand what happened to his or her family, and more broadly, to the country. The narrative takes the reader back to the time and space of the genocide through a series of flashbacks, as for instance in Diop's *Murambi*. The use of amnesia and of a protagonist waiting to be tried, as in Monénembo's *L'aîné des orphelins*, is another device enabling both a progressive reenactment of the past and the piecing together of a fragmented memory, which in turn forces us to confront the present and future for the Rwandan youth. In contrast, other writers have chosen to focus on the post-traumatic effects of the genocide, how the survivors may now live alongside their tormentors and join in the effort not only of reconstruction but of restitution of the past. *L'aîné des orphelins* and Ilboudo's *Murekatete* are particularly representative of that approach.

We analyze *Murambi* more closely in Chapter 3, but we wanted to provide a few elements of analysis in relation to its development of history and memory. *Murambi* is based on actual historical moments also present in the works of the other participants in the project: April 6, 1994, date of the downing of the plane of the then Rwandan president, Juvénal Habyarimana, and the genocides of 1959 and 1973. The novel shares a number of characters with the project's other works, characters that bear the names of actors in the genocide, for instance the Italian nun Antonia Locatelli, and the Rwandan Thérèse Mukandori, who, in *Murambi*, is a friend of one of the main characters, Jessica Kamanza. Because of its topographical progression, the novel pays gradual tribute to the people who lost their lives. Its characters pointedly manifest the necessity of a commitment to change and of a "spiritual strength" to listen, speak, and reckon with history (175).[36]

When *Murambi* came out, it was criticized by some for being, unlike Diop's other works, too factual and descriptive.[37] Somehow, Diop seems to have tried to piece together all the information he has gathered, and, through his characters, he has highlighted all the possible scenarios experienced by the Tutsis and moderate Hutus who had been massacred in Rwanda. Thus that Cornelius, an expatriate, both an insider and outsider, is his protagonist, justifies the questions and the attempt to understand, and parallels Diop's situation as an African writer not from Rwanda who is trying to understand the context of the genocide in that country.

Murambi's style is strikingly different from that of *Le cavalier et son ombre*: it is very sober, and its sentences short and bare. Asked about this change in style, the author has said, "I toned my narrative down, one pitch below reality. In order to be convincing and efficient, mindful of not overdoing it, I avoided any novelistic artifice that could justify the reader in saying: 'This is exaggerated.' I kept the storyline simple so that the reader would have no way out."[38]

In "Génocide et devoir d'imaginaire," Diop comes back to the differences of approach between *Murambi* and *Le cavalier et son ombre*.

> I believe . . . I am in a good position to speak of what distinguishes a novel on genocide, written far away in the comfort of our daily habits, from another novel, written in the surrounding smell of death. In the first instance, it is very tempting to overuse shocking images. . . . The African writer who is well aware of this, often needs to insist on the fantastic in order to keep pace. . . . Before going to Rwanda, I did not feel bound to any respect for the facts. It was difficult for me to understand those for whom writing means: "Here is the truth." Looking to generate doubts was much more exciting to me. (27)

Adopting a minimalist style enabled Diop to write the genocide into fiction, to let the testimonies transpire and the tragedy reveal its rawness. Unlike Ken Bugul, who uses fictional memories (moving away from personal testimony) in *La folie et la mort* (2000), Diop used real testimonies to reconstruct a collective memory, thereby forcing the readers to confront a traumatic episode of African history. Although a few years ago, Diop was saying that engagement had become somewhat obsolete,[39] and that if there were any engagement, it had to emanate from the text itself, *Murambi* goes the opposite way. Reasserting the currency of Mongo Beti's words in his preface to *Le temps de Tamango*, the type of commitment that permeates the text is borrowed directly from reality: "I disciplined myself to match up the testimonies that had been gathered with the known facts of the genocide. Each time I found unconfirmed facts, I eliminated them."[40]

Memory serves here as "a discursive terrain," as a crucial element in the historicized construction of the self (Bhabha, *The Location of Culture*, 7). It is less an attempt to make the present more viable— whereby compared with the past, the present would be more comfortable—than it is a crucial exercise in confronting the present as a direct outcome of the past. Until now, writers engaged in denouncing a dictatorship, nepotism, civil wars, injustice in general, did so mostly by creating a fictitious country, thus remaining within the space of the mythic or of the legendary.[41] Here, for the first time, mostly non-Rwandan writers write the Rwandan genocide into fiction, participating in and taking charge of (re-)constructing a collective memory. In the very act of participating in the representation and construction of memory and history, they push African literature to new limits and renew the meaning of *engagés* writers. A number of questions persist, however: whose collective memory is it? Should we assume that this construction of a new Rwandan memory is accepted by Rwandans and unproblematic because it is the product of pan-African efforts? We come back to this in the concluding section of this chapter.

We now explore the impact of memory in the following texts: Tadjo's *L'ombre d'Imana* (2000), Ilboudo's *Murekatete* (2000), and Lamko's *La phalène des collines* (2000).[42] *L'ombre d'Imana: voyages jusqu'au bout du Rwanda* takes the form of a diary of the author's personal thoughts. This unusual travelogue includes places, dates, and direct testimonies or accounts by survivors and perpetrators of the genocide. The section titled "La colère des morts" deals specifically with the victims' bodies exhumed and exposed on the sites of the genocide, and endeavors to bring a sense of peace to both the dead and the living. Tadjo points to the paradox of remembering the dead *and* forgetting them through the symbolism of such sites, at once visible signs of the genocide and places of erasure where one may forget about fundamental respect for the dead by not burying them. Thus, she indirectly questions the exhumation of bodies as another possible act of violence toward the victims, denied the right to rest in peace.

L'ombre d'Imana, *Murekatete*, and *La phalène des collines* deal with the same issue: how the sites aim to remind people of the genocide and place each person in front of the reality of death, but also to confront each person with her or his responsibilities regarding what happened—not only on the scale of Rwanda and Rwandans, but also on a global scale, face-to-face with the West—which looked the other way. Tadjo points to the bizarre form of tourism the visits to the sites of the genocide have created.[43] Even though these sites were meant to be a memorial for the unburied corpses left there as such, naked, profaned, and mutilated, they kept the wounds open and prevented healing.

> The guide invites me to come and write in the register.
> I am number 7317.
> I write my surname and my first name.
> My address in Rwanda.
> My address abroad.
> In the column headed "remarks," I have difficulty in gathering my thoughts. I jot down a phrase about the horror of genocide.

> Before getting into the vehicle which brought us here, I wonder if I
> should give money to the guide. Yes. (13–14)

In Ntarama, Tadjo directs her gaze not at the site itself, but rather, at
the guide, observing the visitors: "White-haired and serene, the little
old man has a quizzical look. He is observing his visitors, weighing
them up, studying them closely, stripping them of their masks. He can
categorize them straight away: those who will avert their gaze from the
spectacle of death, laid out before them, those who will remain silent,
those who will ask questions, pen in hand, those who seek to rational-
ize, to understand, those who will give him money, and those who won't
dare, those who will write: 'Never again!'" (14). Through the evocation
of the guide, Tadjo poses the fundamental question of why these sites
exist and what motivates people to come and visit them: "Why is he
there, amid these human remains, these bones? He explains, replies
to questions, without betraying any emotions. . . . He displays them as
he would display anything else, as if he were in a museum. . . . Deep
down, he does not understand why we come to stir up Evil. Perhaps in
the end all this will turn against him as he guards the evidence of our
inhumanity. He cannot understand what we have come here to seek,
what is concealed in our hearts. What hidden motive drives us to gaze
wide-eyed at death distorted by hatred?" (15).

It is precisely this point—the genocide sites and their hold on the
guests, these guests' motivations, the consequences of their visit—that
Ilboudo's novel, *Murekatete*, articulates. The book's title is also the
name of the protagonist and means: "Let her live." Even though the
protagonist, Murekatete, and Venant, her husband, have nursed each
other back to life after the genocide, visiting the sites triggers something within him, leading him to a hopeless descent into hell: alcohol-
ism, violence, the rape of Murekatete, and finally, his departure. Murekatete, who had already lost everything, her former husband, and
her child left to die after being hacked, once again finds herself utterly
alone, having to start over again and to find the strength to survive
(71–72). Through the fictional account of this couple's story and the
challenges they face, Ilboudo explores the role played by the memorial
sites and their possible effects on Rwandans. Do they provide an opportunity to heal, to free oneself from nightmares and exorcise ghosts
and fears? Or are they somehow rekindling pains and "accelerating
the apocalypse"? Through Muraketete's words, it is Ilboudo herself
who is trying to "comprehend the incomprehensible" (52): "I wanted

to understand the mechanism by which men, women, and children were persuaded to massacre other men, other women, other children, neighbors, yesterday's friends, spouses, sons, daughters, strangers. How had it been possible to persuade them that killing was not sufficient, that they had to dismember with hatchets, machetes? . . . I wanted to understand the genocide!" (52).

Through this couple's story, Ilboudo broaches the issue of the relationship between the sites and memory, between collective and individual memory, between amnesia, trauma, and memory. "We can't, we mustn't forget. But individually, how do you go on living without trying to forget these horrible sights? And can they be forgotten when every day these dried-out corpses are displayed? Such is this country's dilemma. An entire country is struggling between death and life, between memory and reconciliation" (59). Here the dilemma is laid out for us: distinguishing between individual and collective memory, between awakening individual memory and preserving collective memory. But what constitutes a collective memory?

Looking at memory and history, at death and sacrifice, and at the individual and the collective, the historian David Blight makes the following distinctions: memory is generally treated as sacred, as owned, passed down from generation to generation, articulated through the commemoration of sites and monuments.[44] Considered an intrinsic part of people's identity, it is predicated on the notion of the individual. History, in contrast, is part of a reasoned construction of the past; it is more secular than memory, more contingent. History demands more participation, and, borrowing from Pierre Morot, Blight adds: "Memory dictates, History just writes." He also argues that although people remember individually rather than collectively, the process of remembering has a powerful social dimension. Developing his point, he insists that "nations do not remember; people do."[45] And reconciliations may come at a high cost.[46]

The Chadian Lamko reacts to this issue of the role of the genocide sites turned into museums with virulent anger. During the 2000 Fest'Africa festival in Lille, Lamko explained how the idea for his text came about: during his visit to Nyamata, Thérèse Mukandori's exposed body impaled on a wooden post stupefied him, and her image has since haunted him, as it has the other writers. To someone such as Lamko, who lives in a country where the tree holds fundamental importance and is the very symbol of life, such an image represented an utmost absurdity and the most extreme of horrors. That such a symbol of life would be planted in a woman's womb highlighted the drama and the obscenity of genocide—life killing life.

The issue of what happens to a society when its dead are not buried is a central preoccupation to someone from an animist culture, and Lamko was assailed by the following questions, which are at the core of *La phalène des collines*: How can a society rebuild when its wounds are still open? How does one not see in a flying butterfly the expression of a pained, wandering soul in search of rest? How does one react to the genocide sites, which are organized, staged, and transformed into "museums of human carcasses"?

In Lamko's book, the butterfly, "la phalène," is the reincarnation of this anonymous woman, who endured unimaginable violence. Now a butterfly, she follows Pelouse, her young niece who has come to visit the site. In following the wanderings of the butterfly, the narration journeys to the past, back to the scenes of this woman's life, to her rape and torture. In parallel, the reader also observes the floods of visitors who come, walk through the sites, and disturb the resting dead. Through the butterfly, Lamko lets the dead's upsurge of anger flow. It is an anger directed at those hungry for sensationalism: "The crippled century, irresistibly avid for all that is sensational and virtual; this century greedy for the misery of people, savored through screens and camera lenses. An unavowed cannibalism" (17).

La phalène des collines, however, goes beyond explosive anger to become a long incantation that allows Queen Gicanda to finally rest peacefully. It calls for appeasement, pointing to the necessity of burying the dead and paying them due respect. It becomes a cathartic song for the butterfly and therefore for readers. A symbolic effort to remember a place of irrefutable evidence, a piece of the story's puzzle, Lamko's book points out that these sites may have led to a form of a modern-day voyeurism. Finally, it should be pointed out that *La phalène des collines* is an allusion to Queen Gicanda's horrific assassination in 1994, during the genocide. Her death and suffering are not only emblematic of the destruction of Tutsi women but also of the will to eradicate the royal Tutsi lineage.

All the texts that are part of the Duty of Memory Project raise fundamental and universal questions. "Who can say," notes Tadjo, "what makes up the memory of a whole nation? What images carpet its unconscious mind? Who can know what slaughter, hidden behind the centuries gone by, is even now sculpting the future of a nation?" (19). By highlighting issues related to posttraumatic stress disorder

and effects of the genocide, the authors examine the relationship between memory and history, and between individual and collective
memory.

CONCLUSION

In many countries around the world, commemoration and the "duty
of memory" have become prescriptive and profitable notions. They
have often been politically instrumentalized. Today, memory is both
the subject of serious research and a lever for fashioned consensus.

As noted, the publication of the Rwanda: écrire par devoir de mémoire works, including *L'aîné des orphelins* and *Murambi*, generated controversies, notably about the notions of "devoir" (duty) versus "travail" (work on/commitment to) of memory, about the type
of political commitment the project seemed to imply and the ethical
problems raised by the creation of a de facto literary corpus on the
1994 genocide in Rwanda. The 1994 genocide in Rwanda has been
the subject of a great many works, creative and theoretical, in a variety of disciplines, and by authors, artists, and critics the world over.
To stay with literature, the Belgian journalist Jean Hatzfeld published
in 2000 the first of his two haunting essays/volumes of interviews on
the 1994 genocide in Rwanda, *Dans le nu de la vie: Récits des marais rwandais* (translated as both *Into the Quick of Life*, 2005, and
Life Laid Bare: The Survivors in Rwanda Speak, 2006).[47] His second
book on the subject, *Une saison de machettes* (*Machete Season: The
Killers in Rwanda Speak*, 2005), appeared in 2003 and received the
Prix Fémina. He published a third and more controversial book, *La
stratégie des antilopes* (2007; *The Strategy of Antelopes: Living in
Rwanda after the Genocide*, 2009), in which he addresses reconciliation and how survivors live today side by side with killers. Critics,
including Diop, took exception to what they considered the recycling
of stereotypical representations of Tutsis and Hutus, and Africans in
general, as well as Hatzfeld's self-staging. In 2000, the Quebecois Gil
Courtemanche published in Canada a novel on the topic, *Un dimanche à la piscine à Kigali* (*A Sunday at the Pool in Kigali*, 2004), a book
that was released in France in 2003 and later adapted to the screen
under the same title.[48] Since then, several novels and testimonies by
Rwandans have been published, such as Mujawayo and Belhaddad's
SurVivantes: Rwanda, 10 ans après le génocide (2004), Annick Kayitesi's *Nous existons encore* (We still exist, 2004), Benjamin Sehene's

Le feu sous la soutane (The fire under the cassock, 2005), and Scholastique Mukasonga's *Inyenzi ou les Cafards* (Inyenzi or the cock-
roaches, 2006) and *La femme aux pieds nus* (The barefoot woman,
2008). More political essays have come out since the tenth anniversary in 2004, revisiting the role of Western countries, especially France,
among them Patrick de Saint-Exupéry's *L'inavouable* (What cannot
be told, 2004).[49] This work is a direct address to Dominique de Vil-
lepin, France's minister of foreign affairs in 2004, and it evidences
a number of contradictions (to say the least) in France's Opération
Turquoise. Alain Tasma's feature film *Opération Turquoise* (2007),
shown on Canal+ November 19, 2007, and, since then, publication
of the Mucyo report on France's role in Rwanda before, during, and
after the 1994 genocide (August 2008), question further the real objectives of this military mission and the larger implications of the role
of the French intervention in Rwanda. In 2005, Pierre Péan's essay
Noires fureurs, Blancs menteurs (Black rages, white liars) countered
Saint-Exupéry's thesis, trying to exonerate France at a time when the
French military's role in Rwanda was beginning to be examined more
closely.[50] The history of the 1994 genocide in Rwanda continues to be
written and rewritten. Revisionist theses such as Péan's hinder reconciliation and make the process of moving forward more difficult.
Derrida's notion of *hantologie*, of "the return of the repressed in the
event" is still an issue. It is particularly difficult if one considers the
ways in which memory is constructed and its discourses disseminat-
ed. Indeed, who holds memory today? Revisionist theories make the
acknowledgment of history and memory still very fragile. New publications appeared in 2009 that underline the tensions inherent to this
issue, among them Saint-Exupéry's *Complices de l'inavouable: la
France au Rwanda*, a revised edition of *L'inavouable*, and Péan's *Le
Monde selon K.* (The world according to K.).

As Carol Bellamy, UNICEF executive director, emphasized in April
2004, "Ten years later, the children of Rwanda are still suffering the
consequences of a conflict caused entirely by adults. . . . For them, the
genocide is not just a historical event but an inescapable part of daily
life today and tomorrow."[51]

Although the Duty of Memory Project has been criticized, the novels that are part of its corpus elicited key questions regarding writing
about genocide, especially in the light of the many testimonial narratives that have come out since 2000. The project has helped expand
the representational system and the textual strategies hitherto essen-

tially defined by Holocaust literature. It may also be construed as having provided an initial venue for the expression and the conceptualization of the suffering endured during and after the genocide.

In "Génocide et devoir d'imaginaire," Diop reflects on the meaning and possible outcomes of the project.

> Our only merit is to have tried to do our best, despite the ambiguities of the task. In my opinion, we were successful in expressing what in the suffering of the Rwandan people calls out to every human being. This aspiration for the universal allowed us to inscribe the genocide more strongly in time. Destined to be read by and commented on by high school and university students, our novels are beginning a long journey through time and space. . . . However, I am convinced that the great literary works on the April 1994 genocide will be written later, and by Rwandans themselves. (34–35)

As will be analyzed more closely in our next chapter, the writing of the genocide has had long-term transformative consequences on the authors' choices of narrative techniques and focus. In an indirect reference to Coquio's *Rwanda: le réel et les récits,* Tirthankar Chanda underlines the importance of memory in the fashioning of new aesthetic models for francophone African literature: "Having experienced what cannot be told and what is silenced marked a turning point in African literary history, because it demonstrated both the necessity and the impossibility of engagement. This is a major moment of awareness for the African writer who, after a half-century of messianic discourse on literature, comes to question the correlation between reality and narrative" (31).

The novels and authors we have discussed in this chapter demonstrate the renewed interest in exploring history and the past. In their questioning and rewriting of foundational myths, their crafting of an archaeology of silenced episodes of history, their writing of narratives of violence and affliction, these authors do three things: First, they connect colonial and postcolonial history. Second, they raise questions about (new) representational modes of history. Third, they open up the range of possibilities to ask about reality, realism, and their relationship to the narrative. Our next chapter examines the implications for *engagée* literature and the textuality of African novels. It also analyzes how these authors contribute to shaping new politics of form and defining what engagement signifies today.

CHAPTER THREE

Lifting the Burden?

*Francophone African Writers Engaging in
New Aesthetics*

The longevity of a book written feverishly and literally does not extend more than a few weeks. The more politically committed the discourse, the more it is necessary to work on form—otherwise, the book will miss its goal.

BOUALEM SANSAL, "Untitled"

Art is an exercise in fruitful infidelity.

MARIE-JOSÉ MONDZAIN, "Quelle éthique, esthétique
et politique de la représentation?"

In this chapter we evaluate how the need to be emancipated from the old notion of engagement has led African writers creatively, and how it may have been related to the change in the relationship between France and Africa from the late 1980s on.[1] As pointed out by Raharimanana in the following quote, the younger generations have been confronted more crucially than before with the question of defining themselves in relation to both African and French literatures.

> I imagine how surprised literary critics were when we all turned up, between 1987 and 1990. We were only promising young authors then . . . but also filled with revolt, with a desire to abscond from the legacy of our elders, a legacy that was hard to bear, the whole continent's pain, in fact. Our only wish was to write, to be good writers, to play with aesthetics or just tell a story, and here we were, twenty years old, and summoned to save Africa!
>   We discovered the wealth of literary life in France, in the West. The illusive feeling of resuming the primordial act of writing: the intense pleasure of words, the vertigo caused by creation, and the stylistic pride. Where did we fit? In French literature? In francophone African literature? In national literatures? In the literature of the African diaspora? Salons, colloquia, conferences followed one another

> where these questions were discussed, but we knew full well that the
> fault line from which our writing had burst was in our countries of
> origin. Were we to run away, we could not escape from ourselves for
> too long. (50)[2]

Our first and second chapters, "Enduring Commitments" and "The
Practice of Memory" highlighted some recurring characteristics in
the textualizing of commitment: First, a rewriting and revamping of
myths and history; second, a transformation of the heroic figure (hero,
anti-hero, and non-hero); and third, a new aesthetic of the scream and
of violence.

In *Nouvelles écritures africaines: romanciers de la seconde génération* (1986), Sewanou Dabla identified the conceptual shifts
undergone by the African novel in the 1980s, pointing to a polyphonic system of narrative voices, a fragmentation and disruption
of both the spatial and temporal axes, and the use of magic realism, derisive humor and satire, intertwined representations of
death and sexuality, and violence, as part of recurrent aesthetic
changes. As discussed previously, Phyllis Taoua traced the shift
from realism to experimental fiction to the impact of decolonization through chaotic narratives, fragmented plots, and disruption
of time and space.[3]

One of the shifts currently undergone by francophone African literature is the multiplication of intertextual references. In "La littérature en miroir: création, critique et intertextualité," Boniface Mongo-Mboussa lists Abdourahman Waberi, Sami Tchak, and Alain
Mabanckou as most representative of this trend and explains this phenomenon as an "almost pathological obsession with fitting into world
literature [that] can be explained by the rejection of a certain type of
literary criticism that often only proposes cultural and political interpretations of francophone African literature" (53). Intertextuality is
not, however, a new phenomenon in francophone African literature,
and it has gone through different phases, with reappropriations of
masterpieces, such as Aimé Césaire's rewriting of Shakespeare's *The
Tempest* or Boubacar Boris Diop's *Le temps de Tamango*, a rewrite
of Prosper Merimée's *Tamango*. Other practices of intertextuality
have included Ouologuem's borrowing from Julien Green's and André Schwarz-Bart's texts in *Le devoir de violence*, or more recently,
Calixthe Beyala's forms of plagiarism in *Le petit prince de Belleville*
and *Les honneurs perdus* (The lost honors, 1996).[4] What is new in the
current practice of intertextuality is its tactical inclusion of foreign

literatures in an attempt to inscribe the African novel in the field of world literature and to manifest other literary genealogies, as can be seen in Sami Tchak's *Hermina* (2003) and *La fête des masques* (The masks' celebration, 2004), and Waberi's *Passage des larmes* (The passage of tears, 2009). The multiplication of narrative spaces and the new geographies in francophone African literatures add to that trend and evidence the fact that new maps of knowledge are being drawn and claimed.

Many narratives, such as Monénembo's *Un attiéké pour Elgass* (1993), open up to another African country or represent a diasporic space. With *Pelhourinho* (1995), Monénembo configures Brazil as an African space, as does Couao-Zotti with *Les fantômes du Brésil* (The ghost of Brazil, 2006) and Kangni Alem with *Esclaves* (2009). Achille Ngoye's *Yaba terminus* (1998) and the short story by the same title take place in Lagos, Nigeria. *Yaba terminus* opens up francophone African fiction to include an intra-African space, an anglophone African country, and addresses immigration across national African borders (South/South). Lopès's *Sur l'autre rive* (1992) and Mabanckou's *Et Dieu seul sait comment je dors* (1998), with their narratives set in the French Caribbean, and *Lettre à Jimmy* (2007), a conversation with James Baldwin, are other examples of a similar phenomenon.

Other writers, however, circumscribe the geography of their narratives in an attempt to make the local express a redefined universal. Nganang's *La promesse des fleurs* (1997), *Temps de chien* (2001), and *L'invention du beau regard* (2005), for instance, proceed out from a neighborhood or even just a street. Mabanckou's *Verre cassé* (2005; *Broken Glass*, 2009) and *Mémoires de porc-épic* (Memories of a porcupine, 2006) do so as well.

These configurations are indicative of new trajectories and directions in the writers' gaze. Among these, violence and immigration have emerged as salient and recurrent features. This fact deserves critical scrutiny because violence and immigration have become inevitable analytical categories since the 1990s, with critics reducing their readings of the texts to these two interpretative parameters. Such a tendency has often obscured the diversification of this literary production and the fact that immigration is a site of postcolonial violence. The following section thus focuses on, first, textualizing and engendering violence; second, migration, immigration, and the writing of dis-location (including an examination of the new politics of form pertaining to the figure of the anti-hero, crime fiction, and the use of provocation through sex and gender configurations); and third, the diversification of textual strategies and aesthetics in the past decade.

TEXTUALIZING AND ENGENDERING VIOLENCE

A foundational notion in African literature, violence is being queried anew both in literary and critical works. This reassessment sheds new light on the patterns of violence in texts by previous generations of writers.

A literary representation of violence rests on the elaboration of an aesthetic, of a grammar and rhetoric.[5] Paradoxically, even if a writer intends to denounce it, he or she commits to "do violence": s/he creates violence, selects and constructs its components to make them readable, intelligible, and instrumental—that these components may be unbearable or not is secondary to the issue of representation. In this sense, violence is inscribed in an epistemological system: the success of its representation depends on the writer's ability to make it conceivable to the reader and to force the reader to integrate the violence into his or her understanding of the "story" told by the text. Thus, violence becomes a recognizable and familiar element of the narrative and is one of the tools that ensure the dynamic energy of the plot. Literary violence seeks to elicit fear of (or revolt against) an oppressive social or political regime the parameters of which it concomitantly elaborates. Writing (on) violence is tantamount to constructing it semantically, to ascribing meaning to it. Because fictional violence generates multiple scripts and interpretations, it turns the question of morality, of good and evil, on its head. The characters in this type of narrative have a particular status because they are co-substantial to the violence in the text. They are a function of the rhetoric and the system of violence. Violence provides them with a narrative *in-existence* that clashes with the social *non-existence* the story seems to denounce.

Since the early 1980s, depictions of violence have been much more graphic, taking the readers to the limits of the unbearable. Pius Ngandu Nkashama's early novels, in particular *Le fils de la tribu* (The son of the tribe, 1983) and *Le pacte de sang* (The blood pact, 1984), illustrate this point, and Bolya Baenga's *Cannibale* (1986) may be said to constitute the epitome of abjection and horror in the depiction of violence.[6] As seen previously, violence has become more abject and sacrilegious, and women and children are more frequently represented as its first victims: women are raped, bodies dismembered, guts gushing out, pregnant women torn open, and their babies killed under their eyes. Taken to the extreme, violence is now an obvious metaphor for the dislocation of postcolonial societies, families, and community structures.

In "Des formes variées du discours rebelle," Jacques Chevrier distinguished different phases in the writing of violence. A first phase consisted in rebelling against the colonial authority and claiming one's identity and space. It was successively represented by such texts as Aimé Césaire's *Cahier d'un retour au pays natal* (1956; *Return to My Native Land*, 1969)[7] and Frantz Fanon's *Les damnés de la terre* (1961). A second phase followed, more bitter and disillusioned, whereby writers gave an account of all their disillusionments. Alioum Fantouré's *Le cercle des tropiques* (1972; *Tropical Circle*, 1981), Monénembo's *Les crapauds-brousse* (1979) or Sassine's *Wirriyamu* (1976; translation, 1980) belong to that vein. However, writers soon realized the limitations of "pathos," and this is when the oneiric, derisive, and parodic narratives started to appear and translate neocolonial violence. From then on, texts operated on the basis of subversion, betraying a complex form of both disengagement and renewed artistic commitment. In "Langue volée, langue violée: pouvoir, écriture et violence dans le roman africain," Elisabeth Boyi notes that such representations enact violence on the texts themselves and participate in the Fanonian liberatory process of resisting power. From the 1990s on, therefore, violence is ever more central to the narration, but there is a new twist to its textualization: children and youth who traditionally were the objects of violence have become its agents.[8] This is especially true in novels authored by men.[9]

The increase of violence has led to the *ré-ensauvagement* (re-casting of Africa as the dark continent) of the idea of Africa in world opinion, a *ré-ensauvagement* frequently instrumentalized for profitable commercial use. Shown on television, discussed in all media, and inscribed in books, violence sells. It is relayed, encoded, and diffused for purposes that largely go beyond moral outrage and the will for change. Thus, violence is still a prevailing issue in African letters, but it is deployed by contemporary francophone African writers in increasingly complex ways.

In *Rêves sous le linceul* (1998), Jean-Luc Raharimanana represents Madagascar, and Africa, as a nightmarish place, the characterization of which becomes even more unbearable after the 1994 genocide in

Rwanda. The nightmare is decidedly no longer external to the narrator's immediate experience; his psyche is imbued with it.

> April 29, 1994
> A sofa floating in the fog. Inside, sinking into it, I gently founder. Six hours. One feels good here. A head hacked by a machete. In pre-recorded time. Too bad. Foul-smelling pants on dirty black flesh, green flies on the red of blood. . . .
> A child on the grass, on the rug, feels good here. A naked woman-negress slashed by a thousand insults, a thousand insults. . . . To be raped. To be raped alongside my grave. Alongside my sofa. In pre-recorded time. Too bad. To be pre-recorded in my dreams. (15–16)

"Le canapé" (The couch) and "Le canapé (retour en terre opulente)" (The couch [return to the opulent land]), two echoing short stories in the volume, are parts of Raharimanana's reflection on the status and effect of the images of victimization broadcast by international media. They raise a number of questions, such as: What do such representations signify in a context of a "tele-intimacy with death and destruction"? (Sontag, *Regarding the Pain of Others,* 21). Is the filmic narration of the genocide intended to jar viewers out of their supposed passivity? Do such assaults on their sensibility answer to an imperative for high television ratings? Or are they an attempt at raising our consciousness? Are viewers understood as voyeurs or potential comrades-in-arms? Conveyed by the written word, are violence and its manifestations more easily conceivable and less problematic than on the screen? Is the process of recognizing violence different from that of protesting against it? (40). Finally, in such a context, can the African writer continue to believe in the cathartic quality of his "devoir de violence" (duty of violence) (Ouologuem) and to envision her/himself as a moral authority?

Noting that "the frankest representations of war, and of disaster-injured bodies, are of those who seem most foreign, therefore least likely to be known" (61–62), Susan Sontag underlines that "postcolonial Africa exists in the consciousness of the general public in the rich world—besides through its sexy music—mainly as a succession of unforgettable photographs of large-eyed victims, starting with figures in the famine lands of Biafra in the late 1960s to the survivors of the genocide of nearly a million Rwandan Tutsis in 1994 and, a few years later, the children and adults whose limbs were hacked off during the program of mass terror conducted by the RUF, the rebel forces in Sierra Leone." Sontag also points out that the spectacle of an Africa *in suffering*, the alleged purpose of which is to denounce injustice, is in fact affiliated to the colonial practice of exhibiting exotic and colonized human beings and human bodies, and to the corollary idea that the Other "is regarded only as someone to be seen, not someone . . . who also sees" (71–72).

Thus, the "Canapé[s]" dramatize the violence of the contradictions experienced by the narrator (and possibly the writer, since this is a first-person narrative), an African witness to the representation of the rape of Rwandan Tutsi women and an unwilling participant in the media circus the genocide has become, whose faltering consciousness is caught in a morbid and distancing scopic drive. Of the women on the screen, he says: "To be raped. To be raped alongside my grave. Alongside my sofa."[10]

Boubacar Boris Diop's *Murambi: le livre des ossements* (2000), Tierno Monénembo's *L'aîné des orphelins* (2000), Alain Mabanckou's *Les petits-fils nègres de Vercingétorix* (The Negro grandchildren of Vercingétorix, 2002), and Emmanuel Dongala's *Johnny chien méchant* (2002) allow us to consider how the shaping of violence in francophone African literature stems from a metaphorical tradition that is currently being rethought along new lines. Categories in which such "creative" violence was grounded (the universal scope of violence, a broken historicity, genealogy, memory, utopia, and gender) are being reshaped by others, notably the child soldier, rape, ethnic polarization, humanitarianism, and the media.

These four works (along with Ahmadou Kourouma's 2000 novel, *Allah n'est pas obligé*) carved a new space in the francophone African literary landscape, pushing the representation of violence further. Although Kourouma's and Dongala's works are more clearly thematically related to a form of violence associated with the child soldier, Monénembo's protagonist, Faustin, is similarly inscribed in a violating present. That *Murambi* and *L'aîné* are parts of the Duty of Memory Project should not limit our understanding to that frame alone nor obscure the fact that they too participate in the general reconfiguring of the inscriptions of violence in francophone African literature. Although the titles of the four works seem to put them in two different categories, one resolutely tragic (*L'aîné, Murambi*), the other more ironic (*Johnny, Les petits-fils*), all of these books are pressing interrogations about a possible future for the young generations in the war-torn regions of Central Africa.

L'aîné is the most concise of the four books and contains no chapters. It is a first-person narrative recounted by Faustin Nsenghimana, a fifteen-year-old native of Nyamata, who has been imprisoned at Kigali's Prison Centrale for three years when the book opens. Sentenced to death, he is awaiting execution. The story scans his existence from age ten when he lost his parents to the genocide (although he refuses to acknowledge the fact of their death) to age fifteen. It proposes various avenues for trying to understand who Faustin is, what his choices might have been or meant. His is the story of a life denied by violence, of a denial enforced from the outside but also internalized by the protagonist, and put to use, at times as a posture. That denial is therefore not a simple sign of violent oppression but also the basic element of Faustin's increasingly sharp understanding of the world he finds himself in. We follow him as he evokes the rawness of life in the prison, his meeting with Claudine Karemera, a Tutsi born "at the border" in 1959 in Uganda while her family was fleeing the first genocide (31). Claudine wants to rescue Faustin from his marginality and then from jail. Through her intervention, Faustin, who has become a member of a gang of homeless children, a family of sorts in Kigali, is taken to an orphanage and reunited with his traumatized younger siblings. But, unwilling to adapt to the rules of the orphanage, Faustin runs away and meets his destiny as his past slowly unravels. *L'aîné* closes on one of the most gripping representations of violence in African literature, a provocative reworking of a nativity scene: Faustin remembers and acknowledges the death of his parents in the Nyamata massacre as well as the circumstances in which an old woman found him alive, under a pile of corpses, sucking on his dead mother's bloody breasts "like a newborn" (157).

Dongala's *Johnny* is also a first-person narrative, and takes place in forty-eight hours. The two fifteen-year-old protagonists, Laokolé and Johnny, speak alternately in one chapter after another, one vision of the civil war—and of life—following, introducing, and contrasting with the other. Laokolé represents the experience of the common people, women and children mostly; Johnny represents a young manhood gone astray, at once horrendously and pathetically cruel. Dongala offsets the regularity of the double voice through an intricate system. First, Lao and Johnny enter each other's story (chapters 7 and 10). Second, at times two chapters in a row are in Lao's or Johnny's voices, thus disrupting the alternation between their respective discourses. Third, the opening and closing chapters of the book transmit Lao's voice so that the narrative is framed by her evolving perspective.

And fourth, Lao and Johnny pronounce the same three sentences at different times in the story with the results that either their unique circumstances are enhanced or the universal quality of their human frailty is brought to the foreground, beyond moralistic judgment (70, 157, 230–31).

Through its story of the displaced and their pursuers, *Johnny chien méchant* features the human tragedy and fractiousness that are the products of civil war. Johnny, the out-of-control "mean dog," sows despair and feeds on it. He lives in a virtual reality. His points of reference and those of his motley crew of fellow murderers, Caïman, Idi Amin, Mâle-lourd, Double-têtes, and other such nicknames, are so Rambo-like that they have a cartoon quality (31). Johnny wants recognition, no matter how, and no matter the cost to others. Overdetermined by his drives, Johnny vaguely justifies his destructive aimlessness, and that of his gang's, the Mata-Mata, by the necessity of ethnic struggle, an obvious excuse for looting.

Laokolé is the counterpoint to Johnny's utter craziness. An excellent student before the war and an affectionate daughter, she is a female example to be added to the positive set of young male characters found in other books by Dongala, notably the young Matapari in *Les petits garçons naissent aussi des étoiles* (1998). Like Matapari, Laokolé delights in science and abstraction; left-handed like him—which will save her life in the end—she loves to gaze at the stars, a symbol of transcendence and the future in Dongala's work. Trying to flee the fighting with her brother and her injured mother, she pushes her mother around in a wheelbarrow from one ordeal to the next until Laokolé loses both family members and fights alone for her life.

Johnny's and Lao's characters are means through which Dongola expresses a number of critical ideas about his country's and Africa's civil wars. Through Johnny, Dongala evokes the theme of the responsibility of African intellectuals. Lao serves to articulate the political state of the country (178) and the aspirations of its youth. Her character gives a blunt edge to the theme of immigration, as she relays many African youths' desire to leave: "To leave, to get out of this godforsaken country—this was the dream of every young person of my generation" (159).

Boubacar Boris Diop has said that, for him, there is a before and an after Rwanda, and *Murambi* marks a critical moment in his career. The title of the book refers to the site of Murambi's Ecole Technique in Gikongoro, a school that successively served as a refuge for many Tutsis, as the scene of the massacre of about 45,000 people, mostly Tutsis, and finally as the headquarters of the French Opération Turquoise. As a place, then, Murambi holds a crucial symbolic value (223).

Murambi: le livre des ossements consists of four disparate chapters; the first and the third, respectively titled "La peur et la colère" (The fear and the anger) and "Génocide," offering two series of character sketches that represent the victims, perpetrators, and actors of the genocide. The second and fourth chapters are formally different from the others. Longer (fifty-three and fifty-four pages), they frame the short character sketches mentioned above. More complete, closer to the novel in form, they highlight the writer's preference for an iconoclastic style in this text. They signal his intention to favor clarity and strength of evocation over a more sophisticated novelistic discourse. Respectively titled "Le retour de Cornelius" and "Murambi," chapters 2 and 4 describe Cornelius's evolution. Cornelius, whom we will learn is Dr. Karekezi's son, is a so-called "Hutsi" who fled Rwanda in 1971 as a child and comes back at age thirty-seven from Djibouti where he had been living in exile and where his fiancée lives. Cornelius's return in 1998, four years after the genocide, symbolically coincides with the *Résidence d'Ecriture* of the Duty of Memory Project in Kigali and with the period when Diop began the book.

Murambi's structure reveals Diop's preoccupation with mixing points of view on, and experiences of, the genocide. As mentioned in Chapter 2, the novel shares a number of characters with the project's other works, characters who bear the names of actors in the genocide, such as the "Italienne," and the Rwandan Thérèse Mukandori, who has become the archetype of the violated woman and who, in *Murambi*, is a friend of Jessica's. Because of its topographical progression, the novel seems to pay gradual tribute to the range of people who lost their lives. Its characters pointedly manifest the necessity of a commitment for change and of the "spiritual strength" to listen, speak, and reckon with history (175).

Mabanckou's *Les petits-fils* is a novel at once extensive and carefully organized, with a deliberately demanding liminal apparatus. The title of the book is also its last sentence. Dedicated to Henri Lopès and Emmanuel Dongala, and in memory of Mongo Beti, the volume is anchored from the start in a specific Congolese and literary lineage. A "notebook" written by Hortense Iloki and sent by Léopold Mpassi-Mpassi to a Parisian publishing house, *Les petits-fils* begins with a "Note de l'éditeur" pointing to the importance of an introductory page by Hortense in which she situates her country, Viétongo, geographically, politically, and economically. There is also an "Avant-Cahier" in which Hortense signals her work as a narration of past events where characters once familiar to her are staged through her memory. The narrator expresses her concern that what happened to her country not be forgotten. She indicates that she has written since she was a teenager, but that her motivation for doing so now has evolved from a habit of confession (diary writing) to a desire to produce a fictional testimony.

The core of the novel is made of four parts: "L'adieu à Christiane" (Farewell to Christiane), "D'Oweto [nord] à Batalébé [sud]" (From Oweto [north] to Batalébé [south]), "L'affaire d'Okonongo et ses suites" (The Okonongo affair and its aftermath), and "Derniers Feuillets: Le départ pour Pointe-Rouge" (Last pages: The departure to Pointe-Rouge). The main characters of the book are two mixed couples. Hortense Iloki, a native of the north of Viétongo, married Kimbembé, from Batalébé in the south, before the civil war, when he was a thirty-one-year-old teacher doing his required time in the north and she his sixteen-year-old student. Christiane Kengué and Gaston Okemba present both a parallel and counterexample to the first couple. They met in the economic capital, Pointe-Rouge, not in the village. Christiane is a native of Batalébé and Gaston is from the north. Whereas Hortense and Kimbembé have a child, their daughter Maribé, Gaston and Christiane do not, because of the latter's alleged infertility.

Les petits-fils, L'aîné, Murambi, and *Johnny* have a universal scope. They deal with issues that are resurgent in our contemporary world: memory, resistance to terror, humanitarian aid, and the meaning of "urgency." They raise the question of what is humanely acceptable or unacceptable in the absence of democratic law. They represent absolute evil in the face of a sacrificial morality, disorder as order, and violence as organizational system. They discuss the nature of love and desire, the meaning of origin, and definitions of an acceptable social structure and of a sustaining social fabric.

The four books depict an African world in which historicity is in crisis, where intelligibility no longer comes from the past, from heroic figures born of tradition or nationalist struggle. Grounded in violence, in a present exhausted by it, the four novels display a literary treatment of time with both shared and distinct characteristics. Although all the books aim at denouncing violence and feature a disjointed reality and unstructured lives, *L'aîné* and *Johnny* tend to be more incisive and restless in tone. Despite similar representations of unbearable cruelty, *Les petits-fils* and *Murambi* make more room for silence, for a reflection on the ultimately inexpressible experience of violation. Mabanckou's and Diop's works display a yearning for transcendence. Time stretches out more in *Murambi* and *Les petits-fils*, and memory imposes itself as a theme, unlike in *L'aîné* and *Johnny*, where the clatter of chaos is dominant throughout. That clatter comes to a full stop in *Johnny*, at the end, with Laokolé's symbolic castration of the protagonist.

L'aîné, *Johnny*, *Les petits-fils*, and *Murambi* are all works in which the present has been replaced by a *futur antérieur*, a stasis whereby what was and what could be have no actual foundation, where one's future is behind. *Les petits-fils* and *Murambi* are more evidently concerned with the reinscription of time and memory than the other two books. The two novels present, however, a different treatment of memory. *Murambi* is more closely related to Pierre Nora's concept of *lieux de mémoire* (realms of memory),[11] whereby official memorial sites participate in the construction of the Nation, and to the spirit of the Duty of Memory Project, which included visits to the "main" sites of the genocide. *Les petits-fils* corresponds to the idea of the *non-lieux de la mémoire* (the blank/whitewashed places of memory), as illustrated by Claude Lanzmann in his documentary film, *Shoah* (1985). As is the case in *Murambi*, the geography of *Les petits-fils* is marked by trauma, but the rise of fear, the ethnic carving of the country, the steady erasure of common experience and history, and the creation of the hated Other are shown through Hortense's inner world, through the fictionalized truth of her personal diary. Her writing of a diary is an act of resistance, a reinscription of the authority of the subject, and, as she says, a weapon.[12] It can be viewed as a reaffirmation, albeit tragic, of individual critical potential in a world "dumbed" by cruelty. Recording her fate, her losses and her thoughts, Hortense denormalizes suffering. She reclaims her subjectivity. She posits an "after" to her existence.

L'aîné shows still another use of this apparently problematic opposition between *lieux de mémoire* and *non-lieux de la mémoire*. It takes place mostly in Kigali, with occasional allusions to different parts of Rwanda. Among the four books' different versions of the no-past/no-future question, *L'aîné* is the darker, and perhaps the more desperate: we know from page one that Faustin, little Faust, is compromised. Claudine's tenderness for him comes too late and verges on the farcical because it is expressed at cross-purposes, never fully making sense. Faustin's cards have been dealt: he will die, a social waste, vaguely dignified by the tragedy of his destiny, with no memories to keep and no dreams to uphold.

Murambi, *Johnny*, and *Les petits-fils*, make space for a future that would not resemble the *futur antérieur* previously referred to. Unlike in *L'aîné*, that future is made possible by the suffering and sacrifice of women, the more frequent agents of awareness. *Murambi* is the more utopian work, the one that attempts specifically to reconstruct an intelligible historical discourse and to reinstill the positive universal values represented by the old uncle, Siméon Habineza, Jessica Kamanzi, the young R.P.F. (Rwandan Patriotic Front) fighter, Cornelius, and more indirectly by the allegorical figure of the young shepherd whose soothing music spreads across the land and beyond. Three redeeming notions are at play in *Murambi*: remembrance, accountability, and the restoration of humanity. There are desperate characters in Diop's book, but heroically so. An example of this is provided through Jessica's evocation of a beautiful and nameless Tutsi woman surrendering to her fate and facing the certain gang rape that awaits her in order to walk the sunny streets of Kigali one last time (124).

This idea of a desperate attempt to carve a measure of agency and self-respect runs through all the novels, although as mentioned before, in *Johnny*, the young heroine who faces rape defends herself, matches the violence menacing her, and triumphs. *Murambi*'s considerations about the "pitiful" quality of the "assassins" are dismissed in Dongala's novel. Laokolé's liberation, her intended departure to the United States to study, and the survival of her adopted daughter, Kiessé (joy), come to be possibilities through her eradication of Johnny.

None of these books holds tradition to be a lost Eden. In *Les petits-fils*, although Massengo, the hunter and Mam'Soko's husband, is believed by his wife to have been killed by his double, he more likely committed suicide, a taboo in traditional society. In *Johnny*, Laokolé's castration of Johnny is a clear break in the order of things, a symbolically definite crushing of a destructive male supremacy. Yet, the four novels' relation to a revolutionary utopia is at times contradictory. Going back to *Les petits-fils*, the construction of France as a refuge where Hortense's diary may be published, so that her spirit of endurance and love might possibly live on, is not unproblematic.

Like *Murambi, Les petits-fils*, makes room for protagonists whose extreme suffering has not blinded them to their priorities toward those they love. Christiane, whose husband has been kidnapped and killed by the militia, and who has been raped by them, gives her wedding picture to Hortense, after she has decided not to flee and to face the continuing violence that awaits her. In turn, Hortense emulates her friend's symbolic resistance to the destruction of her humanity. She faces her future rapists and killers so as to save her daughter, who jumps out of the window holding her mother's record of their ordeal. Maribé's jump can be interpreted as a leap of faith toward the future, out of the reality of oppression. It is a defining moment in that the diary will become a book once it has reached Christiane's long-lost brother. Ironically, a "southerner" will see to it that a book by a "northerner" is published.

Johnny, Les petits-fils, and *Murambi* attempt to signal the mechanisms of mass identification and violent discrimination. This is not true for *L'aîné,* where ethnicity remains an unarticulated issue that signals the writer's unwillingness to "think ethnically," as well as his desire to have readers take responsibility for their understanding of the 1994 genocide in Rwanda. Faustin's background is clearly mentioned for the first time only on page 139, almost at the end of the book, as he slowly lifts the curtain of his memory and remembers posing the question of his ethnicity to his father, Théoneste. Théoneste's answer represents that question as beside the point and thus likens his character to Mabanckou's Mam'Soko. Both Théoneste and Mam'Soko are impervious to the notion of ethnicity. As deaf as Théoneste is allegedly simple-minded, Mam'Soko just cannot *hear* Hortense when the latter tries to explain her daughter's and her own situation.

Dongala's and Mabanckou's books present a similar narrative construction of the root causes of ethnic prejudice. *Johnny* and *Les petits-fils* portray ethnic prejudice as the uncontrolled need for personal enrichment and power, and attempt to dismantle the logic of "tribalism." However, whereas Mabanckou does so through "worthy" characters such as Christiane, Hortense, and Mam'Soko, Dongala deconstructs that logic through both Lao and Johnny, and at different levels. Indeed, Johnny can alternatively deliver a clear judgment of what is happening to his society and fall prey to delusional beliefs (104–5).

Literary representations of violence, these texts raise the question of the characterization of abused women as heroines, and, in the case of *Les petits-fils*, the nature of the message conveyed by Christiane's and Hortense's surrendering to rape. The texts also invite the reader to evaluate the qualitative distance separating Christiane or Hortense from other iconic tragic heroines such as Mongo Beti's Perpétue (*Perpétue et l'habitude du malheur*, 1974). Is the idea of a female character facing and surrendering to rape more powerful than that of another castrating her potential rapist, as in *Johnny*? Likewise, does Diop's inclusion of the beautiful Tutsi woman's similar choice to face her certain gang rape in the streets of Kigali constitute a problematic romanticizing in *Murambi*? If through her sacrifice Hortense makes her daughter move from one symbolic order to another, namely from a world of violence to a world of freedom from oppression, is this freedom not tinged with messianic Christian(e)ity?

With the martyr-like figures of Hortense and Christiane, it is tempting to interpret suffering and sacrifice as the essential characteristics of women's memory. However, seeing "Hortense's" narrative as a letter, an investigation, and a book to be published prevents it from being encapsulated by the idea of oppression. The creative interplay between the various narrative forms reinjects a measure of life and movement to a doomed atmosphere. Hortense's compulsive writing can be understood both as a desire for lost time and as a desire to have the last word. Manifesting the power of the (written) word, *Les petits-fils* can thus be read as a poetics of memory articulated through female consciousness. Hortense's reminiscing is a sort of purification that symbolically counters the profusion and excess of violence. Her writing is a re-ritualizing of life, best exemplified when she and her daughter, Maribé, give Mam'Soko a dignified burial in the middle of a civil war, and when Maribé puts the old woman's cane and the loincloth she and her mother had offered her in her coffin. In so doing, they honor their elder and grant her her wish to meet her husband in beautiful garb in another form of life. This respectful observance of reappropriated rituals and customs—all the more significant since Mam'Soko's ethnic origin is never directly alluded to—posits another form of mourning that has nothing to do with violence, rape, or crime, but with the natural process of human existence.

Hortense does not succumb to the extreme exclusion to which she is driven. To her, writing is a signifying activity closely related to what Marc Augé sees as the affirmation of "the shared (reciprocal) consciousness of the bond represented and instituted towards the Other" (102). Hortense's ritualistic writing, in the leveled landscape of violence, aims at recalling that bond, rooted in the family, but also in neighborly commerce, friendship, and work, a bond that belies (and defies) ethnicization.

In the world the four books construct, the child soldier is the other signifier of social and ontological collapse. Both he and adult women are the primary markers of the violence born of economic plunder, and forced ethnic and gender identification. In *Johnny* the child soldier serves as the emblematic figure of a world riddled by the obsession of domination. He is the scapegoat of a society increasingly blind to its humanity. Because childhood tends to be universally equated with innocence and thus holds a sacred value, the child soldier paradoxically represents both the radicalization of evil and the profanation of childhood. The child soldier blurs the social reference points culturally associated with age: childhood, adolescence, youth, and maturity. A child by age, he is a man through oppression and murder. He is the ultimate figure of victimization and cruelty, of the oppressor/oppressed dyad that haunts African literatures. He makes no sense and will not be explained away through moralistic reasoning. Johnny and Faustin are two strong illustrations of this phenomenon, and Monénembo has succeeded in creating in Faustin a particularly subtle literary example of this schizophrenic conglomerate of "values." Through his dealings with Claudine, his benefactor, Faustin shows that kindness and righteousness are no longer points of reference in the life he has had to live. Claudine's wanting to adopt Faustin and her certainty that that should—naturally—be his desire as well, demonstrate how privilege qualifies the meaning of childhood. Her failure to see that he is not a child but an adolescent forced to grow up too fast and her denial of his sexuality represent other forms of violation, albeit contextually more benign.

A narrative reality where the sexual norm is rape may cause the reader to wonder about the perverse and voyeuristic implications of the story. What indeed guarantees a critical interpretation of the type of sexual violence permeating these books? How does the writer ensure that the narration does not eroticize evil? One obvious answer to these questions is that these books are not mere testimonials, but artistic interrogations of complex situations. Another answer is that they contain definite instances whereby the problematic of a literary use of violence is staged through a cataclysm of narrative events halting the reader's progression by their puzzling and tragic incoherence. This causes a double reaction on the part of the reader: first, the suspension of her/his critical sense, and then the beginning of a questioning process to explain what it signifies. This is best represented in *Johnny* when Lovelita, Johnny's girlfriend, wakes up and does not know if she has made love with him or been raped by him, and in *L'aîné*, when Faustin, who routinely sleeps with the young girls in his gang, kills his accomplice and alter ego, Musinkôro, when he finds him having sex with his younger sister. Faustin's unquestioned exercise of *droit de cuissage* (free and legal sexual access to women) coupled with his righteous revolt against it when it concerns his sister could be explained away as a classic instance of male supremacist confusion, but other characteristics of the protagonist, notably the fact that he is twelve years old when he kills his friend, as well as an orphaned survivor of a genocide, complicate the issue and make it hard for the reader to come to a clear-cut moral evaluation of him. This near-impossibility of judgment is played out on another level through Faustin's trial and its preparation. Determined to save the adolescent, Claudine has hired a lawyer Faustin despises at first sight for the law, lies, and social class he vainly represents. As Faustin sabotages his chances for a lesser prison sentence, the reader is left to wonder if Faustin's last revolt was prompted by his understanding of his historical circumstances and his conscious refusal to be further degraded by the system, or if his insults to the lawyer and to the court constitute a symbolic form of suicide, a violent peroration by which he paradoxically confirms himself as the emblematic Other of his society.

Humanitarian aid workers and foreign media operatives constitute a new set of characters in francophone African literature's dramatization of violence. As the foreign expert was one of the supporting characters denoting neocolonialism earlier on in African literature (see, for example, Mongo Beti's *Dzewatama* chronicle), aid workers and media operatives represent the current context of globalization. They provide a broader imaginary background, one where the role and presence of international institutions signify the current tensions between North and South and question the meaning of progress and conflict resolution anew.

Whereas *L'aîné, Johnny,* and *Murambi* propose a range of fictional constructions of such themes, *Les petits-fils* does not. This text constructs the foreign as a process of othering that is internal to the protagonists' society and born of the violent instrumentalization of ethnicity by ruthless and ignorant opportunists.

Diop circumscribes his evocation of foreign "assistance" to the

French Opération Turquoise in 1998, through the tense confrontation between Doctor Karekezi and Colonel Etienne Perrin, as narrated by the latter. The main idea resulting from their dialogue is that their respective interests, that of the French and that of the Hutus in power, were not that far apart. The symbolic proof of their collusion is the installation of the Opération Turquoise headquarters in Murambi's Ecole Technique, the site of the massacre (148). Denouncing France as a neocolonial power, that chapter also identifies the 1994 genocide in Rwanda as one of the historic benchmarks marking the gradual end of its influence in "francophone" Africa (166).

Monénembo's evocation of humanitarian aid and human rights workers bears the same testy skepticism that permeates his characterization of Claudine. His book conveys the idea that the very notion of human rights is predicated on a concept of the universal engineered by, enforced by, and mostly benefiting economically dominant countries. The book manifests a critical understanding of the fact that human rights discourse is a major factor in modern politics. At best, it represents "aid" as a sort of temporary bandage; more generally, it is featured as an empty *beau discours* (empty, mostly rhetorical, speeches) supporting the status quo and having little effect on the daily lives of the people in need. Claudine's friend, Una Flannery O'Flaherty, also known as "la Hirlandaise" (94) and "Miss Human Rights" (63–64, 170), illustrates that point. Her efforts to welcome Faustin to her orphanage outside of Kigali, La Cité des Anges Bleus (the City of Blue Angels), and to keep him there, fail because she holds him hostage to her own sense of what he should do. Her character signals a connection between human rights discourse and a fallacious international moral order.

Yet Miss Human Rights is an innocuous character compared to Rodney, the cameraman Faustin meets in Kigali. Through Rodney and the Western media, the issue of how one looks at Africa and Africans is discussed. An actor of the type of Western modernity that reports, fashions, and broadcasts violent images of Africa internationally, Rodney came to Rwanda for work, that is, to make money (98). Faustin catches on to Rodney's "pragmatism" fast, and heeding his advice, lies so as to obtain a bit of money by becoming a guide to the memorial sites of the genocide, and by staging different versions of his victimization for foreign consumption. A posturing victim, he becomes "interesting" to the foreign media and thus underlines their perverse ways of functioning (105). Faustin's adventures among the media also give another twist to the issue of memory. Since modern events are conceived of by the news media as occurring and being staged simultaneously, the process of memorialization is no longer an a posteriori matter; it is already in the act. Thus the genocide can be replayed and reframed at will.

Overall, Dongala's work shows a more nuanced outlook on the issue. On the one hand, he represents the indignity of the so-called developed world through the outcry by Laokolé as she and other displaced people running for safety and trying to enter a foreign embassy are driven off: "Would we happen to be the new barbarians storming the fortresses erected by the new masters of the world?" (126). Yet, Dongala's protagonist praises the dedication of individual foreign human rights workers—almost exclusively women (181). In *Johnny*, responsibilities for the state of the country are shared between foreigners and nationals, although Laokolé's dream for her future rests abroad, and her "ticket" to go to the United States and study is symbolized by the business card the African American human rights worker has given her.

Violence has remained a fundamental notion in contemporary francophone African literature. It is still articulated around themes that are traditional to it: broken historicity, memory, utopia and change, gender, and immigration. However, the 1994 genocide in Rwanda as well as the civil wars in West and Central Africa have induced the reworking of such themes as memory and gender in significant new directions. The violence born of the narrative opposition between tradition and modernity is no longer obviously operative. Figures of tradition are more often sketched than carefully elaborated. A subject of much contemporary debate and research, the theme of memory seems to have relayed that of tradition/modernity. The future of the youth and the nature of future relationships between women and men, between Africa and the rest of the world, are recast through the representations of the child soldier, of mixed origins as opposed to ethnicity, of human rights workers and humanitarian discourse. Violence is woven in more complex ways in the texts and no longer the expression of a straightforward denunciation. *L'aîné, Murambi, Johnny*, and *Les petits-fils* push African literature's dramatization of violence further, and their authors use a great variety of narrative tools to that end. The self-referentiality of the books is carefully problematized and thought of in global terms.

MIGRATION, IMMIGRATION, AND THE WRITING
OF DIS-LOCATION

The thematics of immigration are not new to African literature either. They date back to the 1960s, with Ousmane Sembène's *Le docker noir* (1956), Bernard Dadié's *Un nègre à Paris* (1959; *An African in Paris*, 1994), and Cheikh Hamidou Kane's *L'aventure ambiguë* (1961)—all testifying to the experience of migration. However, except for Sembène's novels and short stories, especially "La noire de . . . ," they mostly represent the experience of African students during short-term stays in France. The issues raised in these early books pertain to alienation and trying to find a balance between two different cultural worlds, values, and modes of thinking. In the 1990s, the African writers' gaze shifts to African immigrants living in France, and immigration becomes one of the prevalent themes in the works by the new Afrique sur Seine generation. Until recently, immigration was explored mostly by African writers living in France and, more broadly, Europe.

Although her early works centered on Africa and on gendered relationships, Calixthe Beyala's Parisian novels[13] were key in shifting the narrative focus to the community of Africans in France, notably in the Parisian neighborhood of Belleville. In these works, Beyala explores immigration in terms of its potential and its risks for the family, and particularly women. Her novels creatively map out the transformation of gender roles and the redefinition of power that ensues.

Presenting the experience of immigration enables Beyala to construct Belleville, a popular Parisian neighborhood, as a site of displacement. She exposes the stereotypical images attached to African and non-European immigrants by linking them to the stereotypes held about the French working class. Through a multiplication of voices and experiences, Beyala places her characters in the uncomfortable position of insiders/outsiders. In that regard, and as analyzed by Nicki Hitchcott in *Calixthe Beyala: Performances of Migration* (2006), she plays on the ambivalence and ambiguities of her characters, including through gender and code switching, and a construction of the erotic-exotic Other. Beyala furthermore presents us with a comparative view of social exclusion in French society. Based on inversion, her perspective features an ex-colonizer who is objectified and an ex-colonized now in the position of subject, the "I" speaking and reflecting.

Whereas Beyala opted for a humoristic vein and focused first on family, then on women coming into their own, male writers introduced issues of clandestine immigration. The representation of clandestine immigration caused new protagonists to appear: the clandestine, the marginals, the "noceurs" (partygoers) and the dilettantes (Moudileno, "Le droit d'exister: trafic et nausée postcoloniale" [The right to exist: traffic and postcolonial nausea, 2002]). The gradual disappearance of heroic figures corresponds to the disintegration of a congruent vision. A new aesthetics of struggle emerges in the process, one no longer predicated on the collective. If these types of antiheroes are not necessarily original or specific to the new voices in Paris (see, for instance, Sassine's 1985 *Le zéhéros n'est pas n'importe qui*), writers such as J. R. Essomba, with *Le paradis du nord* (The northern paradise, 1996) and *Le destin volé* (The stolen destiny, 2003), Alain Mabanckou with *Bleu blanc rouge* (1998), and Daniel Biyaoula with *L'impasse* (The one-way street, 1996), *Agonies* (1998), and *La source des joies* (2003) have further developed such characterization and settings.

Ambroise Kom has said that "there is no happy return home,"[14] and indeed, Biyaoula's *La source des joies* gives a somber portrayal of Africans' return to their countries of origin. Through his protagonist, Basile's, return to the Congo after many years of absence and his reunion with his closest childhood friends, Biyaoula explores issues of change and location. Back in Congo and forced to reassess reality, Basile realizes that his former group of friends has split along class lines: Raphaël and Sébastien have become financially and politically successful and grown distant from Jean-Luc and Laurent, who can barely make ends meet. Jean-Luc's disappearance and subsequent death in prison act as a catalyst for Basile's waking up to the symbolic violence of social differences.

La source des joies closes the trilogy formed by *L'impasse* and *Agonies*. Indeed, this book taps into some of the main elements of his first two novels. As in *L'impasse*, the narrative is articulated on the sharp differentiation, in behavior and mentality, between the protagonist who lives in France and the other characters that stayed in Africa. Each party holds a stereotypical view of the other but is soon forced to confront its contradictions. Biyaoula's protagonists, Joseph (in *L'impasse*) and Basile (in *La source des joies*), demonstrate the author's critical perception of his country of origin, emphasizing the stalemate of its citizens' daily lives as well as the ways in which they have changed and parted from their ideals. To a certain extent, Biyaoula revisits the central motif of Mongo Beti's *Trop de soleil tue l'amour.* Essomba's, Biyaoula's, and Mabanckou's protagonists feature the anxiety at the core of the experience of migration, particularly the negotiations between their own expectations and those of their communities.

Since these novels came out, the reality of migration has caught up with fiction. Today, at the risk of their lives, thousands of young Africans embark on small boats toward the shores of Spain and Italy, invested with their families' hopes for a brighter future.[15] From the nineties on, the literary production has thus seen a change in the treatment of immigration: from Beyala to Biyaoula, Mabanckou to Bessora, Sow Fall to Fatou Diome and Leonora Miano, African writers have contributed to the shaping of different facets of this issue. Women writers such as Beyala, Bessora, and Diome have used humor and irony, subverting stereotypical representations of the African immigrant, even if, arguably, in the case of Beyala for instance, her works have also participated in a certain "folklorization" of the African immigrant community.[16]

As outlined in our introduction and earlier in the section on violence, the younger generation of women writers (Diome, Etoke, Miano, Bessora) has approached the issue of migration, displacement, and postcolonial identities from a different angle, raising first the issue of youth within a postcolonial urban environment. Bessora's *53 cm* (1999) and *Les taches d'encre* (Ink blots, 2000) mark a significant moment in francophone African literature in that they allow for a deeper problematization of *littérature d'immigration*. They make us reflect on the implications of this literature, not only in sociological terms, but also in relation to the broader context of cultural studies and the notion of diaspora. The structuring principle of these texts is to provocatively challenge norms (national, social, moral, epistemological, and literary) by creating a proliferation of viewpoints that entice the reader to examine contemporary values and the discourses that sustain them. Compared with the books by other African women writers currently living in France, such as Beyala's or Diome's, Bessora's novels are more subversive because they exoticize the "Franco-French" to ironically deconstruct the exoticization of the "others" of French society.

The novels *53 cm* and *Les taches d'encre* are clearly informed by the work of theorists of the postcolonial condition such as Frantz Fanon, and also by contemporary Anglophone scholars such as Paul Gilroy.[17] In Bessora's texts, the main articulations of Fanonian thought are easily recognizable, as they represent a universe where "the complete reassessment of the colonial situation"[18]—i.e., decolonization—is not achieved, and where social "environmental pathologies" (345) continue to be at work. Political and cultural oversimplifications, racism and violence, and the appropriation of history are other notions at the core of *53 cm* and *Les taches d'encre*. Numerous questions raised by Gilroy are echoed in Bessora's texts: questions pertaining to citizenship and cultural affiliation; relations between race, ethnicity, and culture; the dialectics of diasporic identification; and the critical vigilance a romantic linking of the notions of race, people, and nation calls for.

Both *53 cm* and *Les taches d'encre* are peopled with a variety and a hierarchy of lunatics who are oblivious to their condition. Each character has a specific obsession, more or less lethal for himself or herself and others. The novels are concerned with the (ironic) staging of these obsessions and with the representation of the factors that trigger these characters' *passage à l'acte* (acting out). Both books deal with the racial, political, and sexual order, the types of identities it generates, and the systems of identification it proposes/imposes. They present two complementary sides of this problematic: *53 cm* discusses immigration, that is, issues of racial, ethnic, and national identifications; *Les taches d'encre* picks apart (with vengeful glee) the perverse fixedness of the institution of heterosexuality, as it indirectly addresses the question of métissage, raised in *53 cm*.

Referring to anthropometry, a nineteenth-century pseudoscientific technique used to measure the human body and evaluate its proportions, the title *53 cm* raises the issue of the categorization of individuals, the ways and reasons they are classified, and by extension, the types of data gathered, notably in the management of immigration. Evidently, this title also has a salacious connotation. Together with the inclusion of the Saartje Boorman (the so-called Hottentot Venus) character, it refers the reader to the more general problematic of (Western) sexual fantasies and their history.

The narrator of *53 cm* is identified only in the fifth chapter when she introduces herself as Zara Sem Andock, "born on December 25, 1968, of a Swiss Roman mother and a Gabonese Fang father" (28). Before Zara is named, what is important is her function as an urban "gaulologue" (51) who is both an observer and a participant. It is the scope of her gaze onto the chaotic world surrounding her that is the operating principle of her character, a gaze at once ironic and cosmopolitan, critical and objectifying, at times distancing, but always far from authoritative: "I am a learned indigene as well as a candid ethnologist. . . . I observe your people without interfering because a civilized observer is invisible to the indigenes' naked eye, and to the fully clothed eye of the urbanicized. . . . Of course, what is at stake here is not what I think of Gaulois, but what you think of yourself. This is the great mission of ethnology" (37).

Bessora mockingly represents postcolonial France as a disturbed social space that has not yet taken stock of its evolution and is frozen in a reality where the plural vocabulary of the people is out of sync with the prescriptive official appeal to the Nation, a nation that reveals itself as a dangerously controversial myth. The argument illustrated by the novel is that racial identification and profiling is still a factor in the conduct of French political, social, and economic affairs. While postcolonial realities such as immigration, globalization, and métissage seem to bring about a reconceptualization of the notion of race and its applications, the very epistemological bases that inform the conduct of the State have remained the same.

A "primitive" conducting research on primitivism, a candid intellectual, a métisse, a single mother, and a very Parisian undocumented foreigner, Zara is on the side of ambiguity and relativism, not truth. Multifaceted and paradoxical, she represents a particular space at the crossroads of many stereotypes and "ethnic absolutisms" (Gilroy, 3), yet she is also closely linked to the type of reflexive cultural consciousness Gilroy discusses in *The Black Atlantic: Modernity and Double Consciousness* (1993). "The specificity of the modern political and cultural formation I want to call the black Atlantic," says Gilroy, "can be defined . . . through this desire to transcend both the structures of the nation state and the constraints of ethnicity and national particularity" (19).

Diome's first book, *La préférence nationale* (2001), is a collection of six short stories taking place both in Senegal and in France. "La préférence nationale" is also the title of the fourth short story in the book. Like Bessora's, Diome's style is often irreverently humorous and biting, but it is less elaborate in its subversion. Diome is more explicit in her critical and fictional portraiture of modern-day France and Senegal, whereas Bessora progresses with a stick of literary dynamite in hand.

La préférence nationale is a clear allusion to the debates raging in France since the 1980s regarding questions of citizenship, preferential employment policies, and cultural specificity. "The notion of na-tional preference, invented by Jean-Yves Le Gallou and the Club de l'Horloge, a New Right think tank, is at the root of a strategic revolu-tion in the Front National's way to showcase itself. After the slogan, 'Immigrants: Go Away,' here is a more polished and presentable no-tion that recalls Le Pen's seemingly sensible words: 'I prefer my sisters to my cousins, etc.' It does not appear to suggest any hatred or dis-dain, but only to convey an order of preference. Today, this sentence has become the cornerstone of the FN program."[19]

Diome's fiction (like Bessora's) moves away from identity politics by systematically laying out the complexities of citizenship, as ad-dressed by Etienne Balibar, Nacira Guénif Souilamas, and Pap Ndi-aye. Her spirited query of the nuances between assimilation and in-tegration allows for a sharper examination and representation of the question of migration.

That title is also an ironic marker of the conundrum of contempo-rary French national identity. But beyond that, if one considers that some of the short stories in this volume take place in Senegal and that the book title applies to them also, one wonders if "la préférence na-tionale" does not indirectly refer to Senegal's national reality. "What signifies France?" thus calls for a corollary question: "What signi-fies Senegal?" Both questions indicate that immigration politically and culturally affects both the country of origin and the country of destination.

La préférence nationale figures the journey of an immigrant and her cultural transformation, culminating in "Mariage volé" when the protagonist renounces her Senegalese lover, marries a Frenchman, and prepares to move to France with him. Another short story in the volume, "Le visage de l'emploi," features her arrival in France, in Strasbourg, and her awakening to that country's stark racial and so-cial realities. The tone of the book becomes markedly more ironic and diffident from that story on. It communicates the narrator's stalwart resistance to the racialized position she is constantly assigned to, and it speaks to her struggle to free her life from this constraint.

"La préférence nationale" derisively refers to the period in the late 1980s and the early 1990s when the Pasqua laws were in full effect. Diome spins satirical circles around France's *racisme ordinaire* and the range of its pathetic exercises, thereby communicating the im-migrant narrator's bottled-up pain in a manner that allows her to retain discursive control. At times, however, Diome's critique backfires, especially when she overexploits stereotypes, albeit for critical purposes. Diome's literary deconstruction of the immigrant's realities is organized through a three-pronged thematic approach: the racist "national" versus the racialized immigrant Other, the white male native versus the objectified black female immigrant, the white female "national" versus the black female immigrant. Diome depicts situations whereby racism is not mitigated by any possibilities for interracial feminist solidarity, notably through the narrator's allusion to her white *copine de fac* (fellow female university student). Representing white peoples' fundamental blindness to their own "color" and racial privileges, this *copine* manifests the skewed quality of interracial friendships under such conditions.

"Cunégonde à la bibliothèque" situates the Senegalese writer in a specific literary and philosophical tradition, that of Voltaire and the Enlightenment. Akin to Voltaire's Candide, Diome's narrator and heroine also resembles Bessora's Zara, the falsely naive protagonist of *53 cm*. But Diome's and Bessora's candid heroines also consolidate and, because of their gender, problematize what has become of the literary motif of the African Candide epitomized by Mongo Beti's Mezda in *Le pauvre Christ de Bomba* (1956). With an ironic reference to Racine and clear allusions to Fanon, "Cunégonde à la bibliothèque" provides a vignette of the (absence of) relationship between an African student, who looks for solace in books and survives economically through her job as a maid, and her employers, the infamous Dupires (literally, of the worst). It is at once an account of ordinary survival and an admirable, if twisted, struggle for one's dignity, and intellectual and emotional sanity.

The book closes with "Le dîner du professeur" which presents another aspect of the white male native versus the objectified black female immigrant theme we shall call *la consommation du fantasme* (the consumption of desire). The young African female narrator describes the unpleasurable evening she spends at her professor's place, his misreading of her as well as his cultivated blindness to her situation as an immigrant. In this short story, Diome tackles the subject of women's commodification by men on the levels of the commodification of younger women by older, professionally established (dominant and immature) men and the sexual objectification of black women by white men. This feminist agenda is also present in Bessora's work, in *53 cm*, through the character of the immigration inspector and his sexual "consumption" of Zara, and in *Les taches d'encre*, through the neurotic married couple, Bernard and Bianca, and the loving relationship between the Rwandan, Muriel, and the French Jew, Azraël.

Diome's immediate editorial success and the remarkable reception to her first novel, *Le ventre de l'Atlantique*, a best seller for the 2003 fall *rentrée littéraire*, demonstrates that she struck a chord. *Le ventre de l'Atlantique* is original in that it is articulated around two axes, a geographical one (here/there) and a temporal one (past/present), and thus proposes a new narrative of immigration. Furthermore, the author offers her readers two concurrent visions of time and space, through a juxtaposition of her own perceptions and remembrances as well as the perceptions of her brother, who dreams of coming to Europe via the opportunity granted by sports.[20] Through the narrator's brother's dream of becoming a soccer player on an Italian or a French team, Diome evokes the dreams of an entire generation of African youth. Soccer is not a new theme in itself; it already appears in novels such as Mongo Beti's *Les deux mères de Guillaume Ismaël Dzewatama, futur camionneur* (1983) and the sequel, *La revanche de Guillaume Ismaël Dzewatama* (1984), Angèle Rawiri's *Elonga* (1986), and more recently, Eugène Ebodé's *La divine colère* (2003). This theme was analyzed by André Ntonfo in *Football et politique du football au Cameroun* (1994).

Diome's novel proposes a critical rereading of the myth of France as a haven for immigrants, the path to social recognition, and the exit-door to thwarted possibilities on the continent. Here she also addresses the notion of economic interaction, something explored at length in Effa's *Nous, enfants de la tradition* (We, children of tradition, 2008).

Furthermore, Diome's narrative proceeds through both collective and individual memories. To save her brother from the difficult realities of clandestine immigration and denounce the myth of sport as the promise for an easy, fast, and sure success, the narrator reconnects with her own painful memories, addressing the attraction of France and its clichés.

Textually, the trans-Atlantic phone conversations between the brother and sister, and their respective commentaries on soccer games during the European Cup represent both the fragmentation of their exchanges and the dislocation of her experiences. The contacts between the siblings show an array of paradoxical features. On the one hand, their relationship develops from the fragmentary quality of their conversations; on the other, the brother never really hears what the sister is saying, that is, that his dreams of soccer fame are unrealistic and even dangerous, and that he should settle for a small business at home, with her financial assistance. On yet another level, these different inferences can be read as signs of globalization on the African continent. With a gaze that encompasses both the past and the present, Diome undoes a number of the myths and stereotypical representations of migration and immigrants that operate both in Europe and in Africa.

With *Ketala*, a novel written in 2006, Diome further explores the enduring myth of France as a *terre d'accueil* (the land of welcome) but addresses this issue from a different angle, adding family pressures and taboos about homosexuality to the equation. In a revamped version of Mariama Bâ's subversion of the Mirasse tradition (an Islamic principle by which a deceased person's material possessions are distributed), *Une si longue lettre* (1979; *So Long a Letter*, 1981), Diome draws up an inventory of the protagonist's life, Memoria, giving voice to her different belongings before they are shared between her relatives after her death. Each of Memoria's former possessions testifies to her past life, and the reader gradually discovers how she has been doubly sacrificed. Married out of convenience so that her husband's homosexuality is covered up, she follows him to Strasbourg, France. She is then separated from her husband and forced to manage on her own, resorting to prostitution to be able to keep sending money back home.[21] Subsequently, this financial burden is responsible for her illness (AIDS) and her death. Despite the sub-theme of homosexuality, the novel remains first and foremost emblematic of the question of financial dependence and the ways young immigrants' futures often remain tied to the betterment of their families back home. It is noteworthy that filmmakers are also engaged with this issue, as illustrated by Jean-Marie Teno's *Clando* (1996), Mweze Ngangura's *La pièce d'identité* (1998), and Moussa Sene Absa's *Teranga Blues* (2007).

The exploration of migration and the expression of displacement and transculturation have redefined the writing of postcolonial identities. As pointed out by Derek Wright in "African Literature and Post-Independence Disillusionment," disenchantment has been a key characteristic of this aesthetic redefinition.[22]

Miano's writing of disenchantment carves a new space. Although her trilogy—made up of *L'intérieur de la nuit* (The inside of the night, 2005), *Contours du jour qui vient* (Contours of the coming day, 2006), and *Tels des astres éteints* (Like extinguished stars, 2008)—

and her 2009 novel, *Les aubes écarlates "Sankofa cry"* (The scarlet dawns "Sankofa cry") were set on the African continent and marked by violence, wars, and their ensuing traumas, *Afropean soul et autres nouvelles* (2008) is anchored in Paris. This in itself is not original, as Beyala had walked a similar path. However, Miano brings in a number of innovative elements: working her narrative like soul music and improvising freely from a core structure, the writer lets disenchantment seep through each short story and invites her readers to interrogate the causes of a persistent pain. Each piece evokes the impossibility of going back home and, in the process, denounces the myth of Paris/France as the land of plenty. In "Depuis la première heure," the first short story of her collection, for instance, Miano shows that fifty years after most African countries' independence, the dreams of young women such as Diouana, Sembene's protagonist in *La Noire de . . .* , remain tainted by (post)colonial imagery. Each short story reveals (in the photographic sense) the misperception and stereotypical representations about Paris, wherein center and margins, inner city and suburbs are merged together. In a rising style reminiscent of Aimé Césaire's *Cahier d'un retour au pays natal*, Miano exposes the underbelly of migration to Paris/France, revisiting for the youth the dreams that have shaped generations of Africans. She powerfully evokes images of exploitation, racial profiling, daily humiliations, and thwarted hopes, and highlights the contradictions of the French Republic, particularly with regard to its educational system.

> I would describe under-the-sleeve work, for which one is not always paid. The unhealthy squats one is forced to accept as if condemned to crawl through France's bowels. Until the foggy early morning when one is thrown into a plane and sent back home. Handcuffed. This ominous dusk keeps haunting us. I would tell of the unemployed about to fall into illegality. The homeless. The beggar. . . . This country cannot do anything for us; and certainly not allow us to dream: what is there to expect from someone who produces nothing but feelings of emptiness and exclusion. Such a country cannot teach us anything. Such a country has no lesson to teach. It's time we turn our eyes away and invent ourselves. (28–29)

Each narrative reasserts French society's refusal to deal with the postcolonial subject and her/his agency. As explored by Michel Laronde in "Représentation du sujet postcolonial et effets d'institution: Les silences de l'Immigré"[23] (Representation of the postcolonial subject and institutional effects: the silences of the immigrant), the French establishment has been slow to articulate a coherent discourse that would seriously take into account the postcolonial situation/context in France with regard to the notions of immigration and citizenship. The pervasiveness of clichéd images of Paris and African immigrants today evidence the palimpsestic nature of the French postcolonial imaginary, whereby the colonial lurks behind the postcolonial.

Yet, Miano's short stories in this collection seek to go beyond the mere expression of an individual identity crisis. Rather, they focus on mapping out the situation in France and on the narrator's positioning in relation to that nation. Laying claim to a larger identity, the narrator is no longer an immigrant exiled from his native country, he is an "Afropéen."

> He did not feel particularly close to those who were speaking out; he did not live like an African exiled in France. He was Afropean, a European of African descent. Nothing had changed. Yet, the social climate in the country was hurting his feelings, forcing him to wonder. They spoke of national identity. There was talk of circumscribing it clearly, of making it an administrative entity. As was the case for Justice, Health, Education. The young man was wondering whether Afropeans' identity was national. (53)

Asked about the motivation behind this collection of short stories, Miano says the following: "For years I have wanted to produce a series of snapshot narratives, slices of life taken from what nobody dares yet call Black France. There are Blacks in France. The literature of this country does not really speak of them, as featuring them means bringing them closer to others. I believe we need to do so, especially these days" (*Afropean Soul*, 92). Her statement is in line with Pap N'diaye's *La condition noire. Essai sur une minorité française* (2008).[24]

> We must reveal this paradox: black people in France are individually visible, but they are invisible as a social group and have not yet received particular attention from researchers. . . . We could rejoice in the invisibility of France's black populations, or at least consider that it does not constitute a problem in itself, if some of the specific social difficulties affecting them were evaluated, known, and recognized. This is not the case. And so, rather than being the peaceful consequence of an absence of particular problems, this invisibility can be considered as a wrong. (17)

Through *Afropean Soul* and her most recent collection of short stories, *Soulfood Equatoriale* (2009), Miano aims at breaking away from the usual representations of postcolonial identities, especially representations of Africans and Africa. At the same time, while highlighting the necessity for French society to redefine itself and be more inclusive of Black France, she tries to move away from the ghettoization of a literature of migration through new aesthetics.

The exploration of migrancy, displacement, and the writing of new postcolonial identities has prompted new aesthetic forms and opened up new registers of language in the representation of sex and sexuality. Among women writers, Beyala has given representations of sexuality a central place in her writing. Immigration has reconfigured gender roles and issues of power. Despite this, however, Beyala's female characters appear progressively more at a loss, destabilized, and experiencing meaningless sexual lives. And although Beyala's declared search for a new sexual ethics seems to have failed, she did attempt with *Femme nue, femme noire* (Naked woman, black woman, 2003) to open a new phase in her writing of sexuality even though the back cover of that book, presenting it as an erotic novel, actually reinforced the exoticizing, objectification, and essentializing of "the" black woman.

Among the diasporic writers in Paris, Sami Tchak's use of representations of sex and sexuality is particularly provocative. Tchak's *Place des fêtes* created quite a stir when it came out in 2001. A transgressive novel, it attacks the ultimate taboos governing the understanding and practice of sex, such as desiring a parent, thinking of one's mother, sister, or cousin in sexual terms, and imagining relatives as sexual agents. Under the cover of a humorous and playful tone, *Place des fêtes* conveys a lucid picture of the consequences of immigration on second-generation African youth, their loss of bearings and their search for a sense of being through sex. This approach is new to sub-Saharan literature and brings the text closer to considerations raised especially in the "Beur" or Franco-Maghrebi novel (for instance, finding one's place in society, unemployment, and generational conflicts). In that regard, *Place des fêtes* contributes to the decentering of diasporic writing in Paris.

Tchak's next book, *Hermina* (2003), uses some of the same sexual imagery as *Place des fêtes*. The narrator, a writer, fantasizes about a young adolescent, named Hermina, his landlord's daughter. His sexual fantasies feed his imagination anew and become the pretext for his writing again. Eventually, scared by the intensity of his desires, the narrator lets Hermina fictitiously die, stung by a snake (and the evident phallic image it stands for).

Unlike most francophone African novels,[25] *Hermina* starts in the Caribbean, in Cuba.[26] That island, however, remains a generic entity for tropicalism and insularity, a pre-text. The narrator, Heberto, moves from one sexual encounter to the next—from Cuba to Europe, to Miami, back to Europe and finally to Miami—and the intertextuality of the narrative, with multiple references to world literature, enables the author to address a phenomenon of globalization of both the experience of immigration and literature. Thus, the narrative leads the reader to reflect on the multiple layering and opacities in the shaping of postcolonial identities. The economic and political factors accounting for migration are relegated to the background, so that the narrative focus is placed on the issue of personal disconnection. Heberto is ready to follow anybody, any woman, Hermina, Ingrid, Mira, any fantasy and dream. He will go to any place in the hope of finding an anchoring that continues to elude him. Finally, the inclusion of excerpts from *Pagli* (2001) and *Soupir* (Sigh, 2002) by the Mauritian author Ananda Devi, interspersed with Tchak's own literary analysis of Devi's writing, contributes to a decentering of the novel as a genre.

In Tchak's following novel, *La fête des masques* (2004), the location becomes even more incidental. The text addresses issues of power and dictatorship without necessarily giving any specific geographical or cultural reference or alluding to the African continent. Tchak's highly eroticized writing, whereby the borders between the erotic and the pornographic become blurry, is utterly provocative within the configurations of the African novel and, in that sense, contributes to shaking its foundational bases. Ironically, *La fête des masques*, a text where Africa and Africans have disappeared, was awarded the Grand Prix de l'Afrique Francophone in 2004 for its criticism of dictatorship. Tchak is a writer who has defined himself as more preoccupied with world literature than with African literature per se. His more recent novels, *Le paradis des chiots* (2006) and *Filles de Mexico* (2008), take place in Colombia and Mexico. Acknowledging *La fête des masques* as a politically committed text reopens the debate on the *engagé* novel and the extent to which writers such as Tchak participate in questioning the literary establishment while becoming more established in France.

In contemporary francophone African literature, the theme of migrancy often dovetails with the vein of crime fiction. Just as memory is instrumental to revamping and subverting traditional myths, criminal fiction revamps the myths of modernity, particularly in the urban context. A corpus of francophone African detective novels has been shaping up for the past twenty years with such writers as Mongo Beti, but also Simon Njami, Yodi Karone, Bolya Baenga, Achille Ngoye, Moussa Konaté, J. R. Essomba, and younger, less seasoned writers such as Aïda Mady Diallo. The detective novel explores the postcolonial urban landscape particularly well. Bolya's *La polyandre* (1998) and *Les cocus posthumes* (Posthumous cuckold, 2001), Achille Ngoye's *Kin-la-joie Kin-la-folie* (Happy Kinshasa, crazy Kinshasa, 1993), *Agence black bafoussa* (1996), *Sorcellerie à bout portant* (Point-blank sorcery, 1998), and *Ballet noir à Chateau-Rouge* (Black ballet in the Château-Rouge neighborhood, 2001) alternate settings between Paris and Kinshasa, Paris and Brazzaville. Corruption, trafficking of all kinds, prostitution, and urban dangers are the basic ingredients of the plot. In these works, the viewpoint is always male even when the narrative voice may be identified as female. The male detectives also fit the profile of the antihero, most being akin to the protagonist in the American television series *Columbo*. It is also noteworthy that Moussa Konaté's Commissaire Habib has common characteristics with Yasmina Khadra's Superintendent Llob, and Boualem Sansal's Si Larbi in *Le serment des barbares* (The barbarians' oath, 1999). Along with Mongo Beti, Bolya and Ngoye cross linguistic borders, incorporating slang, but also vulgar, crude, and violent language as well as graphic scenes.

Under the cover of irony, laughter, and entertainment, these crime novels deliver a harsh criticism of postcolonial Africa and Africans, thus approaching engagement from a different, less dogmatic, angle. The codified structure of crime fiction functions paradoxically: while it presents readers with a plot construction that they recognize readily, it offers more potential for unorthodox transgressions and playful explorations than does the committed novel. These transgressions and explorations, however, are not devoid of ambiguities. Inasmuch as they at times lean on folksy and cartoon-like clichés, they can be said to be predicated on a replacement of the colonial imaginary with a problematic imaginary of the common people.

Ambroise Kom in "Littérature africaine: l'avènement du polar" (African literature: the advent of the detective novel, 1999), Françoise Naudillon in "Black Polar" (2002), and Pim Higginson in "Mayhem at the Crossroads: Francophone African Fiction and the Rise of the Crime Novel" (2005) and "A Descent into Crime: Explaining Mongo Beti's Last Two Novels" (2007) have traced the emergence of the African polar (detective novel) and explained it as a process of appropriation ranging from African American literature to a larger, international, cultural context. In a later article, "Tortured Bodies, Loved Bodies: Gendering African Popular Fiction" (2008), Higginson underlines the crime novel's "capacity to explicate local scenes through transnational and transsubjective prisms constructed from an assemblage of genre-specific tropes: urban settings, movement and migration, vernacular language, senseless violence" (133–34).

As alluded to in Chapter 1, Mongo Beti gave significant consideration to what was called at the time the detective novel, partly because he associated it with popular literature, a genre he claimed offered closer ties to readers, and partly also because *littérature noire* foregrounded the underdog.[27] Additionally, the detective novel allowed Mongo Beti to recontextualize political commitment in a postcolonial context where the figure of the militant had lost both its luster and relevance. In Chapter 1, we pointed to the hollowing out of the figure of the heroic militant through the character of the lawyer. A similar parallel can be drawn between Perpétue in *Perpétue et l'habitude du malheur* and Bébette in *Trop de soleil tue l'amour* and *Branle-bas en noir et blanc*, that is, from a heroic victim to a street-savvy "chick." As is the case in the works of younger Cameroonian authors, such as J. R. Essomba's *Le dernier gardien de l'arbre*, Patrice Nganang's *Temps de chien,* and Eugène Ebodé's *La divine colère* (The divine anger, 2003), no character is capable or ready to take charge of the people's destiny.

To understand the implications of the detective novel in Mongo Beti's work, one needs to put it in a broader, pan-African and diasporic, perspective, one metaphorically conveyed through his evocation of jazz. Therefore, his use of the detective novel represents a politically appropriative move, and the crafting and assertion of a Black literary lineage. One must also take into consideration another factor though: detective novels sell. Mongo Beti squarely acknowledged that he wanted his books to sell so as to have money for his other projects, which included his bookstore, the agricultural development of his village, and the project of an independent radio. In *Mongo Beti parle*, he admits that the literary vein of his last two novels was in part a marketing strategy.[28]

Apart from these books that have a distinctive crime fiction style and are part of crime fiction series, African literature is rich in narratives that have a detective feel: Bessora's *Les taches d'encre* (2000),

Henri Lopès's *Dossier classé* (2002), Mabanckou's *African psycho* (2003; *African Psycho: A Novel*, 2007), Couao-Zotti's *Notre pain de chaque nuit* (Our nightly bread, 1998), and *Le cantique des cannibales* (The cannibals' hymn, 2004), Ken Bugul's *Rue Félix-Faure* (2005), and to some extent, Boni's *Matins de couvre-feu* (Mornings of curfew, 2005) and Diop's *Kaveena* (2006). In these works the detective novel atmosphere is a pretext for investigating social issues.

A DIVERSIFICATION OF TEXTUAL STRATEGIES AND AESTHETICS

The different forms of aesthetics that we have seen thus far reveal alternative forms of literary commitment. They attest to issues of shifting power and establish, as Andrew Smith underlines in "Migrancy, Hybridity, and Postcolonial studies," that "there is a link between the loss of hope in anti-colonialism and migration" (245). Discussing Ben Okri's work, Smith extrapolates as follows: "As we can infer from Okri, much of the hope and optimism that *had* been invested in the new nations at decolonization is being transferred to a traveling cosmopolitan position in which the nation no longer seems a vehicle for any kind of social or historical progress. Hand in hand with the disappointments of the post-independence era there emerges a crisis of confidence in oppositional political movements generally" (247). That disappointment is at the root of the plurality of aesthetics that have emerged in the past twenty years. The violence, whether strident or trivialized, that emanates from these works betrays the writers' own disillusionment and their own ways of positioning themselves vis-à-vis the question of literary engagement.[29] Expatriate writers, especially those living in London and in Paris, have shown a desire to dissociate themselves in one way or another from Africa—interestingly, this is not true of francophone African writers living in the United States, whose narratives are still predominantly set on the continent. As Femi Osofisan notes in "Warriors of a Failed Utopia: West African Writers since the 70s":

> Almost all authors of the new movement are living in exile, either outside the continent, or in some other country than that of their birth. . . . All of them are published abroad, on the list of the publishing houses in the capitalist centers of Europe and America. That first point, about their enforced exile, positions them as disillusioned fugitives; and the second, their place of publication, dictates that their

audience will largely be foreign. These two factors determine their chosen style—a disjointed, postmodern prose, dissonant and delirious, in conformity with the current respectable literary fashion to the west (confirmed by their ability to win these glittering prizes); and an a-historical, un-ideological vocation, in celebration of their escape from, and abandonment of, the African predicament. (261)

Having experienced issues of dislocation, relocation, and citizenship, these expatriate writers have queried their belonging to a nation. Fredric Jameson's postulate about writing as a metaphor for the nation and the foundational basis for political consciousness no longer necessarily holds. There has been an increasing rift between writers on the continent who perceive the "children of the postcolony" writers as disengaged, and the latter who claim the right to their craft. Yet, there is another paradox at work here. In their exploration of the self and of displacement, these expatriate writers are in fact addressing urgent questions related to the agency of Africans, and particularly that of African youth today. Although their narratives of immigration and violence may have corresponded to pragmatic marketing strategies, and could be faulted for a certain creative exhaustion of francophone African literature, they also articulated new aesthetics of engagement. This is part of a process to lift the burden of commitment. Alain Mabanckou, for instance, who makes no qualms about his refusal to be "le pompier de l'Afrique" (Africa's firefighter) and wonders if it is not cliché to always think of the African writer as speaking for the collective,[30] has a novel evoking the war in Congo, the previously mentioned *Les petits-fils nègres de Vercingétorix,* and, more to the point, contributed a short story to *Dernières nouvelles du colonialisme* (Latest news on colonialism, 2006), the volume edited by Raharimanana. This is something that Tanella Boni had previously addressed in "Ecritures et savoirs: écrire en Afrique a-t-il un sens?" (Writing and knowledge: Does writing in Africa mean anything?).[31]

Abdourahman Waberi is another interesting example of a writer whose work displays aesthetic forms that reposition francophone African literature in relation to the question of engagement. With *Balbala* (1997), Waberi received new critical attention, not only as a poet but as a novelist. Like Dongala and Mabanckou, Waberi weaves together several (subversive) narrative voices and characters: Wais, "le marathonien" (the marathon runner); Dilleyta, the poet; Yonis, the doctor; and Anab, the sister. Each part brings each character to the possibility of a confrontation with death. Through these four separate sections and different narrative voices, the author enables himself to express a fierce criticism of the regime, and its subversion and distortion of the concept of tradition and clan wisdom. In his polyphonic treatment of the narrative voice as well as his articulation of individual responsibility to the collective, Waberi inscribes himself in the Somalian Nuruddin Farah's literary lineage. Sketching the predicament of Djibouti, its economic immigration to Qatar, Kuwait, and Jeddah, Saudi Arabia, his fiction moves away from the familiar scenarios of francophone African literature. Likewise, through his evocation of the history of the region and several coups d'états (Libya, Sudan, Somalia), he renews the definition of memory to portray it paradoxically as a means to mask and forget the past: "For the longest time, I thought that memory was a way to remember the past, to go back in time, to peregrinate in the little streets of the present. What a gross mistake! I finally came to realize that memory mostly serves to occult the past, to forget the wounds that are still too fresh, by crowding it with memories that upset the initial order of events. Indeed, memory serves to forget" (21).

With *Balbala*, Waberi reexamines the political terminology, particularly that of the civil war, highlighting its euphemistic language: "an unprecedented mis-adventure, with its retinue of corpses, demolitions, driftings, and ambushes" (119). Finally, through Yonis and Anab, Waberi renews the language of love and death, and of war and politics.

A few years later, the Chadian poet and critic Nimrod, also in his first novel, *Les jambes d'Alice* (2001), addresses the Chadian civil war through an unusual lens, focusing on the legs of Alice, the student narrator, and thus decentering the language and picturing of war, exodus, and refugees. Interestingly, in his second novel, *Le départ*, the notion of engagement disappears. The narrative becomes a tool in the quest for the inner self and in the reclaiming of the language of the imaginary. Thus Nimrod proposes new relationships between aesthetics and politics, recalling Jacques Rancière's idea of a new "partage du sensible," which we evoked in Chapter 1.[32]

Through the intersection of cultural and geographical spaces (Djibouti, Montreal, Paris, Berlin), and the conflation of different historical and personal times, Waberi's *Passage des larmes* (2009) also features an innovative and decentered narrative of self-writing. Several layers of intertextuality and modes of writing are crafted to that effect. An obvious rewriting of Michel Leiris's evocation of Djibouti in

L'Afrique fantôme (1934), the first pages invite the reader to simultaneously embark on a quest for her/his inner self and a detective story. The genre of self-portrait writing is thus subverted. Under the guise of the travelogue/diary, Waberi constructs a criminal fiction narrative. Returning to his native Djibouti, Djib, the narrator who works for a mysterious North American company, is to gather information about terrorist activities related to "the horn of Africa." A third layer to the narrative is provided as Djib's diary/investigative writing is juxtaposed with that of an unknown Muslim character following him around. Two types of self-writing alternate within the larger narrative. Yet, to these contiguous narratives are superimposed a fourth and fifth strata: with the mysterious Muslim's own notebook, in which he consigns both his *maître*'s words and his prayers to God, and within that notebook, an invisible text the signs of which progressively reappear. In turn, this invisible text, "le livre de Ben," introduces both an additional addressee, the philosopher and writer, Walter Benjamin, with whom Djib happens to imaginarily converse, and Benjamin's own writing and views on History. Through these textual relays, to which should be added Denise, Djib's Canadian lover who had introduced him to Benjamin's works, the narrative is showcased as multilayered. Increasing the text's amplitude, Waberi appeals to a transcendental, yet iconoclastic, (intellectual) consciousness. Waberi invites the reader to reflect historically and culturally on the idea of terrorism and the prevalent literary and political views of Islam.

Subverting and playing with genres and texts, *Passage des larmes* addresses the lingering effect of colonial imagery on postcolonial Djibouti and the Horn of Africa. Djib's character allows Waberi to move beyond the dilemma of cross-cultural heritage and identity quest, and interrogate the politics of form in an innovative manner.

In "Réflexions sur le champ littéraire africain dans la période 1988–1998: Enjeux et perspectives de la production littéraire francophone" (Reflections on the field of African literature from 1988 to 1998: Challenges and perspectives on the francophone literary production), Bernard Mouralis confirms that, since the 1980s, the figure of the francophone African writer has been characterized by an increasing diversification (56). That diversification, however, is not necessarily reflected by literary criticism. Earlier criticism tended to frame the reading of francophone African novels within the Sartrian context of the *roman engagé*. As we have seen earlier in this chapter, critics since the 1990s have focused mainly on issues of migration, displacement, and postcolonial identities, and progressively turned to issues of violence. Yet, the new generations invite us to approach the francophone literary production differently.

If we include Werewere Liking, Kangni Alem,[33] Efoui, Raharimananana, Lamko, Koffi Kwahulé, and Ouaga Bale Danai, who were playwrights before turning to the novel, and if we think of Monénembo's and Diop's recent plays, theater appears as an active ferment in the current renewal of aesthetics, especially with regard to language and the crafting of dialogue. Evidencing a "new aesthetic based on a dialogue between the arts" (Mondzain and Lehmann, 368), this trend also testifies to a rethinking of the relationship between aesthetic and ethics. Inasmuch as they are the creative and hybrid products of writers who explore different literary genres and they dramatize the position and status of the reader/viewer of their work, they lead us to reflect on the terrain art occupies in our consciousness and how it speaks to us at a time when new technologies of communication are rapidly developing.

Kwahulé is an author whose creative itinerary is akin to that of the South African Zakes Mda. A prolific dramatist, Kwahulé authored more than twenty plays before publishing his first novel, *Babyface* (2006). What is interesting in this work is not merely the literary crossover of genres but the inventiveness of his text. In an interview with Yvan Amar,[34] Kwahulé explained that the structure of *Babyface* is based on a paneling effect of four frames that can be read in isolation or simultaneously. Each frame deals with one of the following aspects: history, foundational legend, romance, and a metadiscourse on fiction. An essential element of Kwahulé's narrative, and of his plays, is music, and most particularly jazz. In *Babyface*, Kwahulé borrows from jazz its improvisational techniques, its plays on a range of polyphonic voices, and its effacing of hierarchy between players and characters. Because of his experience as a dramatist, Kwahulé engages his readers differently, allowing each of them to choose his score. Kwahulé has the same expectations of his readers as he does of his audience. He invites them to participate actively, to be "present to the act of reading." His plays, especially *Scat, Jazz,* and *Mysterioso 119,* have had considerable influence on the composition of *Babyface*. Although that book is foregrounded in the lasting crisis in Ivory Coast and stages elements of the realities experienced there by characters we may recognize, the amorphous quality of the protagonist, Babyface, offsets the verisimilitude of the story. In Kwahulé's words, Babyface is "a character that does not exist . . . a mirror in which one sees one's own reflection." *Babyface*, although a first novel, represents an interesting example of both engagement and renewal of aesthetics, a space in which new intentions and inventions are manifested by the artist.

Kossi Efoui, a dramatist, chronicler, and the author of three novels, *La polka* (1998), *La fabrique des cérémonies* (2001), and *Solo d'un revenant* (Solo of a ghost, 2008), has also crafted an original aesthetics using his experience in theater. Like Kwahulé, he is a playwright who seeks to reinvent and expand the range of language. To Efoui, the word is sound/music and gesture/movement/dance. Writing is intrinsically linked to the activity of reading and to the act of rehearsing, that is, interpreting and incorporating. The written text must resonate. The oral quality that is customarily lent to African literature is therefore both present and transformed in Efoui's novels. His novels partake in a *gestuelle,* whereby the reader is constantly invited to renegotiate the protocols of understanding s/he generally applies to the deciphering of a novel. The *aventure des mots* is more important than the story being told. The novel is an activity in which the writer as novelist exercises his art.

La polka and *La fabrique des cérémonies* release their meaning through two apparently contradictory prerequisites on the part of the reader who must accept to aimlessly progress, yet be present to the moment when a sign will manifest itself. The metaphor of the photographs in *La polka* shows literature (life) to be the production of signifying moments to be reckoned with. In that novel, the narrator/ writer is akin to a collector of snapshots. He is the one who, flipping through the photos, sees/seizes meaning and frames the image/the scene into context.[35]

On the African continent, Couao-Zotti, also a dramatist and a cartoonist, has likewise contributed to a renewal in aesthetics. Whether in his plays or his novels, Couao-Zotti excels in rendering the atmosphere of the urban underground, including in his use of the vernacular. Both *Notre pain de chaque nuit* (1998) and *Le cantique des cannibales* (2004) illustrate the ways in which the state manipulates the underprivileged, trying to corrupt relationships and erase trust. Taking the Indian legend of the Bandit Queen, Phonan Devi, as a point of departure and combining it with a Beninois female impersonation of the legendary Robin Hood, Couao-Zotti creates a narrative in which a female prostitute and thief, Gloh, is sought after by the State so that she can help reelect the president, Kere-

Kere. Couao-Zotti frames the daily life of Benin in the visual style of comics. His dynamic style has drawn attention beyond francophone Africa, as demonstrated by his nomination for the 2002 Caine Prize for African creative writing, for a short story taken from *Thieves and Other Dreamers: Stories from Francophone Africa*, a collection resulting from a collaboration between professional translators (in this case, Tava Gwanzura and Veronique Wakerly) and students at the 2001 Zimbabwe Book Fair.

This type of narrative is indicative of a recent development in the crafting of dialogue in francophone African literature. Examples of other writers participating in that trend are Kourouma with *Allah n'est pas obligé* (2000), Nganang with *Temps de chien* (2001), and Mabanckou with *Verre cassé* (2005) and *Black Bazaar* (2009).

The way African novelists have been revisiting and subverting the iconic images of traditional oral literature and coming up with a new literary bestiary proceeds from a similar spirit. In the late 1970s and 1980s, animals were figures of corruption and infestation. They were linked to the idea of social degeneration and illness, as, for instance, in Monénembo's *Les crapauds-brousse* (1979), Massa Makan Diabaté's *L'aigle et l'épervier ou la geste de Soundjata* (The eagle and the sparrow hawk or Soundjata's gest, 1975), *Comme une piqûre de guêpe* (Like a wasp's sting, 1980), and *Le lion à l'arc* (The lion with the bow, 1986), Bernard Nanga's *Les chauves-souris* (The bats, 1980), and Nga Ngando's *Les puces* (The fleas, 1984).[36] Since the mid-1990s, works such as Lamko's *La phalène des collines* (2000), Nganang's *Temps de chien* (2001) and *L'invention du beau regard* (2005), and Mabanckou's *Mémoires de porc-épic* (2006) have given animals more than a mere metaphorical and symbolic presence. Animals such as dogs, butterflies, and porcupines have, at times, become intrinsic characters and narrative voices in these texts, enabling the authors to set their gaze from a different perspective. At times bitingly humorous, cynical, or blasé, they give a finer rendering of the daily grind of urban postcolonial life.

These different writers are pushing the limits set by the novel as a genre. The polyphonic quality of their works, the use of music and the specular, and the development of dialogue are constitutive elements of what becomes a multidimensional representation. To a certain extent, this diversification of aesthetics has made it possible for the writers to lift the burden of Engagement and to shift from an *engagée* literature to an engaging literature. However, critical issues have emerged regarding the status of francophone literature, notably its relationship to French and world literatures, the shaping of francophone African literature outside the continent, and the marketing of African literature as a global product. This is examined in detail in our final chapter.

CHAPTER FOUR

The Fashioning of an Engaging Literature

The Publishing Industry, the Internet, and Criticism

Writers entertain among themselves relationships and exchanges that defy borders and time. . . . Artistic creation evades its author and the society in which it sprouted, to propel itself beyond borders and languages. It is impervious to the wrinkles of time.

HENRI LOPÈS, Ma grand-mère bantoue et mes ancêtres les Gaulois

Despite its increased visibility, the production of African art continues to be burdened by adverse market forces and cultural stereotyping. This is especially true for African literatures and visual arts. Despite great creative output and the international recognition of some individual artists such as the Senegalese sculptor Ousmane Sow and the conceptual artist Yinka Shonibare, and despite the collaborative efforts deployed by various critics/scholars/artists such as Simon Njami and Salah Hassan, African visual arts are yet to be fully appreciated. Internationally acclaimed exhibits of African visual arts, such as the 2005 Africa Remix[1] at the Centre Pompidou in Paris, continue to happen largely outside the continent. Although Malian photographers such as the late Seydou Keïta (1921–2001) and Malick Sidibé (born in 1936), and the Congolese painter Chéri Samba (born in 1956)[2] have been acknowledged since the nineties, the richness and range of the artistic forms being generated by other African artists—particularly younger African artists—on the continent call for more attention.

In France, the success encountered by the comic book *Aya de Yopougon*, the brainchild of the Franco-Ivorian Marguerite Abouet (text) and the French Clément Oubrerie (illustrations), is quite symptomatic of the fact that, in general, international recognition still comes through Europe and the West. Awarded the 2006 Prix du Premier Album at Angoulême's Festival International de la Bande Dessinée, *Aya* was applauded for breaking away from the usual clichés associating the continent with war and famine. Portraying a nineteen-year-old girl living a "normal" life in an Abidjan neighborhood characterized by its solidarity and sense of fun, *Aya* was praised for its "fraîcheur" (freshness) by French critics from *Le Figaro* to *Télérama* and has become a regular fixture in *Libération*. It enjoyed the same consensual reception as Marjane Satrapi's series *Persepolis*.

Four aspects are interesting to reflect on, however: First, *Aya* is often critically isolated from the wider context of African cartoon production in Europe and on the continent.[3] Second, that popular cultural references such as the Senegalese Alphonse Mendy's (pseudonym: T. T. Fons) cartoon character Goorgoorlu have not gained recognition outside the continent demonstrates an imbalance in distribution, readership, and reception. This is all the more telling since both *Aya* and *Goorgoorlu* use a comparable narrative device, that of the hero of daily life. Furthermore, it should be noted that Goorgoorlu's adventures appeared regularly in the Senegalese satirical magazine *Le cafard libéré* and have been adapted for the theater and television, notably by Moussa Sene Absa, who included skits in both Wolof and French. Third, a more serious vein tends to be categorized as "cliché" or fails to attract sustained attention. Edimo Simon-Pierre Mbembo's *Malamine, un Africain à Paris* (2009) is a case in point: it has enjoyed a *succès d'estime* in France, but one limited by the social criticism it expressed. To take things further, politically committed cartoons, such as the Senegalese Samba Ndar Cissé's *Oulaï*, addressing female genital mutilation, tend to be overlooked by critics outside the continent, while at the same time being used by international NGOs working on site.

African visual productions, including Nigeria's thriving video industry and the development of African "soap operas" in Nigeria and in Mali also attest to the inventiveness and vitality of contemporary African cultures, underscoring the fact that "some of the most dynamic examples of cultural production come from what we are now defining as the collapsed state" (Gikandi, 7).

As Simon Gikandi has pointed out, literature is far from being the most important cultural production in Africa (see "Postcolonialism's Ethical [Re-]Turn: An Interview with Gikandi," 11). Music is much more immediately central to most African cultures. For the past twenty-five years, the creation of new forms of African music has been remarkable, as has its rising accessibility to wider popular and international audiences. With the expansion of African urban youth culture since the end of the eighties, Hip-hop has been important in creating new forms of artistic engagement. In Senegal, for example, Positive Black Soul (PBS), the hip-hop *posse* (group) created by Didier Awadi (DJ Awadi) and Amadou Barry (Doug E. Tee) in 1989 was key in bringing about new committed forms of music and inspiring many young African rappers. Didier Awadi's solo track "Parole d'Afrique" (2001) and album "Sunugaal" (2006), a plea to young Senegalese not to leave their country and risk their lives on *pirogues*, have been significant contributions.

Against the backdrop of a perceived cultural context whereby, despite these developments, Africa continues to be linked to poverty with regard to cultural significance, the reception of African literature has undergone notable changes. French literary awards and *succès de librairie* (best sellers) have conferred francophone literature some visibility. Diome's *Le ventre de l'Atlantique* (2003) sold very well, and *Ketala* (2006), her second novel, was placed on the *Nouvel Observateur* selection of titles in the months following its publication. In July 2006 Mabanckou's *Verre cassé* (2005) was listed as the twenty-fourth best-selling work in France. Most of Mabanckou's novels are now available in paperback, and Beyala has been able to live on her book royalties, despite the charges of plagiarism levied against her.

The market has opened up slightly for African writers, and publishers are trying to capitalize on that by creating new series. The Internet has also had an impact on the ways writers and their books are recognized, as well as on the writers' interactions with each other and their readers. New parameters have emerged with authors writing directly online and critics adjusting to other modes of electronic dissemination and analysis. The development of technology and the increasing accessibility of the Internet on the African continent have also affected the understanding and contextualization of African literature. These parameters have, however, brought their own contradictions, including risks of literary ghettoization, an increased divide between francophone African writers on and outside the continent, and a fashioning of African literature along the lines of cultural prescriptions set by global markets.

FRANCOPHONE AFRICAN LITERATURE:
A LITERARY GHETTO?

As demonstrated in our previous chapter, there has been a shift from *engagé* to engaging literature, and recent best sellers show that francophone African literature is engaging to readers. Yet, the visibility of francophone African literature has come at a price and often implied limiting editorial politics. Currently, three basic contradictory configurations emerge with regard to francophone African literature in France: the ghettoization of that literature, the broadening of its reach, and the role of new series in bridging francophone and French literatures.

In "La Francophonie, oui, le ghetto: non!," an op-ed piece in *Le Monde* (March 18) following the 2006 Salon du Livre in Paris, Mabanckou reacts to that year's showcasing of francophone literatures by saying:

> We need to erase our prejudices, to reflect on certain definitions and recognize that it is suicidal to pitch French literature against francophone literature.
>   This categorization is most frequently supported by French publishers who create literary series for Africans, alleging that they must be visible. Yet, one day or another, this dangerous ghettoization reaches its limits. It devalues the expression of an entire continent and constructs a literature of the herd legitimized by the color of the writers' skin and the place where they were born. Shut away, balkanized, cooped up, and isolated, these authors are thus irremediably condemned to carry the burden of an ideology incompatible with literary creation. (15)

Mabanckou's statement corresponds to a stand that marks a new form of engagement, at once inclusive, confrontational, and open-ended. Indeed, the "nous" and the "nos" of "il *nous* faut effacer *nos* préjugés" (we have to erase our biases) seem to (rhetorically?) point to a shared responsibility of French publishers and "African authors." On the other end, the term "ideology" mentioned at the end of the passage is not so defined as to clearly convey what it means.

In 2006, after an unprecedented number of francophone writers were awarded the more prestigious French literary prizes (Prix de l'Académie Française for the novel, Prix Renaudot, Prix Femina, Prix Goncourt, and Goncourt des Lycéens), forty-four French-speaking writers issued a manifesto titled "Pour une 'littérature-monde' en français," published in *Le Monde des Livres* (March 16, 2007, 1–3).[4] This manifesto voiced concerns similar to those expressed by Mabanckou in the preceding quote, concerns that were further articulated in the essays gathered by Michel Le Bris and Michel Rouaud in *Pour une littérature-monde* (2007). Both the manifesto and the book affirm these writers' desire to no longer be seen as "the products of decolonisation" ("Pour une 'littérature-monde' en français," 2) and to rightfully be acknowledged as creative innovators with regard to the novel. Stressing that France is no longer the only cultural center for French speakers and, conversely, that francophone authors no longer represent its margins, they situate themselves within the new continuum of a world literature in French: "*Littérature-monde* because today, French-speaking literatures are clearly numerous and diverse throughout the world and form a vast corpus with branches reaching out on several continents. But *littérature-monde* also because they prefigure the world that emerges in front of us" (3). This provocative theoretical repositioning of French-speaking literatures rests on a rejection of Francophonie, and most specifically of the French literary establishment's arbitrary distinction between French and francophone literatures: "Let's be clear: the emergence of a consciously articulated world literature in French, open to the outside world and transnational, seals Francophonie's death certificate" (3).[5] Celebrating "the task of giving voice to the world's unknown," the manifesto concludes on the idea of a "renaissance . . . a dialogue in a vast polyphonic space, unconcerned by the fight for or against the pre-eminence of any language or 'cultural imperialism'" (3).

Raising new questions on what it means to write in French today, the manifesto triggered many reactions on different continents and lit up the blogosphere. Political proponents of Francophonie tried to counter and reframe the manifesto's arguments via the French press. Abdou Diouf, the former president of Senegal and current Secretary General of the Organisation Internationale de la Francophonie contributed a sinuous rebuttal, titled "La Guerre de Cent Ans" (The hundred years' war), to *Le Monde* (March 19, 2007) in which he exclaimed:

> All of us share in the same resounding and stimulating acknowledgment, namely that "contemporary literatures in French are diverse." It is also clear that we have the same objective of "a dialogue in a vast and polyphonic space." But allow me to disrespectfully demonstrate to you, ladies and gentlemen writers, that in this manifesto, you contribute to entertain the gravest misinterpretation regarding Francophonie, by mistaking cultural exception with cultural diversity, albeit with all the authority that your talent confers to your words.

In turn, Nicolas Sarkozy, who was then a candidate for president, produced an opinion column, "Pour une francophonie vibrante et populaire," published in *Le Figaro* (March 22, 2007),[6] in which he argued for "a Francophonie in Senghor's image" and denied that it is "a colonial concept," while tenuously insisting that "a language also conveys a political message, a certain vision of the world. Spoken by people as diverse as those living in Lebanon, Niger or Vietnam, the French language is the story of a common destiny between 'us and them.'" It is worth recalling that this opinion column appeared four months before the newly elected Sarkozy's widely decried speech at the Université Cheikh Anta Diop in Dakar, Senegal. It is also noteworthy that Sarkozy mentioned Maryse Condé, Mabanckou, and Mbembe by name in his address. Not only did he thus recognize them as interlocutors, he also called for the creation of new positions ("Chaires") for such writers/intellectuals in the French universities. As of 2010, however, there are still only a handful of academic positions officially dedicated to African literatures.

The posting of Mbembe's subsequent article, "Francophonie et politique du monde" (Francophonie and world politics, March 24, 2007),[7] in Mabanckou's blog opened up the debate—which continues to this day through an array of conferences and literary events.[8] In this article, Mbembe marked his agreement with the *Manifeste*'s authors, reinforcing that "the French language is, nowadays, more widely spoken outside of France than in the country itself. France no longer holds exclusive rights to French. It is a plural language." He then linked France's "decline" to its inability "to conceive of what Edouard Glissant calls the 'Tout-Monde'" to its cultural narcissism and Parisian elitism, born of "the complete identification of the French language with the French republic" and its corollary "monolingual reflex."

"Pour une 'littérature-monde' en français" and *Pour une littérature-monde* attempt to configure new forms of literary commitment that eschew ideology, respect each individual writer's right to retreat to a creative tower and speak for himself or herself, while empowering writers with the freedom to define their aesthetics collectively, and in relation to a broader universe. To what extent is this going to affect the long-term realities of French publishing? Is this phenomenon merely marking a shift to a new intellectual elite or a remapping of the influence of the old Parisian elite? Will the *Manifeste* and *Pour une littérature-monde* enable "younger generations," lacking the connections to the Parisian publishing world that the better-established authors have, to get published more easily? How will their production be framed by critics? Will (international) structures of publication emerge that allow this new production to flourish, in French, beyond the cultural prescriptions set by Francophonie? Finally, are (French) literary awards the correct gauge for progress? Although the number of francophone recipients of the Goncourt has increased since Tahar Ben Jelloun won that award in 1987 for *La nuit sacrée* (1987; *The Sacred Night*, 1989), no francophone *African* author has been granted it since then. Time will tell, but with the October 2008 attribution of the Nobel Prize in Literature to J. M. G. Le Clézio, one of the signatories of the *Manifeste*, the impetus seemed to be there and the issue front and center.

Conversely, several articles in French newspapers commented negatively on the attribution of the Nobel Prize to Le Clézio, the Renaudot to Monénembo, and the Goncourt to the Franco-Afghan Atiq Rahimi. Regardless of the literary prize and the author, the consensus appeared to be, as Frédéric-Yves Jeannet put it, that "finer feelings and noble causes don't necessarily produce good sentences, and literature does not belong to the realm of sentiment" ("Jean-Marie Le Clézio ou le Nobel Immérité," 18). This was followed by a series of responses, notably by Mabanckou in *Le Monde* (October 25, 2008) with "Le Clézio, Nobel mérité" and by Waberi, on their blogs, both reacting very strongly to Jeannet's criticism that "Le Clézio's Nobel Prize causes French literature to regress by several decades" (19).

Reactions such as Jeannet's reinforce an implicit hierarchy between French and francophone literatures, which posits that francophone writers have the potential to become great classic writers, but come short of it. In "Un exotisme de cape et d'épée" (A swashbuckler exoticism), Raphaëlle Rérolle said, regarding Monénembo's *Le roi de Kahel*, for which he obtained the 2008 Renaudot: "The style of this novel, very elegant, but often artificial in the dialogues, further reinforces the reader's frustration, leaving him or her wondering what more a writer so obviously skilled with language might have done with such a beautiful topic" (4).

Many writers and critics converge in their acknowledgment of francophone African literature's increasing visibility, yet stress that this recognition is largely happening outside France. They note that an international demand for francophone African literature does exist, but that the French publishing world has not necessarily understood or is still resistant to this fact. In that respect, Mabanckou has repeatedly argued against the marginalization of African literature in France compared with other literatures written in French, notably Quebecois literature or literature by Chinese writers in French. With Serpent à Plumes, Pierre Astier tried to remedy the elitist context of the French publishing world (including people in the press, critics and editors on panels awarding literary prizes), which, in his opinion, perpetuates a form of segregation, and constitutes a historical mistake. In an interview with Mabanckou, titled "Le métier d'éditeur est l'un des plus beaux métiers du monde quand on découvre un auteur" (Working as a publisher is one of the most rewarding jobs when you discover an author) and posted on Mabanckou's blog on June 16, 2006, Astier clarifies that, in France, the "collection-ghetto" has not been specific to francophone African literature.[9] Series identified as "French" were closed to writers from Belgium or Switzerland, unless they had blended into the Parisian literary landscape. Astier rounds up his argument by showing that such series will eventually disappear. As for the new series, they have helped give this literature more visibility but at the price of a certain exoticism, as appears in Schiffano's initial postface to Editions Gallimard's Continents Noirs series.

Diop pushes Mabanckou's argument about ghettoization and the *politique du livre* further by situating the issue within the context of globalization. In *L'Afrique au-delà du miroir* (2007), he addresses the role of globalization in the shaping of Negro-African arts, especially film and literature. He argues that although globalization is supposed to open new markets for African art, specifically literature and cinema, it perpetuates neocolonial dynamics of economic and cultural dispossession.

> Today, African cinema is almost totally controlled by foreign interests. In its former colonies, France continues to finance films through its Ministère de la Coopération. Under the same pretext of francophone solidarity, private producers, Canadian or French, manage the industry. This has drastically affected the thematic and aesthetic approach of the African filmmakers who are currently most recognized. Their films, conceived to be shown in Western festivals, are almost never seen in Yaoundé or Libreville. Although authored by Africans, they cast a foreign glance on the continent. (204)

Diop sees in these changes what could be equated with an "appropriation of the imagination" (204), with many African writers favoring a Western readership and the West as *the* space for publishing, and the readership becoming more fragmented. For Diop, globalization has in fact "narrowed a pool of readers that had already been dramatically affected by the drop in purchasing power" (206). He sees a risk in artists abiding by a trend that increasingly disconnects them from their creative process: "An artist is nothing and has nothing to say if he does not first and foremost strive to be himself" (208).

Heeding Diop's critical evaluation of the state of (francophone) African cultural production, should one consider that littérature-monde is yet another Western market strategy, rather than a self-conscious attempt on the part of the writers to go beyond the confines of the aesthetic and editorial politics inherited from Francophonie? An unequivocal answer to this question cannot yet be provided, as it is part of the complicated and paradoxical process of lifting the burden of Engagement. One could say, however, that, to a certain extent, the aesthetic Diop is experimenting with in his novel, *Kaveena* (2006)—a disruption of the story line, a fragmentation of narrative voices, and barren sentences—recalls similar textual strategies by other writers, such as Raharimanana's *Nour, 1947*, Essomba's *L'enfant aux larmes de sang*, Edem's *Port-Mélo*, and Kwahulé's *Babyface*.

Although Boubacar Boris Diop paints a grim picture of the publishing market on the African continent, underlining that most existing publishing houses are struggling financially, closing, or being bought by Western major publishers (as is the case of Senegal's Nouvelles Editions Africaines and the Nouvelles Editions Ivoiriennes, both bought by Havas and Hachette),[10] he insists that globalization should not mask other causes for the crisis. He also notes that some of the difficulties may potentially have a stimulating effect on African literatures.

> The fact that it is difficult for an African author to penetrate the global market is not necessarily a bad thing. Knowing that he cannot live from his pen, he can make aesthetic experiments and write for the future. However, one should not be content with a situation that, in fact, is a step backward. The extent to which the publishing crisis has weakened the circulation of ideas in Africa is fascinating. It is significant that one no longer hears the great African voices, as was the case with the journal *Présence africaine*. Soyinka's 1986 Nobel Prize seems to have marked the end of an era. The editorial market was much more open when an anthology could include the names of Mongo Beti, Amos Tutuola, Mario Andrade, and Langston Hughes. Texts were promptly translated and the names of Senghor, Achebe, and Richard Wright were known throughout Africa. Today franco-

phone intellectuals know almost nothing of Pepetela, Chenjerai Hove or Ayi Kwei Armah. (205–6)

This *politique du livre* goes beyond the issue of the nature of the structures of publication. Other factors have to be taken into consideration, such as the price of books and their availability. In Africa, books are often unavailable, including at the university level where most instructors use photocopied material in their classrooms. When books are available, as for instance at Librairie des Quatre Vents and Librairie Claire d'Afrique in Dakar, Senegal, their price is often a deterrent. How many people can afford Diome's novel, *Ketala*, when it costs 12,000 to 14,000 CFA (about 24 euros) or one of the recently released essays on Senghor (Philippe Dijean's, Nimrod's, or Njami's)? The fact is that, currently, the Librairie des Quatre Vents and the Librairie Claire d'Afrique are predominantly patronized by expatriates. Most Senegalese are only able to afford books published locally (at NEAS-Nouvelles Editions du Sénégal, or NEI) where novels are more likely to be in the 2000–4000 CFA (4 to 8 euros) range. Furthermore, there are generally very few public libraries, and readers are not sought after, particularly early on. Véronique Tadjo pointed out at the 2006 ALA conference in Accra, Ghana, that this is indeed a problem to be heeded by African writers and that the production base must be broadened. She appealed for African writers to produce books for children at all levels of their schooling in order to increase the readership. To Tadjo, it is essential to teach African literature as early on as possible.

It is still easier and cheaper to publish books in Europe than in Africa, not entirely because of a lack of infrastructure, but because the publishing industry is locked. In Senegal, for example, the lucrative textbook market is in the hands of Hachette, and European textbooks are generally more valued.

While the *librairies par terre* (informal sidewalk or market "bookstores") sell used books that are affordable, these are most often textbooks, African classics in paperback, and alternatively, works published by local presses. African youth on the continent are essentially cut off from their own current literature. The irony and paradox is that Africans have to leave their countries to be able to read African literature.[11]

The same can be said with regard to films. As stressed by Patrick Schmitt and Joe Sciarrillo in "Where Has the Cinema in Dakar Gone?" (5), with only a handful of theaters remaining open in downtown Dakar, one of which is at the French Cultural Center, the general public tends to favor a neighborhood theater at a more reasonable 500 CFA ticket (compared to 2,500 CFA at Le Paris) or, more likely, gather around a video, TV film, or soccer game at someone's house. With the exception of the FESPACO, African films can be seen mostly outside the continent, through a network of international festivals.

Although problems of cash flow and distribution remain the norm, there are some hopeful signs for the future, primarily regarding the local market. A country such as Mali, for instance, has developed a system of *wagons bibliothèques* (library vans) that travel to rural areas. Generally, though, private initiatives tend to work better. Moussa Konaté's publishing house, Editions Le Figuier, in Mali, and a number of small presses in Burkina Faso, have shown a rethinking of the question of book marketing. Offering different qualities of paper and a range of prices depending on the intended format, Le Figuier has aimed at reversing global market differentials: books sold on the continent are cheaper than the ones that are exported. This said, Konaté's Le Figuier and other ventures, such as Mongo Beti's bookstore in Quartier Nzinga in Yaoundé, Cameroon, have never been financially profitable, although they clearly put the issue on the map. Interestingly, Mongo Beti had also entertained the idea of library vans for Cameroon.

Individual writers, such as Diop, Raharimanana, Rakotoson, and Nganang, have occasionally chosen to have their books published on the continent and in Europe through *co-éditions*. Furthermore, they, and a few others, have developed close relationships with independent French publishing houses (Vents d'Ailleurs, Joëlle Losfeld Editions, Editions Philippe Rey, and Elytis) that give them more creative and intellectual latitude. In 2008, Rakotoson founded Opération Bokiko, an organization promoting the revival of the publishing industry and reading in Madagascar.

However, despite the many signs of a new dynamism in the production of francophone African literature on the continent, the situation may seem regressive when compared with the period immediately following independence. It bears remembering that, after independence, francophone African countries saw the birth of several publishing ventures, notably Nouvelles Editions Africaines (NEA), an initiative by Senghor, financed by the Republic of Senegal for a number of years. NEA extended from Dakar to Abidjan and Lomé. For various reasons, including poor management, an untargeted editorial policy, and local pressures, NEA had to stop its activities. NEI (Nouvelles Éditions Ivoiriennes) was the second largest publishing house in Ivory Coast after CEDA (Centre de l'Edition et Diffusion Africaine). Established in 1961, CEDA was privatized in 1992 and saw 75 percent of its operations taken over by Editions Hatier in Paris in 1992. Eighty-five percent of NEI's publications consist of school textbooks and educational works, and 15 percent are general literature and children's/youth literature. A similar observation can be made regarding literary journals currently being published in francophone Africa. Of the following three publications, *Abbia-Revue culturelle camerounaise*, created in Yaoundé in 1963, *Ethiopiques-Revue socialiste de culture négro-africaine*, created in Dakar in 1975, and *Revue de littérature et d'esthétique négro-africaine*, created in Abidjan in 1977, only *Ethiopiques* (barely) survives (see Guy Ossito Midiohouan's "Le Devoir de penser: Mongo Beti et la passionnante aventure de *Peuples noirs-Peuples africains*").

Both Présence Africaine and NEA have had financial difficulties since 1985. They remain a place for African writers to publish on the continent, but overall they have lacked in adequate management and budget. Liking's most recent novel, *La mémoire amputée* (2004), for which she was awarded the NOMA prize, is a case in point. Published by NEI, it ran out of stock fairly quickly and became unavailable for a while. A few authors, such as Diop, who generally publishes in France, occasionally choose to publish some of their works with NEI. This was the case for the paperback edition of Diop's *Le cavalier et son ombre*, for instance. As for *Doomi Golo*, it was published by a small independent publishing house in Dakar, Editions Papyrus. Finally, it should be noted that although NEI is always in a state of financial difficulty, and despite the political turmoil in Ivory Coast, it has managed to keep afloat thanks to some of its popular series, such as Calliope, Plaisir de Lire, Enigmas, and Adoras. Some titles published in the Adoras series have been adapted for television in Ivory Coast, which has paradoxically resulted in a wider readership. Even if the models they represent are problematic (because of gender, social, and political stereotypes), these adaptations have had some positive outcomes in terms of literacy. The same parallel can be drawn regarding the new phenomenon of video production, in Nigeria and Madagascar, for example. Although the *cinéma d'auteur* is experiencing serious difficulties in terms of production and distribution, the independent and African-centered video industry is enjoying a healthy success. As pointed out by Olivier Barlet in "Grandeur et ambivalences de la révolution numérique" (May 16, 2008), more than twelve hundred video films are produced in Nigeria each year.

The Editions CLE (which Jacques Chevrier has compared to Monde Noir Poche, the imprint he currently directs for Hatier) was founded in the 1960s in Yaoundé, Cameroon, and its initial focus was the publication of religious material. This African publishing house strove to publish affordable and accessible texts. Gradually it extended its production to literary works. Today, CLE continues to publish and remains one of the few possible outlets for francophone African authors on the continent.

In France, the production of francophone African literature has also undergone notable changes, but new literary series, tools, and networks of production have not always resulted in progressive developments. They have sometimes reinforced a number of contradictions, not to mention demonstrated a certain regression in the reach of African literature.

Présence Africaine, which later grew into a library and a literary journal, was the first African publishing house to be created in France in 1949 and to focus solely on African writing. In his evocation of Présence Africaine, Daniel Maximin remembers the congenial atmosphere of the bookstore where people could, for example, come and meet Césaire back from his parliamentary sessions at the Assemblée Nationale. For the younger generation of writers to whom Maximin belonged, this accessibility of black artists and black cultural and literary figures encouraged discussions and a new creativity.[12]

A number of publishing houses, such as Julliard, Plon, Seuil, Gallimard, Hatier, and Buchet-Chastel, also produced works by African writers, poets, and scholars. As emphasized by Bernard Mouralis in *Littérature et développement* (149), this testified to a significant degree of integration of black writing into French literary life, which is not necessarily the case today. In "Qu'est-ce qu'un classique africain?" (What is an African classic?), Mouralis also reminds us that a series such as Les Classiques Africains, created in 1963 by Julliard, offered a bilingual edition of a "literary text produced in an African language." Another series, Littérature Africaine, also founded in 1963, but this time by Fernand Nathan, offered short volumes containing excerpts from the work of an African author in the context of his life and production, with suggested elements for analysis, paper topics, and a critical bibliography, aimed at high school students.

Whereas Les Classiques Larousse continues to be a key element in the dissemination of Franco-French literature, the type of edition Nathan offered for francophone African literature no longer exists. This is intriguing if we consider that anglophone publishing houses such as Norton are currently selling books by African writers containing a "reading-group guide"—for example, Helon Habila's 2003 *Waiting for an Angel*. To sum up, there existed right after independence publishing policies that seemed more progressive than what exists today, that is, policies that addressed the conditions of creation and readership in francophone Africa and France.

To a certain extent, and as pointed out by Célestin Monga, Mongo Beti's *Peuples Noirs-Peuples Africains* (*PN-PA*) can be understood as having filled a void for an African youth that, by 1978, had grown tired of *Présence Africaine*'s culturalist perspective of the continent. Mongo Beti tried to redefine the concept of culture as applied to Africa, against the grain of colonial and neocolonial ethnographic discourse. A pluralistic journal, *PN-PA*'s objective was the "complete appropriation of our present and our destiny, by contributing, each one within one's area of expertise, to make culture, no longer this kind of magic word as the source of all the ailments of Africa for the past centuries, but to make it a lively dynamic reality, a space for an awakening of consciousness to confront the crucial issues of our times, and a ferment of progress" (*Remember Mongo Beti*, 212). As mentioned in Chapter 1, Mongo Beti's vision regarding the distribution of ideas and books in Africa extended to the creation of a publishing house, Editions des Peuples Noirs, in Rouen, France, and in 1994, of a bookstore, Librairie des Peuples Noirs, in Yaoundé, Cameroon. It involved other forms of cultural production, including, notably, the project of an independent radio that Mongo Beti was not able to concretize.

Another publishing house of note is L'Harmattan, which was created in 1975 in Paris for African writers and scholars in African studies as an alternative to Présence Africaine. In 2006, Editions L'Harmattan considered about 6,500 submitted manuscripts per year and published 1,500 titles yearly. Of these 1,500 titles, 30 percent concerned literature, with books on Africa representing 34.6 percent of the total volume of publication. L'Harmattan has frequently been a springboard to more visible, French-based, publishing houses. Several of the well-established francophone African authors, such as Effa, Sami Tchak, and Eugène Ebodé, had their first novel published by L'Harmattan. Sami Tchak's first novel, *Femme infidèle* (Unfaithful woman, 1988), was published by L'Harmattan, but under his birth name, Tcha Koura Sadamba. Interestingly, although Effa's first two novels were published by L'Harmattan, *Tout ce bleu*, published by Grasset, is always presented and listed as his first novel. Ebodé first published at L'Harmattan under the name of Jean-Jacques Nkollo, and Mabanckou's early volumes of poetry appeared there, whereas his first novel was published at Présence Africaine.

Although many writers complain about L'Harmattan, particularly in regard to its distribution procedures and unfavorable contracts, it has provided an outlet in a French editorial context that is tight and network-oriented. Yet, the dearth of publishing houses and the lengthy time of manuscript review have caused writers to stay with L'Harmattan for a while, especially as Présence Africaine faced an increasingly dire financial situation in the 1990s. However, a number of writers chose to remain with Présence Africaine as long as they could, despite the circumstances, because of its historical prestige and cultural relevance. Interestingly, Ken Bugul published her first four novels at Présence Africaine before moving on to Serpent à Plumes and returning to Présence Africaine for *Mes hommes à moi* (My men, 2008).

A number of new literary series, such as Gallimard's Continents Noirs, and publishing houses such as Le Serpent à Plumes, emerged in the 1990s, while other publishing houses and series disappeared. Continents Noirs, Le Serpent à Plumes, Actes Sud (especially in its offering access to translations of anglophone and lusophone texts), and a new journal, *Africultures*, have had a specific impact in the past two decades.

A journal founded in 1988 by Astier, and later a publishing house under his direction, Serpent à Plumes took off in the 1990s. With a strong presence at festivals (La Plume Noire, Fest'Africa, Etonnants Voyageurs and, more recently, in Bamako, Mali, and in Haiti) and at salons (Salon du Livre, Salon Littérature Outre-Mer in Paris), Serpent attracted new talent (Waberi and Raharimanana, among others) and introduced writers such as the Haitian Dany Laferrière to the French readership. Serpent also recruited writers from Présence Africaine and L'Harmattan. In 2004, Serpent was bought by Editions du Rocher.[13] This change prompted writers to leave the series, with Ken Bugul publishing her next novels elsewhere—*Rue Félix-Faure* (2005) with Hoëbeke and *La pièce d'or* (The golden coin, 2006) at UBU Editions. Mabanckou published *Verre cassé* (2005) with Seuil; Waberi moved to Lattès with *Aux Etats-Unis d'Afrique* (2006; *In the United States of Africa*, 2009); and Couao-Zotti to UBU with *Les Fantômes du Brésil* (2006).

One wonders if the disappearance or altering of some classic series is indicative of a normalization in the status and production of francophone African texts in France. Yet, if that is indeed the case, why do specific "black" series such as L'Harmattan's Encres Noires, Gallimard's Continents Noirs, and Homnisphères' recently created Latitudes Noires exist? In fact, there are two concurrent and opposing marketing logics for African literature in France. One such logic is the "collection noire" (the black series), the rationale for which is that the series format gives these works a greater visibility and establishes links between African texts. Yet, the corpus thus created establishes faulty parallels. Indeed, what are the principles that ensure the coherence of such a series? Are they based on aesthetic principles? Are they fortuitous or momentous? The question is especially important if we consider that an author such as Ananda Devi left Gallimard's Continents Noirs to move to Gallimard's general list (a.k.a. "La Blanche") after she had published four novels, *Pagli* (2001), *Soupir* (Sigh, 2002), *Le long désir* (2003), *La vie de Joséphin le fou* (The life of Joséphin the madman, 2003), and gained increased visibility. The other logic is that these series have a ghettoizing impact and that to gain visibility and be acknowledged, writers must leave the series.

Since 2005, certain series, notably Gallimard's Continents Noirs, have further accelerated and diversified their production of African literature. As some writers who were publishing in that series have become known and left for more visible series elsewhere,[14] Continents Noirs has been producing an increasing number of first novels by African writers,[15] many of them living outside the continent: Théo Ananisso's *Lissaholé* (2005), Pascal Béjannin's *Mammo* (2005), Edem's *Port-Mélo*—which was awarded the 2006 Grand Prix de l'Afrique Noire—and Ousmane Diarra's *Vieux lézard* (Old lizard) in 2006. Continents Noirs also publishes first novels by authors confirmed in other literary genres, for instance, *Babyface* by Kwahulé in 2006. Conversely, Lopès, whose novels are published by Seuil, gave his essay *Ma grand-mère bantoue et mes ancêtres les Gaulois* (2003) to Gallimard's Continents Noirs.[16] Since then, this series has published several essays, including three volumes of essays by the late Mongo Beti, in 2007 and 2008.[17]

These shifts highlight the limits of such series and raise the question of literary ghettoization. If they open up possibilities for publication and constitute spaces for experimentation, both aesthetic and editorial, these series regroup their writers according to their perceived origins. This may be construed as a form of *racialization*, problematically reminiscent of France's colonial epistemology and anthropological categorization. One should point out that the "Noir" in L'Harmattan's series, "Encres Noires," and the "Noir" in Continents Noirs do not translate similarly. From its inception, Encres Noires included African authors whose common narrative focus was Africa and bore an implicit committed vision. At first glance, Continents Noirs could be viewed as an africanist type of series, given, for instance, the quote from Michel Leiris on the first page of each volume ("L'Afrique-qui fit-refit-et qui fera" [The Africa that did-redid-and will do]). Until 2004, the volumes also closed with a position statement by Michel Schiffano that emphasized the authors' creativity yet paradoxically grounded it in a fairly exotic understanding of African literature.

> The entire twentieth century has witnessed the transformation of its artistic representations under the influence of African sculpture.
>
> A century during which, in black Africa, sculptural and oral expression has largely dominated the recent advent of written literature.
>
> African writing, from black Africa and the diaspora, laden with *primitive creative force* and taking over from it, *magically* plays on metaphors and metamorphoses, is imbued with freedom, rebellious grace, invention and strength. African writing is unrestrained in its use of words with a linguistic and syntactic fluidity that has often been lost in France and in Europe since the 17th century. It evokes with genius both "the language of Mme de Sévigné and the black man's balls," as the Congolese writer Henri Lopès has phrased it.
>
> Here, we are betting on the Africans, from Africa and elsewhere, on French-speakers and practitioners of any written language, spoken of course, not yet written. We are betting on the written literature of black continents to liberate the literary spirit and the French language of the new century. *We are betting on the fetishes made out of paper to replace the fetishes made of wood.*
>
> These words are spoken from Brazzaville, in *the heart of the first Black continent*. (Emphasis ours)

The argument that these series offer a space for experimentation thus needs to be qualified. Indeed, most of the titles of the novels published so far in Continents Noirs, the authors' backgrounds, and respective careers point to an interest in language and form. In this respect, the series takes francophone African literature away from the premise of engagement. Although these types of series can be said to allow African writers more creative freedom, that freedom is strongly framed by the Parisian publishing structures and marketing strategies. Hence, an ironic situation has emerged whereby the potential ghettoization of such African literature series contributes to ground these texts in a Franco-French literary landscape. And if the recent commercial success of francophone writers as diverse as Nina Bouraoui, Mabanckou, Diome, Jonathan Littel with *Les bienveillantes* (2006; *The Kindly Ones*, 2009), and Yasmina Khadra with *L'attentat* (2005; *The Attack*, 2006) (and to a certain extent Nancy Huston with *Lignes de faille* [2006; *Fault Lines*, 2007]) seems to indicate that France's literary establishment has become more broadly inclusive, that establishment remains predominantly elitist.[18] Ironically, Marie Ndiaye's continuing success in France, capped by her 2009 novel, *Trois femmes puissantes* (Three powerful women), happens as she has relocated in Berlin and uncharacteristically turned her narrative to Senegal.

The French editorial model is often opposed to the Anglo-Saxon model, showcased as promoting a more egalitarian and less racializing world literature. The anglophone African writer, although integrated in a wider and less marginalized field, is, however, more isolated, and Paris still functions as a meeting ground for literary exchanges. Yet, one can say that the anglophone writers have fared better in unstable times because they tend to use literary agents who are able to anticipate editorial shifts. This is not necessarily true for francophone writers, especially those living on the African continent. At this point, they remain largely dependent on festivals such as Etonnants Voyageurs in Bamako and publishing houses such as Présence Africaine and L'Harmattan, and, more recently, Gallimard's Continents Noirs.

However, France's cultural/editorial economics are also changing. Whereas in the past, texts written by Africans were dealt with by one specific editor in a given publishing house (Gilles Carpentier at Seuil, for instance), publishers now give works by Africans to editors who are not necessarily considered specialists in the field. At the same time, and this may seem contradictory, several writers serve as readers for a number of these series. These may be signs that francophone African literature is being mainstreamed, and the future will tell if "black series" will come to pass and how.

If the situation of African writers in France is showing some improvement, with royalties going up and more titles coming out, one should not forget that we are talking about books published in France by writers who, for the most part, live and write outside the African continent. With the exception of well-established writers such as Diop, Tadjo, Boni, Ken Bugul, Couao-Zotti, and Sow Fall, the situation remains most challenging for those trying to publish on the continent, particularly when they send their manuscripts to local presses.

As mentioned earlier, the editorial culture of African writers is also undergoing changes. Anglophone writers are generally represented by literary agents who contact the publishing houses and help market their works. This is not yet the case for francophone African writers living in Europe, and those living on the African continent must devote much time and energy to ensuring that their books are published.

THE UNDERSTANDING OF FRANCOPHONE AFRICAN LITERATURE: ISSUES IN READERSHIP AND CRITICAL APPRAISAL

In "Comment penser l'Afrique? De la famille africaine, des artistes, des intellectuels, de la critique et des évolutions de la création: Entretien d'Achille Mbembe avec Célestin Monga" (How to think about Africa? The African family, artists, intellectuals, criticism and the evolutions of artistic creation: an interview with Achille Mbembe by Célestin Monga, 2006),[19] Mbembe defines criticism as follows: "By criticism, I simply mean the body of work necessary to think differently—but to think differently in order to do something else, to become different from who we are presently." Expanding on this definition, Monga adds:

> Such a criticism does not only take on the political. It goes beyond it to tackle the core of the problem, i.e. the limits we impose on our dreams and imagination. Such a criticism blows up the cover, the wall of silence that several centuries of a deficit in self-appreciation have imposed on Africans. It succeeds in doing so by making us see new possibilities.

Today many African artists and intellectuals are expressing a desire for a new Negro-African episteme, one that would "shake up the grammar of the francophone imagination," propose new aesthetic forms, and think "au-delà du miroir" (beyond the mirror). The grand narrative of Engagement no longer provides the vocabulary and impetus to articulate African ideas and creativity. As Jean-François Lyotard outlined in *The Postmodern Condition: A Report on Knowledge* (1984), the post-Cold War multiplication of communities of meaning and the acceleration of their production and circulation have radically transformed people's apprehension of their reality. Ideological narratives have lost their large-scale epistemological and ethical appeal. In this context, African writers and intellectuals theorize their positions and understanding of the world differently. They refuse to be cast as the foot soldiers of Africa's fight against victimization and to speak of Africa through discourses defined by or in reaction to others. They want to be respected for their contributions to the world, based on terms they participate in defining.

Here again, though, contradictions appear, as this is comparatively easier to do for the African intellectuals and writers living outside of the continent and working at international universities and institutions. Francophone African intellectuals and artists who chose to, or had to (sometimes temporarily), leave the continent have also experienced career and personal paths specific to their generation (as well as to their given historical and geographical contexts). This is translating into a broad spectrum of collective experiences, opinions, and works, ranging from the Cameroonian Monga's *Un Bantou à Washington* (2007) to the Malian Traoré's *L'Afrique humiliée* (2008) and the Malagasy Rakotoson's, *Juillet au pays: Chroniques d'un retour à Madagascar* (2007), to name just a few. Also, whereas in the past, the majority of francophone Africans went abroad to study in the (former) *métropole*, the younger generations have not automatically followed that "logic." Many have gotten degrees in two, three, or four different countries (African, European, and American, for instance) and are familiar with these cultures and languages.

Finally, the nature of the relationship and priorities one cultivates toward one's country/geography of origin varies according to the time and age of emigration, the strength of families ties and familial narratives of belonging, the availability of communication, the affordability of traveling back, and so on. It may therefore be wise not to equate working and living abroad with being divorced from where one comes from.

It can be said that the understanding of African literature in the West has been marked by a persistent illiteracy. In "Ignoring Authentic African Literature Means Ignoring Africans,"[20] Carlin Romano raises the question of American illiteracy regarding African literatures and nonfiction about Africa and Africans. Deploring the scarcity of anthologies of African literatures in the United States, he advances a number of hypotheses explaining the lack of knowledge, and general interest, in African literature (with the exception maybe of South African literature). Quoting an article in *The Times* of London by the Nigerian writer Diran Adebayo, Romano states that "the Golden Age of African Literature is generally held to date from around the publication of Chinua Achebe's *Things Fall Apart* in 1958 to the early 1970s, when Achebe, Ngugi wa Thiong'o and Wole Soyinka bestrode the international stage.... It is worth asking, why, since then, books by black Africans have made so little impression on the Western imagination?"[21] In turn, Adebayo's answer is that "Black Africa's literary high point came during decolonization, and many lauded books were about the effects of that colonial period on African minds and cultures. The West was interested because they were in the story. Africa has moved on, but this Western desire to be in the story is catered to by the interest in white tales of Africa" (see Romano, 13). These considerations are also pertinent to francophone African literature, which, with respect to the question of intended readership, and regarding texts written in France, presents narratives constructed on an alternation between the "here" and "there," the "here" giving an indirect portrayal/reflection of French society.[22] The success of such narratives may therefore be partly attributed to a narcissistic feeling on the part of the readers who find themselves represented in the text.[23] But literature written on the continent has moved on. It gives little space/representation to white characters and has thus decentered France.

There is another dimension to this concept of readership illiteracy regarding Africa in France. That illiteracy has a history and is grounded in France's colonial past. The general illiteracy affecting the understanding of African literatures does not apply homogeneously across "francophone" Africa. As seen in Chapter 3, there are holes in the French collective memory. So far, French readers are more familiar with the historical circumstances surrounding Maghrebi literatures in French. The scars of the Algerian war are still fresh, but they are exposed. Since the mid-1990s, they have been the subjects of a very significant number of novels and essays, notably by Maghrebi writers.[24] In contrast, who knows (or remembers) about the Bamileke's persecution in the 1950s in Cameroon?[25] If there is a correlation between readership literacy and cultural production, one could say that the current French editorial market reflects a partial deficit in the education of the population vis-à-vis its colonial past. True, books on the subject of memory, colonization, and immigration have increasingly been published these past twenty years, and such projects as the Musée des Mémoires de l'Esclavage (Edouard Glissant) may generate new conversations and protocols of understanding. One can also say that (per force) the 2005 "riots" have allowed for original and more in-depth analyses on the part of both French and international intellectuals.[26] Books by Africans and Franco-Africans theorizing the position of Africans in France have been released and continue to appear.[27] While Serge Bilé's and Gaston Kelmann's respective contributions generated controversies, Pap Ndiaye's *La Condition noire* and Patrick Lozès's *Les Noirs sont-ils des Français à part entière?* (Are Blacks full French citizens? 2009) have been praised; and Edouard Glissant's *Réflexions sur la question noire* (Reflections on the idea of blackness, 2009) is attracting attention. Yet, W. E. B. Du Bois's *Souls of Black Folk* was published more than a century earlier, in 1903.

Looking at the strategies and notably at the disruptive aesthetics African writers have been experimenting with—from Kourouma's *Les soleils des indépendances* (1968) and Labou Tansi's *La vie et demie* to, for example, Bessora's *53 cm*, Raharimanana's *Nour, 1947*, and Mabanckou's *Mémoires de porc-épic* (2006)—is thus key to grasping the evolution and changes in francophone African literature.

African writers and intellectuals, and especially those living abroad, are prying themselves from the oppositional politics and aesthetics of Engagement and fashioning other scenarios of involvement. In his preface to *Manifeste d'une nouvelle littérature africaine: Pour une écriture préemptive* (A manifesto for a new African literature: in favor of preemptive writing, 2007), Nganang points out that the critical understanding of African literatures also needs to be freed from stifling past perceptions.

> Any piece of writing is pregnant with its aesthetic project. The critics must identify the nature of this project and, like midwives, free it from the confines of the womb and into the world. Criticism is the daughter is maieutics. Yet, sometimes, critics get distracted, caught as they are in the quagmire of their own presuppositions or swept away by the latest theoretical interpretations. They lend a deaf ear to the deep pulsating rhythms of the texts. And so it goes for the production of contemporary African authors. Their texts are crushed under the reductive applications alleging "engagement," "postmodernity," "postcolony," or even the perpetuation of the "baroque," the "rabelaisian laughter" and the concept of "créolité." (4)

In this book, whose original working title was "L'indépendance d'esprit" (Free thinking), Nganang also affirms the necessity, for writers and scholars alike, to read broadly and venture into books that do not merely pertain to their field of interest but foster new ways of understanding the subject and the world. In doing so, Nganang reminds us that reading and writing fiction have to do with freedom: freedom to create and (make) believe, and freedom to interpret. Casting a comparative glance on the respective meanings of fiction and belief in *The Broken Estate: Essays on Literature and Belief* (2000), James Wood seconds that opinion, underscoring that creative freedom *and* critical freedom are both key to knowledge, and highlighting the relationship between literature and intellectual history: "Despite its being a kind of magic, [fiction] is actually the enemy of superstition, the slayer of religions, the scrutineer of falsity. Fiction moves in the shadow of doubt, knows itself to be a true lie, knows that at any moment it might fail to make its case." He adds further: "In fiction . . . one is always free to choose not to believe, and this very freedom, this shadow of doubt, is what helps to constitute fiction's reality. Furthermore, even when one is believing in fiction, one is 'not quite' believing, one is living 'as if' . . . . Fiction is a special realm of freedom" (xii).

Yet, in "Observations sur la nouvelle génération d'écrivains africains" (Observations on the new generation of African writers, 2007), Kesteloot interprets the increasing visibility of contemporary francophone African literature as a fallacy. She considers the argument that it is currently undergoing an aesthetic renewal, a misnomer because it largely excludes writers from the continent and it is built on an overly systematic opposition to the previous generations of African writers and their beliefs: "This is only the result of an approach, which, at first, consisted in 'liberating' the young writers who, for various reasons, were residing in France, from the moral tutelage of their 'elders' and the objectives they had assigned to the literary exercise" (66). Decrying textual strategies such as the graphic imagery of sex and violence, the erasure of punctuation, the blurring of the story line, and the use of slang, Kesteloot sees this phenomenon as largely opportunistic.[28]

Despite the different changes, Paris remains a hub for many francophone writers, either because they live there or because Paris is where their publishers and some of their professional networks intersect. This means that most francophone African writers know (of) one another. They may not always agree, but most of these writers know what their peers produce and have an understanding of the literary field they contribute to shaping. This is particularly the case for those writers (mostly men, interestingly) who serve as readers in a series (for instance Waberi, Mabanckou, Sami Tchak, Kangni Alem, and Couao-Zotti).

The tradition of having African books prefaced by French writers or intellectuals has also shifted. African writers increasingly preface or postface other African writers' works. *Désir D'Afrique*, Mongo-Mboussa's essay, is prefaced by Kourouma and postfaced by Sami Tchak. In turn, the Rwandan Mukasonga's *Inyenzi ou les cafards* (2006) is postfaced by Mongo-Mboussa. The English translation of Nganang's *Temps de chien* (*Dog Days*, 2006) is prefaced by Dongala.

Another roadblock in the diffusion of this literature can be traced to France's curbing of immigration and the restrictive policies of its university system. With jobs scarcer in France and student visas increasingly difficult to obtain, more and more young francophone Africans leave Africa to pursue their studies on the North American continent. The same holds true for scholars and has resulted in their finding teaching positions at American and Canadian universities. This process has been aided by policies aimed at diversifying the teaching staff at most North American universities. The relocation of these students, scholars, and writers eventually hired as faculty in North American universities is resulting in the decentering of the production of francophone African literature and in a "redrawing of the geographic boundaries of Africa and France in our imagination" (Thomas, *Black France*, 6).

Today, an increasing number of university teachers and writers from the African continent teach not only in French or English departments but also in Comparative Literature, Africana Studies, Ethnic Studies, International Studies, and so on. These African writers meet, dialogue, and network at professional meetings such as the ASA (African Studies Association), the ALA (African Literature Association), the MLA (Modern Languages Association), the APELA (Association pour l'Etude des Littératures Africaines), and the CIEF (Congrès International des Etudes Francophones). The number of writers who have become teachers and critics has thus grown, as have the contacts between writers from different linguistic areas. For these writers and the ones recurrently invited as writers-in-residence or as guest lecturers (for instance, Ken Bugul, Tadjo, Diop, and Waberi), the editorial possibilities have extended to American and Canadian publishing houses. African writing is therefore to be framed in larger terms. Younger writers follow in the footsteps of their elders, such as Pius Ngandu N'Kashama, Ngugi Wa Thiongo, Dongala, and simultaneously produce works of fiction and critical essays, often in different languages. They are an integral part of the American university system and its network of speakers.

The increasing number of francophone writers and scholars in North America has had other consequences. It has given a larger visibility to francophone literature in French/French and Francophone Studies departments. When translated and taught in such departments as Comparative, African, or Diaspora studies, the works are read from different points of entry and summon different protocols of knowledge and understanding.

Today the separation of African literature into distinct fields, compartmentalized according to former colonial languages (Francophonie, Commonwealth literature, Lusophone literature, etc.) is being questioned by scholars and academics who tend to organize their work in multidisciplinary directions, thus collapsing linguistic borders. Some scholars argue that comparative literature is a better framework today because it opens up the different fields of knowledge and allows for richer dialogues beyond national, regional, and linguistic borders (see APELA's international conference in September 2008). Beyond these questions, however, there remains a significant discrepancy between what is being published in French and what is available in translation, and this has had two major implications. Because there is a backlog in the translating of primary sources, the teaching of francophone African literature in English does not reflect the actual production of the writers. In the case of Mongo Beti, and with the exception of *L'histoire du fou*, only his early novels have been translated.[29] His more recent fictional work and his essays have not yet appeared in English. The same situation exists regarding the books of Lopès, Ken Bugul, Sow Fall, Monénembo, and Diop, although the latter's *L'Afrique au-delà du miroir* is forthcoming in English.[30] Consequently, the understanding of the field or of the overall production of a specific writer is fragmented. Few novels by writers of younger generations were translated until recently, with the striking and misleading exception of Beyala. *Le petit prince de Belleville* gave Beyala her visibility in France. It was published in paperback very shortly afterward. By 1994, only three years later, it appeared in English. Soon thereafter, Beyala's first two novels, *C'est le soleil qui m'a brulée* (1987; *The Sun Hath Looked upon Me*, 1996) and *Tu t'appelleras Tanga* (1988; *Your Name Shall Be Tanga*, 1996), also appeared in English. Why was Beyala translated so quickly? Four factors came to bear: the cultural and political context in France, the theme of the novels, their style, and their potential as classroom material. *Le petit prince de Belleville* came out in France in 1992 around the time of the Pasqua laws, when a number of controversies surrounding immigration and cultural perceptions of immigrants made headline news.[31] Beyala's novels deal with complex issues in seemingly simple ways. They are differently exotic to both Franco-French and American readers, and the joviality that permeates the narratives leaves room for different appropriations. Although the Traorés live on the margins of French society, a fact reinforced by the theme of polygamy, for example, they belong to their popular nineteenth *arrondissement* and are a feature of it.

Both *Le petit prince*[32] and *Maman a un amant* have become staples in American universities' introduction to francophone literature courses—as is still Mariama Bâ's *Une si longue lettre* (1979). Straddling the line between social criticism and voyeurism, they are written with verve in an accessible language. They are funny, direct, and light-hearted, which is pleasing to the student body and a welcome contrast to the darker realist African novels.

The specific context of the French-language classroom must be underlined. What is taught there often depends on pragmatic considerations, such as availability of stock, distribution channels, costs, and each university's policy regarding textbook acquisition. From the nineties on, the production by "young" francophone African writers living and/or publishing in France has become more predominant in syllabi because of their visibility on the Parisian literary scene. As mentioned, these texts tend to be translated first. This has driven canon formation in a certain direction, particularly in the United States where older texts tend to disappear from the curriculum, and literary history is thus affected. Additionally, in France, some of the canonical texts of African literature, such as Sembène's *Le docker noir* (1956; *The Black Docker*, 1987), *O pays, mon beau peuple!* (1957), and *Les bouts de bois de Dieu* (1960), Sow Fall's *L'appel des arènes* (1982), are recurrently out of print, which again contributes to a piecemeal understanding of the field. Interestingly, these works are often available in other languages, as Sow Fall's works are in German.[33]

Additionally, literary genres other than the novel (poetry, short stories, and plays) have not been granted the same attention—although Irène d'Almeida's *A Rain of Words: A Bilingual Anthology of Women's Poetry in Francophone Africa/Une pluie de mots: Anthologie de la poésie des femmes en Afrique francophone* (2008) addressed this issue. Thus the backlog in translation is indirectly shaping the perception of francophone African literature and establishing a canon that does not match the production. This is symptomatic of a specific history regarding the structures of publication of francophone African letters.

The fact that the perception of African literature is largely circumscribed by what is accessible in Paris has interfered with the perception of its production. As Mouralis has emphasized, African literature tends to be regarded as cumulative, but also eternally emerging, hence the tendency to introduce contemporary authors as "young" or "new" voices. Positioned by the publishing industry as youthfully energetic and creative, diasporic African writers have been viewed as potential sources for the "renewal" of the French language. The flip side of that "youthful" creativity, however, is that francophone African literature tends to be regarded as immature, that is, still taking shape. In that regard, the colonial infantilizing and exoticizing of Africans is still operative. The boxing in of African literature reveals a hierarchization according to which French literature remains *the* reference and francophone literature still minor.[34]

In Europe and North America today, there is a faster turnover of published texts. Books have a shorter shelf life. Does this fact imply less editorial attention? To what extent is marketing part of the decision to publish a new author? What determined the recent successes of Chinese or Russian authors writing in French? Can it be said that the marketing of novels by Shan-Sa, Dai Sijie, and Andreï Makine capitalized on renewed forms of exoticism and orientalism, the likes of which were present in the reception of Marguerite Duras's *L'amant* (1984; *The Lover*, 1985) and later, Kim Lefèvre's *Métisse blanche* (1989)? Does the current reassessment of France's colonial memory and heritage translate into a different cultural epistemology?

In many respects, the production of novels, at least in the United States and Europe, has entered a seasonal cycle, organized around book fairs, salons, and festivals, and articulated on the notion of *rentrées littéraires*.[35] The fact that the manuscript evaluators of many series are often writers themselves adds to that pressure and cyclical phenomenon, especially given the fact that the more prestigious publishing houses tend to lock their promising authors in contracts asking for more than one book. Within such a context, is the idea of *oeuvre* still conceivable? Can a singular African text or writer become commercially viable outside of this dynamics?[36] Diop's 2003 novel *Doomi Golo* demonstrates that it is a possibility. Written in Wolof, and with over a thousand copies sold within a few days in Dakar, it has been read by the Senegalese community in Paris, Rome, New York, and elsewhere. After *Doomi Golo*, Diop pushed the boundaries of his writing further, translating and liberally adapting his original text from Wolof to French (*Les petits de la guenon*, 2009).

Diop's decision to turn to Wolof resulted from his participation in the Duty of Memory Project. Writing *Murambi* and reflecting on the 1994 genocide in Rwanda prompted him to reassess not only France's political role in Rwanda and in Africa in general, but also the ramifications of Francophonie and the role of the French language as a mode of expression today. While continuing to publish in French, he has published in Wolof as well. The fact that the translation of *Doomi Golo* was delayed gave a symbolic "in" to Wolof critics and created the "effet de miroir" commented on by Diop in his 2007 essay.

Further contradictions emerge that help us evaluate the ways African writers are engaging with the issue of the African intellectuals' responsibility today. In "Le regard de la différence: Réflexions autour du mot 'francophonie'" (2005), Boni points to the conflicts inherent to the publication of francophone literature. She remarks that "enmeshed in a difficult history, the francophone writer finds himself caught between its realities and the demands of various institutions: special-interest associations, publishing houses, networks. . . . The structures that serve as markers for the so-called francophone space are showcased as welcoming, advisory, and offering assistance" (130).

Essentially identified as committed, francophone African writers are caught in a paradoxical situation whereby, in order to benefit from institutional support and be published, they must fashion their writing carefully and make that engagement engaging.[37] A number of collective projects, anthologies, and volumes tackle this problem head-on, notably *Dernières nouvelles de la Françafrique* (2003) and *Dernières nouvelles du colonialisme* (2006), published by Vents d'Ailleurs and edited by Raharimanana. The online an-

nouncement of the latter volume is interesting because of its tenuously poetic rendering of the ambivalent position African writers
may find themselves in.

> In this collection, the authors give of us texts that are serious,
> funny, offbeat, nuanced or roughly chiseled, revolted or scream-
> like. On the edge of time, memory like a tightrope walker. A thread
> across the abyss, ashes vibrating from the tumult of the present. The
> true face of colonialism is frozen and silent, ashes blown into our
> eyes to release the ruins of the "colonial splendors." Whose "splen-
> dors" exactly?
>
> What is to be written of the past today when all that is left is its
> ashes? Can fire tell the same story as charred wood?
>
> Silence is an impossibility because it turns one into an accomplice,
> and refusing to hear serves crime so well. Men's and women's voices
> telling of the multiple facets of a complex reality, indeed, but also tell-
> ing us where power differentials are defined and that the roles of vic-
> tor and vanquished are distributed in advance. . . .
>
> Read theses short stories, laugh or cry, but above all, keep your
> eyes open.[38]

Published barely five months after the 2005 riots in France, these short
stories manifest the return of the *refoulé colonial* and colonization
as a continuing point of reference.[39] The writers are calling for civil
awakening and a fresh awareness. As was the case with Mongo Beti's
Main basse sur le Cameroun (1972), this collection of short stories
represents these African writers' insiders' understanding of French society and articulates the construction of France's Others. The participation of Nganang, known for his *prises de position*, but who had not
hitherto taken part in collective projects such as this, is significant.
The same goes for Mabanckou and Sami Tchak, both known for their
reservations vis-à-vis the question of *littérature engagée*.

Contrary to anglophone African literature (see Romano), francophone African literature has a long practice of showcasing itself in anthologies. As Jean-Marc Moura has highlighted, the anthology is a
distinctive phenomenon in francophone African literature and serves
precise purposes: "The anthology is a dynamic means of constructing
the sites of enunciation of a given text. It invites the reader to discover a
literary and cultural movement in a new coherence. In France, the recognition of Negro-African literature is tied to the phenomenon of the
anthology" (*Littératures francophones et théorie postcoloniale*, 115).

It should be added that African anthologies have mostly featured
short stories, often *engagées* but not exclusively so, and polemical es-

says. They have contributed to showcasing young African literary talents. Because of the economic difficulties experienced by publishing houses on the continent since the eighties, the production of such volumes has shifted to Europe. Anthologies tend to regroup writers who belong to specific networks. Because they have a fast production cycle, the visibility they confer to the writers tends to be more immediate and to highlight their forthcoming books. These anthologies also serve the interest of the publishing houses as they keep their titles in the market and confer an impression of dynamism. As has always been the case for anthologies, the apparatus (titles, prefaces/introductions, afterwords, back cover, etc.) plays a crucial part in their commercial viability and distribution.

Moura has also noted that an anthology "has a practical dimension. . . . It ties . . . literary creation to a cultural or racial community thus calling for a certain understanding of the texts that will influence the scenography of the books to come" (117). The practical dimension of the anthology and the fact that it elicits a certain understanding of the texts it includes are valid characteristics. However, its connecting African literary creation to *a* cultural or racial community is a parameter that no longer seems relevant. Indeed, francophone anthologies of African literatures have traditionally been purposeful instruments for racial and cultural identification. But transnational migrations and globalization have caused these identifications to become diasporic in nature. Furthermore, in France, where state-sponsored Francophonie instrumentalizes the idea and the production of African literature, and where the publishing world remains in the hands of an elite still influenced by colonial representations, identifying with a single racial or cultural notion has perverse consequences. In contrast, *Le huitième péché* (The eighth sin), a volume of short stories published in 2006 by the Franco-Gabonese publisher Ndzé, under the direction of Kangni Alem, regrouped works by francophone writers of various geographical areas (French-speaking Africans, Franco-French, French-speaking Canadians, etc.).

One of the paradoxes of anthologies is that they falsely give an impression of synthesis. In reality, few theoretical studies give a historiography of the field or a thorough mapping of African literature. The field has considerably expanded over a forty-year span, to the point that it is at times difficult to keep track of yearly publications. Furthermore, as shown by Romuald Fonkoua in "Comment appréhender la 'sagesse des barbares'" (How to conceive of the "'barbarians' wisdom," 2005), the critical discourse on African literature has often been constructed around an opposition between a "learned" criticism of African literature (promoted by the academia) and a more "popular" one. Fonkoua stresses that the "learned" criticism ("critique savante") elaborated in the seventies marked a turning point.[40] Constructed as a site of knowledge/power, it bore consequences in terms of cultural agency.

Increasingly, another type of criticism runs parallel to this "critique savante": the "critique chronique," deployed in the literary columns of newspapers and magazines, such as *Le Monde, L'Express, Le Figaro, Le Nouvel Observateur, Télérama,* and *Libération.* As Fonkoua remarks, it "punctuates the daily production of literature . . . the construction of its status and therefore . . . its visibility." This is especially evident during the seasonal cycle of *rentrées littéraires* with its highly selective deployment of marketing strategies. Such "critique chronique" participates in the higher visibility of these works, which, in turn, bears consequences in terms of shaping the canon: "Today more than before, critics exert an influence on the literary practice of African writers who, on closer examination, are sensitive to critical discourses. The literary text has become the locus of a critical exercise. For want of producing a specific work of criticism, the literary text serves as such" (5).

Finally, as Kesteloot underlines in *Histoire de la littérature négro-africaine* (2001), from the nineties on, critics increasingly turned to conceptual tools and models borrowing from political science rather than anthropology and sociology. She points to the influence of such works as Jean-François Bayart's and Stephen Ellis's *Criminalisation de l'état en Afrique* (1997; *The Criminalization of the State in Africa,* 1999), Samir Amin's *L'empire du chaos* (1991; *Empire of Chaos,* 1992), Tsheiyembe Mwayila's *L'état postcolonial, facteur d'insécurité en Afrique* (The postcolonial state: a contributing factor to Africa's insecurity, 1990), Abdou Maliq Simone's *Mutations urbaines en Afrique* (Urban mutations in Africa, 1998), Traoré's *L'Etau: L'Afrique dans un monde sans frontières* (The vice: Africa in a borderless world, 1999), and Mbembe's *De la Postcolonie* (329).

NEW MODES OF CULTURAL DISSEMINATION

Africultures, founded in 1997 and supported and distributed by L'Harmattan, represents a new type of cultural endeavor. Trying to bridge the gap between an academic readership and the general public, between Africans and Europeans, especially urban, cross-disciplinary in spirit, and to showcase as exhaustive as possible a range of African cultural events, *Africultures* aimed at decompartmentalizing the African artistic and literary scene. Structurally, it also represents an effort to decenter the production of African art, with its administrative unit being based in the south of France. The propelling concern was a diversification of the media, a democratization and access to a larger number of readers. There are several stages to *Africultures'* development and visibility. Initially a monthly hard-copy journal, it became accessible on the Internet, both in French and in English.[41] In 2004, it shifted to a quarterly publication. The Internet opened up many new possibilities, among which are a number of more elaborate rubrics (music, cinema, art exhibits, concerts, cultural events, "Infos," Afroblog," etc.), and attracted a larger public. The free weekly subscription to the newsletter further ensures a regular readership. In 2008, another element was added: *Afriscope*, a bimonthly "cultural and socially aware magazine" with a focus on diversity, African cultures, the dissemination of practical information, and intercultural dialogues. *Afriscope* is free and available in and around Paris, at town halls, *associations*, public libraries, community homes/hostels, specific (trendy) cafés, and cultural centers. *Afriscope* can also be read online and downloaded in PDF format.[42] *Africultures'* democratic format is part of what Ayoko Mensah, its chief editor, has called an "almost political pact of commitment."[43]

Thematically organized around specific topics, with a guest editor in charge of each issue, *Africultures* has been working in partnership with different festivals pertaining to Africa, such as Fest'Africa, Etonnants Voyageurs, and the Festival International des Francophonies en Limousin, in Limoges, France. After the Fest'Africa Edition in Rwanda and in Lille, in 2000, *Africultures* produced a special issue on history and memory. Likewise, after the 2003 Fest'Africa festival in N'Djamena, Chad, on political commitment, a special issue came out on "L'écrivain africain et l'engagement." Thus, *Africultures* has increasingly contributed to shaping the political debates between African intellectuals and their readerships. Online, *Africultures* offers a forum where some of the participating writers are able to address, sometimes vigorously, their differences of opinion, which is indicative of new dynamics operative in francophone publishing.

The Radio France Internationale (RFI) competitions for best short story, poetry, and play have also contributed to the recognition and visibility of several writers who started to publish at the end of the 1980s and early 1990s in France. Many of the "enfants de la post-colonie," as Waberi calls them, have been laureates of such RFI competitions: Efoui, Raharimanana, Waberi, Couao-Zotti, and more recently, Ludovic Obiang and Ouaga Balle Danaï, to mention just a few. As discussed in Chapter 3, these "new" voices, noticed through their poetry, plays, and short stories, crossed over genres, and gained recognition through the novel, as was the case, for instance, for Mabanckou.[44]

A whole set of cultural and literary exchanges contributes to shaping the canon along the best-sellers' list. The various salons that have taken place annually over the past fifteen years are, besides the long-standing Salon du Livre in Paris, Etonnants Voyageurs (in Saint-Malo, in Bamako, and in Haiti in 2007), the Limoges Theater Festival, La Plume Noire in Paris[45] (at its peak from the mid-1990s to early 2000), and Fest'Africa in Lille. Today, Fest'Africa is undergoing some restructuring. The festival suffered from Maïmouna Coulibaly's departure in 2004 and is searching for its bearings.

In its conception, Fest'Africa is the only manifestation of the sort. Initiated and spearheaded by Africans, with the Ivorian Coulibaly serving as administrator and the Chadian Djedanoum as director, the festival was born in 1993, around a group of friends, African and French; a core were graduates from the School of Journalism in Lille. A nonprofit organization with a number of volunteers, Fest'Africa was meant to increase the visibility of African literature, arts, and media. The format of this festival was structured around roundtables and *cafés littéraires* where African (as well as French-speaking Caribbean and Indian Ocean) writers present their most recent works. Within a few years, Fest'Africa took off and became one of the more visible literary events about Africa and the diaspora. Fest'Africa was unique in its care for the writers and artists, creating a forum for genuine discussions among writers, including anglophones, and between writers and their readers. It was the point of departure of the Duty of Memory Project, and since then it has worked on several special issues with *Africultures* as well as *Notre Librairie-Revue des Littératures du Sud*.

The Internet has been another contributing factor to the distribution and advertisement of recent works by francophone African writers. It has allowed for a counterbalance to the didactic use of African literatures in school curriculum and books. It promotes a democratic means of distribution by targeting a large audience. Through its pluridisciplinary interactive format, the online version of *Africultures* has contributed to a repositioning of African literature, casting it in a context that transcends the usual geographic boundaries of the Hexagone or the African continent. *Africultures* contributes significantly to the distribution of African ideas and gives African intellectuals and artists a platform to dialogue with different constituencies. A case in point is Mbembe's influential article "La République et sa bête: A propos des émeutes dans les banlieues de France" (The Republic and its beast: on the riots in French suburbs), which was first published in *Africultures* 65 and then posted on its online site. This article has generated a lot of attention and proven central to the ongoing discussion of the riots of October–November 2005. Now linked up to an array of other online sites,[46] it is read and discussed in ever widening circles.

Notre Librairie-Revue des Littératures du Sud's—now *Cultures du Sud*—policy to grant free online access for its most recent publications, while still being mainly geared toward an academic readership, represents another opening up. Other websites, such as Fabula,[47] Thomas Spear's *île en île*,[48] Virginie Coulon's LITAF,[49] and others, constitute new tools for research and offer new forms of both production and critical approaches. They also allow for faster and easier access to centralized databanks.

A number of authors now publish some of their works online, particularly short forms such as essays. The Internet has provided an opportunity for authors like Raharimanana and Nganang to address political issues directly. It has allowed authors such as Ilboudo, Ebodé, Raharimanana, Ken Bugul, Marie-Célie Agnant, Tadjo, and Boni to feature a variety of creative pieces, particularly short stories and poems.[50] It should also be noted that the Internet developed after the expansion of the independent press in Africa in the 1990s. Many faithful readers of such publications as *Le Messager* (Cameroon) now have online access to them, and it is more difficult for the Biya government to control the spread of information. The Internet allows for news to circulate more broadly and quickly.

Mabanckou, Kangni Alem, Waberi, Boni, Devi, and Léonora Miano have gone one step further by developing their own websites[51] and blogs with a number of useful Internet links. Among these blogs, Mabanckou's and Kangni Alem's are the most visible and informative, engaging the reader and blogger with topics current to contemporary French and African events. Topics have included the November 2005 riots in France as well as polygamous marriages (a renewed point of discussion after the French government surreptitiously tied the violence in the *banlieues* to polygenic practices), migrancy, literary awards, and so on.

Mabanckou's blog also features his reviews of some of the most recently published books in African literatures. In that respect, it contributes to shaping the current canon—all the more authoritatively as the blog relays this recognized writer's opinions and introduces his readers to world literature, not just French and francophone literatures. A window onto contemporary cultural events, it popularizes francophone African literature in an immediate manner.

These websites serve as platforms for the writers in different—and more or less useful—ways. Including songs by favorite musicians of hers, Miano attempts to cultivate a sense of proximity with her readers while informing them about African creativity at large. This is also a space for her to present her writing and put it in personal context. Mabanckou's blog aims at a broader reach. For instance, his—albeit oblique—account of his stay in Rwanda and participation in a conference in the summer of 2008 generated reactions that reopened the debate on the issue of engagement. However, it failed to mention that Diop and Waberi were also present at that conference, thereby limiting the scope of that event to his own participation.

The links between some Franco-French blogs, such as Pierre Assouline's La République des Livres,[52] and francophone African blogs, such as Mabanckou's, are also worth noting, as they signal a dialogue or at least an appreciation of the interconnectedness of their readers. Another question raised by these blogs is the extent to which the criticism of African literature is "packaged" according to, "controlled" by, and fashioned after market (including academic) forces.

Together with *Africultures*, these Internet sites give the pulse of the moment and affect the shaping of the canon quite effectively. However, the benefits of the Internet are not evenly distributed in Europe, Asia, the Americas, and the African continent. Anglophone literature now has a literary award for electronic publishing, the Caine Prize, of which the Kenyan Binyavanga Wainaina was the 2002 recipient for his short story "Discovering Home," published on g21, the World's Magazine Website, in 2001.[53] Wainaina, an online journal editor, opted for this type of publishing because he believed that it was the way to reach a larger audience of young readers. Receiving the Caine prize at Oxford, he addressed the issue as follows: "At home we cannot walk into bookshops and see ourselves, and we cannot see ourselves on television. I think it's peculiar that at a time when Kenya is going through a recession a new generation of artists has come up, and young people are finding money they don't have, to go and listen to music, to listen to stand-up comedians, and for the first time they see reflections of themselves. . . . This is the first-born generation of independent Africans, and this voice must come out."[54]

In an interview with the *East African*, speaking about the state of the publishing industry in Kenya, Wainaina addressed some of the transformations he has been witnessing—how young people are redefining themselves today, and the role of the Internet in this transformational process. He added, "I have discovered that there are many, many writers out there, many good ones . . . but the publishers are so far away from them, that they are looking for ways, on the Internet, abroad, to be read, to be heard. This redefinition of who we are is to me the most important thing happening in the country, which, like many other Kenyan things, is part of the 'informal sector.'"[55]

This assessment, however valid, should be put in perspective, as many technological imbalances continue to affect the African continent, in terms of infrastructures, physical access, and skills. While the African telecommunication market has dramatically expanded during the past ten years, there remains a digital divide with the rest of the world, a digital divide that also plays out between individual African countries—with South Africa, Morocco, Egypt, Mauritius, and the Seychelles ahead of the game—and between urban centers and rural areas.[56] Not everyone in Africa can spend money and time in cybercafés. Furthermore, the number of cybercafés varies from country to country. Almost completely absent from N'Djamena, cybercafés can be found on most street corners in Dakar, Kigali, and Lagos. The way people use the Internet also varies. Right now, it primarily serves for emailing and social networking purposes. Fewer people use it to read articles or as a consulting tool. In addition to frequent power outages, downloading is often slow and thus expensive, as is printing.

Initiatives such as *Africultures* and the writers' blogs, as well as access to a great variety of African and international newspapers online represent a step toward the democratization of reading. By being part of more global economies of cultural production, African literature occupies a more visible place. Websites have become important elements in the advertisement of editorial policies. L'Harmattan, for example, has been offering a website for quite a while and has been part of the effort to promote a collaborative site, *Afrilivres*, which lists member publishing houses focusing on Africa and African literature, on the African continent and in Europe. Présence Africaine, on the other hand, has been slow to join in, and just recently started advertising its new titles through an electronic newsletter. Thanks to the fast evolution in technology, websites such as Grioo.com and Netelli.com are allowing for a freer distribution and circulation of news. African newspapers have also added substantial cultural sections, for instance, the "supplément littéraire" in *Les Dépêches de Brazzaville*,[57] featuring sophisticated layouts and photos. M-NET (Electronic Media Network), the subscription-funded television channel established in 1968 in South Africa, is slowly digitalizing African films. And an underwater cable connection may soon allow East Africa broad Internet access.

CONCLUSION

The current configurations in the production and interpretation of African arts are indicative, on the one hand, of a dynamic creativity, and, on the other, of mounting contradictions. Francophone African literature fares better and reaches a broader and more diverse readership. However, although the proliferation of titles, colloquiums, and projects have translated into its recognition at literary salons and book fairs, most of the works are produced outside the continent, reaching first and foremost non-African readers or expatriates. As the Senegalese filmmaker Moussa Sene Absa remarked in an interview with *Wal Fadjri* (June 16, 2006), artists, filmmakers in particular, remain cut off from their own audience. Just as it is easier to see African films outside the continent, it is easier to find African literature outside the continent. The production that is read, and that critics discuss, is still essentially confined to what is available in Europe and the United States. What is available is what is published outside the continent, and this includes criticism of francophone African literature. The result is that young people on the continent are increasingly distanced from both their literature and their cinema, and if they want to read the new voices and works, or watch the latest films, they have to do so outside the continent. This context reinforces the current trend by which many young Africans, including writers, feel they have to leave in order to succeed.

This conflation of contradictory features has an obvious influence on the notion of engagement and the ways writers have channeled it aesthetically. Following Gikandi's argument according to which "postcolonial places need to be recognized as places that theorize the very object they produce" (11), we could suggest that the exhausted notion of engagement has become a burden because it has not yet been fully theorized within the current parameters of postcolonial Africa. And thus, the following remark by Olivier Barlet on African cinema can be extended to literature: "This cinema [and literature] no longer construct truth, they propose to reinvent it."[58]

The Possibilities of Artistic Commitment

Discussing in an interview the function of contemporary art, which he had written about in his essay *Le spectateur émancipé* (2008), Jacques Rancière highlights the following discrepancies:

> There was a time when art clearly carried a political message, and critics tried to discern this message in the works. . . . It was thought that, by pointing out certain representations of power . . . one would elicit in the viewer both a consciousness of the system of domination and the aspiration to fight against it. In my opinion, this tradition in artistic criticism has been running out of steam for the past twenty-five to thirty years. ("L'entretien avec Jacques Rancière," 7)

Rancière does not say that domination has come to an end or that the possibilities of artistic commitment have become nil. Proposing that the old models for political analysis and action are divorced from our contemporary reality, his thinking evidences ongoing attempts among intellectuals to reinvigorate the debate.

Today, the words of *engagé* intellectuals as diverse as Toni Morrison, Arundhati Roy, Noam Chomsky, Salman Rushdie, Wole Soyinka, and Orhan Pamuk carry weight and resound across the world, relayed by the international media. Contemporary francophone African writers and intellectuals participate in these conversations through their fictional and expository work. Tanella Boni's "La spirale de la violence" (2002), Emmanuel Dongala's op-ed contribution to the *New York Times*, "The Genocide Next Door" (2004), Boubacar Boris Diop's collaborative volume with Odile Tobner and François-Xavier Verschave, *Négrophobie* (2004), Patrice Nganang's *Le principe dissident* (2004), and Achille Mbembe's "La république et sa bête: A propos des émeutes dans les banlieues de France" (2005) testify to this. Aminata Traoré's *Le viol de l'imaginaire* (2002) and *Lettre au président des Français à propos de la Côte d'Ivoire et de l'Afrique en général* (2005), Diop's 2007 essay, *L'Afrique au-delà du miroir*, and the collective essays *L'Afrique répond à Sarkozy* and *Petit précis de remise à niveau sur l'histoire africaine à l'usage du Président Sarkozy* (A short refresher course on African history for President Sarkozy's use), both published in 2008, further confirm that African writers and intellectuals are renewing the tradition of speaking out and intervening in the (global) cultural sphere.

In November 2009, Marie Ndiaye, the recipient of the Prix Goncourt, was the target of strong criticism by Eric Raoult, a UMP (Union pour un Mouvement Populaire) deputy, for a statement she had made in an August 2009 interview with Nellie Kaprielan in *les Inrockuptibles*. In that interview, she attributed her move to Berlin to the "monstrous" sociopolitical context following President Sarkozy's election.[1] In his November 2009 letter to Frédéric Mitterrand, France's minister of culture, Raoult stated that Prix Goncourt's awardees should be bound to a "devoir de réserve" (necessary restraint) in an effort to preserve national unity and integrity.[2] Ironically, Ndiaye, born in France of a French mother and a Senegalese father who left the family early on in her childhood, has never self-identified as African or as an *engagé* writer. A close reading of her oeuvre shows, however, that abandonment and the search for roots are central to *Rosie Carpe*, *Les serpents*, and *Hilda*. Furthermore, "Les soeurs," a short story of hers pertaining to métissage, prefaces *La condition noire*, by her brother Pap Ndiaye. Last, *Trois femmes puissantes*, for which she was awarded the Prix Goncourt in 2009, uses Senegal and Senegalese women as background and characters.

What emerges from our analysis is that engagement no longer appears as an unproblematic "form of cultural self-representation" (Spivak, *A Critique of Postcolonial Reason*, 7). Yet, while it may be perceived as programmatic and passé, engagement has allowed for new aesthetics that go beyond the political. Unpacking the meanings of the concept of engagement, our first chapter proposed a more nuanced reading of works by the generation of "enduring militants." We showed that, in an overdetermined historical context, a gradual shift from the poetics of oppression was already in the works. Also highlighted was the role of the critical reception of francophone African writers' texts as *engagé*.

Against the backdrop of an international context in which official histories are being contested and transnational movements elicit a re-thinking of the meaning of citizenship and logics of belonging, Chapter 2 analyzed the renewed importance of history in francophone African literature. Our analysis of the Duty of Memory project enabled us to formulate questions of aesthetics pertaining to the expression of violence, and more broadly, to dialogue on memory, conflict, and conflict resolution. Working on the 1994 genocide in Rwanda, francophone African writers have pushed the boundaries of the *ineffable* (Blanchot). The publication of novels by Rwandans (Benjamin Sehene, Annick Kayitesi, Scholastique Mukasonga, and Gilbert Gatoré) demonstrates that the Duty of Memory Project has created an opening for Rwandans to write about the genocide, their own history and traumas. Along the same lines, authors such as Werewere Liking and Patrice Nganang have devised additional textual strategies to figure (out) silence and define it in terms other than those associated with a crisis in/of representation.

The prevalence of history and memory in contemporary discussions translates into African writers' efforts to explore episodes of the colonial past and more recent events still shrouded in silence. Yet, while the French government and historians seem to be engaged in a similar process of restitution of French history, one cannot fail to be struck by the hardening of political discourse and by the State's resistance to admitting certain historical facts and mistakes. Sarkozy's 2007 speech in Dakar falls into that strategy, as does the canceling of Raharimanana's play, 47, which betrays a refusal to acknowledge France's fierce repression of the 1947 Malagasy rebellion. In "Silence sur 47," with a tone and a style reminiscent of Césaire's *Discours sur le colonialisme*, Raharimanana reacted as follows:

> Silence weighs on memory. People begin to talk. Men and women will want to understand. In a desire, real this time, to live together. Men and women, beyond the borders of history and relationships of power, will want to know. Why in 47, two years after the carnage, two years after "nevermore," why one of the greatest colonial massacres was perpetuated in Madagascar? A massacre committed by those who had defeated Nazism? By those who saw up close the horrors of the war? It is this silence that the play "47" explores. . . . A common history. Violent. Sensitive. . . . But so decided the political wing of the DGGID. Cooperation or development? Silence on 47. Show cancelled. Ban on the expression of these words at the African cultural centers and Alliances Françaises. Stifling memories to perpetuate which tradition? Which domination?[3]

In Chapter 3, we examined francophone African literature's new politics of form, in regard to the textualizing of immigration, gender, human rights, and urban violence. We also showed that the current practice of intertextuality cultivates an aesthetic that goes beyond French and francophone literatures (Monénembo and Couao-Zotti with Brazil, Ngoye with Nigeria, Mabanckou with the Caribbean, etc.), building further onto existing intertextualities with Western and non-Western canonical texts. Also noteworthy is the relationship between the location of writing and the imaginary space for authors living outside the continent, for example, Miano, Tchak, Mabanckou, Nganang, and Waberi. Mabanckou, who now lives in the United States, is paradoxically the writer most connected to the French literary scene, and he is frequently used by French journalists as a resource on American life. Mabanckou's 2009 novel, *Black Bazaar*, shows an innovative practice of intertextuality by featuring a protagonist easily identifiable as the Haitian writer Louis-Philippe Dalembert. Giving Dalembert a fictional life, Mabanckou constructs him as the narrator's mentor, someone he is inspired by and strives to emulate, including in his personal life and in his interactions with other characters in the narrative.

Mabanckou's intertextual tricks are both similar to and different from Sami Tchak's. Whereas, in *Hermina*, Tchak comments on Ananda Devi's writing, Mabanckou lists several of Dalembert's novels and recounts the narrator's encounter with Dalembert at a book signing at Le Rideau Rouge in Paris. As their friendship develops, the narrator comes to speak of his feelings when reading about Dalembert's characters, how they remind him of his compatriots, and how Haiti, Haitian painting, and music speak to him. The narrative becomes a playful adaptation of fictitious conversations with Dalembert, as mentor to the narrator, and of others, between the two writers as friends. Considering that Le Rideau Rouge is an actual bookstore in the eighteenth *arrondissement* of Paris, where Mabanckou has had book signings, and on the website of which an interview of his appears,[4] the text becomes an interesting interplay between what is real and what is fictional. By definition, intertextuality is dependent on the reader's alertness to its contexts and quirks. Mabanckou draws the reader in by multiplying the instances in which s/he is made part of the narrative. It remains to be seen, however, if readers, and particularly women, are convinced by the "truculent" exchanges between the narrator and Dalembert about "face B[s]" (buttocks).

Through a fictional discussion between the narrator and his Antillean neighbor, Mr. Hippocrate, Mabanckou focuses on the debate regarding the "aspects positifs de la colonisation," thus returning to the issue of engagement, but in a manner both serious and offhand that cuts through dogmatism and gives the reader (and author) more freedom of involvement. This strategy proves effective in exposing the layers and motifs of France's *racisme ordinaire*, as was the case with Bessora's *53 cm* and Fatou Diome's *La préférence nationale*.

At the intersection of chorus, song, and novel, "chants-romans" such as Werewere Liking's *Elle sera de jaspe et de corail, Journal d'une misovire,* and *La Mémoire amputée,* and Véronique Tadjo's *A vol d'oiseau, A mi-chemin,* and *Reine Pokou,* are representative of a weaving together of genres. Articulated on a plurality of voices and approaching narratives as performance and re-creation, they manifest an effort to democratize the novel and involve readers in a broader understanding of art.

These different experiments can be read as a way to lift the burden of commitment. Yet, one issue to be raised is that of *lisibilité*[5] (legibility): Are there limits to the aesthetics of experimentation at work in *Nour, 1947,* for instance? How much should be expected of readers? These challenging texts are especially interesting inasmuch as they open up spaces of contradictions: on the one hand, the accent seems to be on formal innovation; on the other, they express a strong political stand against various forms of political, social, and cultural oppression.

Indeed, fruitful paradoxes are arising in the field of francophone African literature. Mabanckou, who once said that he did not want to be "le pompier de l'Afrique" (Africa's fireman) is giving a new spin to the issue of engagement in *Black Bazaar* as is Tierno Monenembo in *Le roi de Kahel* (2008), with its problematic rendition of the colonialist Olivier de Sanderval's quest for a kingdom in Fouta-Djalon at the turn of the nineteenth century. In *Le roi de Kahel*, the paradox lies in the writer's (and reader's) intimacy with the protagonist, whose colonial fantasies are constructed as both utopian and fascinating. A figure of "humanitarian" colonialism, Sanderval should be infuriating. Yet, his "mad scientist" personality, as well as the relentless and almost mystical nature of his dream/delusion, gives him tragic status. In contrast to the other colonialists in the narrative, who are not only brutal but also arrogantly ignorant of indigenous cultures, Sanderval's intellectual curiosity and quixotic sense of mission confer on him an endearing quality that may be read as exonerating. At the same time, Monenembo's fictional reconstruction of Sanderval's life, hubris, and disintegration can be interpreted as a sign of the *indépendance d'esprit (et d'écriture)* such people as Nganang, Mbembe, and Monga have argued for in their respective essays.

These paradoxes reflect other phenomena and junctures happening on the political scene. In France, for example, media and government are paradoxically encouraging an exploration of the past and an acknowledgment of past errors, while the confrontation with history, most particularly colonial history, is subject to supervision. The aesthetic forms francophone African writers are experimenting with, including playing with levels of legibility and intertextuality, are very much part of their renewed efforts to write the political into their narratives and push against that supervision. In that regard, the lack of legibility does not imply a lack of intelligibility.

To continue with the rethinking of the relation between ethics and aesthetics, at a roundtable on exile and return,[6] Kossi Efoui explained that his coming to France had much to do with his idea of democracy, his feeling of estrangement within his own country, and the forms of theater he thought he could explore abroad. Yet, once in France, he was drawn to the underground theater and the possibilities offered by its aesthetics. These possibilities, however, were not devoid of contradictions. One of the dramatic forms he discovered, the *théâtre d'appartement* (apartment theater), had its inception in the former East Germany where it was used to circumvent State control. This was fascinating to Efoui because it seemed to indicate that certain artistic constraints, particularly a lack of freedom of expression, prompted creativity, and thus, that aesthetic experimentation was integral to political engagement. What this means is that the same writer may reject the idea of being political and *engagé* and yet experiment with aesthetics that are central to protest and resistance.

Our analysis also stressed a series of transformational processes, some currently unfolding and others undergoing changes. These changes, and among them the fast-evolving production and distribution of African literatures, need to be taken into consideration when reflecting on the place of the political in the field(s) today.

In Chapter 4, we remarked that francophone writers are more visible, thanks to festivals, literary book fairs, and awards. The Internet increases the distribution of these writers' works and has significantly contributed to their recognition. Yet, a number of festivals, particularly the more established ones, are struggling. The size and audience of Fest'Africa has diminished considerably, going from sixty to seventy writers and artists speaking over two weeks (from the mid-nineties to 2004), to a mere ten writers, traveling from Paris for the day in 2008. This turn of events might be partly attributed to the public's fatigue for structures that have not sufficiently renewed themselves. It can also be explained by the current shift in regional and national funding, from cultural events featuring African arts to more "European" programs. This new orientation in cultural policy is clear in the case of the Festival Francophone de Théâtre en Limousin, which saw its budget reduced by one third in 2008. This is not specific to francophone literatures and arts, however: the French government has been rethinking its overall cultural policies and looking to curb its financial support or channel it in other directions. Tastes and interests are being fashioned differently. Prompted by both financial and artistic concerns, a festival as important as Etonnants Voyageurs in Bamako is becoming more vested in exploring world literature and considering relocating to an environment that is no longer strictly francophone. In the summer of 2008, Etonnants Voyageurs in Israel proved a success to organizers, authors, publishers, and audience. This reconfiguration in tastes and priorities may have several consequences. One is the decrease of the visibility that the African writers living outside the continent had developed through literary awards and festivals. These very writers are often the ones who had been raising the question of the moral responsibility of the African author. Opening up to the larger structure of littérature-monde—which a number of francophone writers have been arguing for in an effort to de-ghettoize francophone literature—means that they will have to struggle for recognition in a much more competitive context.

Writers such as Efoui, who are weary of the label of "African writer" and dissociate themselves from the notion of *engagé* writing, have often erased Africa from their narratives and put the accent on aesthetics. Interestingly, African authors, men and women, who have taken a stand and become vocal about their moral responsibility to Africa and to their country of origin have become more recognized, and the writing of the political has again come to the fore. This is resulting in more dialogical protocols of writing, and an equation whereby new aesthetics = new movements of ideas and a rearticulated/reconceptualized engagement. The writers committed to that process are doing so through experimenting with aesthetics, often using processes similar to those of their peers, rejecting the position of *engagé* intellectuals.

Léonora Miano's first novel, *L'intérieur de la nuit* (2005), has been characterized by critics as *engagée* because of its representation of war. Miano herself, however, has steadfastly refused to be pigeon-holed as "the writer of African wars." The different interviews she has so far given attest to her preoccupation with humanity and the inner chaos generated by armed conflicts and violence. Says Miano in *Afropean soul et autres nouvelles* (2008): "I write to understand what being human means. It seems to me that the personal inevitably meets the universal. Whatever our 'engagement' . . . novels can only make a difference to a few individuals. Novels cannot help prevent wars or the frantic race toward global market growth" (93). Similarly, Miano objects to being considered as primarily focused on women's issues, and this despite crafting powerful female characters that are central to her stories.

All of these factors prompt the following question: Does engagement remain one of the theoretical grids from which to understand francophone African literature and "read" it in its historical context? The writing of the political is still very much part of African literature, but as demonstrated in Chapters 3 and 4, it is now woven differently, in terms more closely related to the notions of *dissidence* and *irrévérence*. Although, today, francophone African writers see political commitment as a matter of personal involvement, many express a deep concern with generating new ideas in Africa and on Africa, going beyond what Rancière defines as "la tradition de l'art critique." If African writers continue to interrogate the notions of power and social proximity as well as the idea and meaning of belonging, their works call for a reevaluation of the critical parameters by which they are gauged. The growing deterritorialization of the African writer's experience needs to be addressed more finely as well as the shifts involved in theorizing francophone African literature through the prism of Francophonie, littérature-monde, comparative literature, and post-colonial studies.

In their efforts to give a synthetic view of the production at the end of the 1990s, critics such as Joubert, Kesteloot, and Mateso focused on the ideas of chaos and fragmentation. Historians, political scientists, and philosophers such as Bidima, Diouf, Mbembe, and Mbokolo shared a similar view but theorized it as a stage toward Africa's self-determination and a transition to a greater integration into the global world. A decade into the twenty-first century, the production of francophone African literature is characterized by the development of aesthetics of commitment in which the accent is put on the engaging quality of the text and in which women's innovative approaches to writing the political are not restricted to gender issues or to a gendered readership.

Finally, the engaging quality of the production of the past decade poses the question of legacy anew, both in terms of transmission and in terms of prospects. Today, as Diop signaled, engagement is met with a measure of both mistrust and respect: " [A]ll writers distrust the word 'engagement.' They are suspicious of it because it seems to imply that they must renounce their freedom of expression. . . . Yet, as much as writers are suspicious of the notion of engagement, they respect it. . . . This freedom that one wants for oneself, I think one wants it first for others."[7] To the new generations of francophone African writers, that freedom extends beyond the world of Francophonie, and their relationship to political commitment is more a matter of personal choice. They no longer feel the notion of literary engagement as binding; nor is it necessarily a burden.

NOTES

1. The dates of publication of the books mentioned in this book correspond to the dates of the original editions, whereas the dates mentioned in the bibliography correspond to the editions that are readily available.

2. During a conversation with one of the authors, Ken Harrow rightfully pointed out that the usefulness of Eagleton's argument is limited by the divide it constructs between the West and Africa, thus failing to recognize that many of the cultural dominants existing in the one sphere are to be found in the other. This remark seems particularly applicable to diasporic African writers.

3. Dramatizing the effects of globalization on Africa, Abdourrahmane Sissako's film, *Bamako* (2006), centers on a mock trial of the West and its models for development and progress in which Traoré herself impersonates an impassioned writer called to the bar to voice her concerns about Mali's increasing poverty.

4. In this book, we use the capitalized form of the word "Engagement" when referring to its French/Sartrian context. In French and italicized, *Littérature engagée* is similarly linked to that historical logic. In its noncapitalized form, "engagement" is understood as synonymous with literary commitment, which is the term most prevalent as the book unfolds.

5. Among others: Noam Chomsky, Cornel West, Edward Said, Michael Moore, Bill Moyers, Bernard Henri Lévy, Alain Finkelkraut, Wole Soyinka, Traoré, and Arundhati Roy.

6. The translation of this quotation corresponds to its English edition.

7. See PDF version prepared by Jean-Marie Tremblay (August 28, 2008, Cegep: Saguenay, Quebec, Canada). The original version of Althusser's article appeared in *La Pensée,* no. 151 (June 1970). A successive version appeared in *Positions* (1964–1975): 67–125. Paris: Les Editions Sociales, 1976.

8. "Mongo Beti," Alexandre Biyidi's pseudonym, is consistently men-

tioned in its entirety since it loses its meaning when "Beti" is used as a family name—"Mongo Beti" meaning "son of the land" in Ewondo.

9. For example, the Papon trial and torture in Algeria during the war of independence.

10. Although this book gives an idea of the contemporary production of francophone African authors, it could not possibly focus on each author's work in detail. Choices were made to highlight our arguments with intelligibility in mind.

11. The same held true for Faïza Guène's *Kiffe kiffe demain* (2004; *Kiffe Kiffe Tomorrow*, 2006), which appeared in translation almost immediately.

12. Available at http://www.univ-paris8.fr/agenda/science2_html.php?id_event=344.

The Prix Edouard Glissant was created in 2002 at the Université Paris 8 with funding from the Agence Universitaire de la Francophonie (AUF) and RFO. It distinguishes works that value métissage, linguistic and cultural interactions, and the sharing of identities and knowledges. Nimrod was its 2008 recipient.

1. ENDURING COMMITMENTS

1. There are numerous, and more recent, instances of writers speaking out on the question of political commitment in literature. Lamenting the declining publication of novels in the vein of John Steinbeck's *Of Mice and Men* (1937) and *The Grapes of Wrath* (1939), and Harper Lee's *To Kill a Mockingbird* (1960), Barbara Kingsolver, the American author best known for her 1998 novel *The Bean Trees*, created the Bellwether prize in 2000 "in support of a literature of social change" to reward books of conscience, social responsibility, and literary merit. See "Defining a Literature of Social Change" online at http://www.bellwetherprize.org/change.html.

2. Midiohouan, *L'idéologie*, 214.

3. "Littérature engagée can be viewed from two different angles: either it is considered as a "moment" in the history of French literature, that is to say as a trend or a doctrine (1945 Sartre and *Les temps modernes*) . . . before it gives way to other ideas or practices of literary writing (Nouveau Roman, Structuralism, New Criticism . . .), or politically committed literature is thought of as a transhistorical literary phenomenon, recurring in other norms and forms throughout the history of literature" (Denis, 17–18).

4. Rancière defines the concept as follows: "I call the distribution of the sensible the system of self-evident facts of sense of perception that simultaneously disclose the existence of something in common and the delimitations that define the respective parts and positions within it" (12).

5. In that respect, Midiohouan shares in the thinking of other African intellectuals, such as Cheikh Anta Diop and Boubacar Boris Diop, who have

expressed the necessity of developing "African languages' ability, like any other language in any other cultural sphere, to sustain a modern education, to serve as a vehicle for in-depth knowledge" (Cheikh M'Backé Diop, *Cheikh Anta Diop: L'homme et l'oeuvre*, 109).

6. See also chapter 2 of Dominic Thomas's "Francocentrism and the Acquisition of Cultural Capital," in *Black France*, 41–81.

7. In "L'engagement de l'écrivain africain."

8. Conference paper, "Hommage national à Ousmane Sembène," under the auspices of the Ministère de la Culture, du Patrimoine Historique Classé, des Langues Nationales et de la Francophonie, (June 10, 2008), Dakar, Senegal.

9. Awam Amkpa, "Hommage national à Ousmane Sembène," ibid.

10. In "Langue volée, langue violée: Pouvoir, écriture et violence dans le roman africain" (Stolen language, violated language: power, writing and violence in the African novel, 1991), Elisabeth Mudimbe-Boyi takes up Fanon's theory of the liberatory function of violence to underline its therapeutic aspect.

11. With the exception of *Cannibale*, all works by Bolya Baenga were published under the name "Bolya."

12. Christopher Miller's point in *Nationalists and Nomads* about "French colonial myth-making efforts" (65) can actually be extended to include post-independence African nationalist myth-making efforts.

13. In Mercer, "Black Art and the Burden of Representation," 235.

14. Miller, *Nationalists and Nomads*, 119–20.

15. See Basil Davidson, in *The Black Man's Burden: Africa and the Curse of the Nation-State* (1992).

16. Nganang's trilogy, *La promesse des fleurs* (1997), *Temps de chien* (1999), and *L'invention du beau regard: contes citadins* (2005), evidences this point.

17. Conversation with the authors, May 2008, Dakar, Senegal.

18. Also see Phyllis Taoua, *Forms of Protest: Anti-Colonialism and Avant-Gardes in Africa, the Caribbean and France*, chap. 6.

19. In "Mongo Beti and the Responsibility of the African Intellectual" (2003), Ambroise Kom underlines the "confusion between notions of elites and intellectuals, [created by] the colonial model obstructing African minds . . . [as well as the fact that] sometimes the role of intellectual is ascribed to individuals who are merely agents of mediation between the sources of knowledge and the consumers of that learning." Kom further expands on this point by saying that "Mongo Beti can be classified in more than one of these categories. An elite in the mandarin sense of the term— he was an *agrégé* in Classical Letters—as well as an agent of the transmission of knowledge (as a journalist, he is a successful political writer), he is also a fierce defender of justice and a speaker of truth. It is the former sense

that beckons to us with a particular urgency because of its ethical dimension" (42–43).

20. Nkashama uses the expression, "dramaturgy," Lopès "martyrologue," and Jean-Marc Moura "scenography."

21. In *Africultures* 60, available online at http://www.africultures.com/index.asp?menu=affiche_article&no=3610.

22. That question would later pit James Baldwin against Richard Wright, generate attacks from Harold Cruse, author of *The Crisis of the Negro Intellectual* (1967), on James Baldwin, and manifest in the Black Arts Movement's virulent discussions on the social use of arts, etc.

23. In W. E. B. Du Bois's "Criteria of Negro Art" and James Weldon Johnson's "The Dilemma of the Negro Author."

24. See Françoise Pfaff, Gadjigo, and a chapter in Thomas's *Black France*.

25. In *Le Quotidien*, June 11, 2008.

26. *Peuples Noirs-Peuples Africains* is hereafter referred to as *PN-PA*.
At the Manifestation d'Encre et d'Exil, 8ème Rencontre Internationale des Ecritures d'Exil, which took place on December 5–7, 2008, at the Centre Pompidou in Paris, France, and focused on "Ahmadou Kourouma et Mongo Beti: deux itinéraires d'exil," Kom compared *PN-PA* with *Les Temps Modernes*, founded in 1945, and underlined that it sought to appeal to the African intelligentsia.

27. *Main basse* was initially intended to be a volume of collected essays.

28. Mongo Beti's exile was "co-substantial but not essential to his oeuvre." It had more to do with an exile inward, in his *imaginaire* and militant activities, than with an exile from Cameroon (Kom, Manifestation d'Encre et d'Exil).

29. Mongo Beti thus kept the label that he had created, from his publishing house to his bookstore.

30. See Patricia Célérier, afterword and selected bibliography to *The Story of the Madman* by Mongo Beti.

31. In a 1995 unpublished interview with Célérier at the Librairie des Peuples Noirs, Mongo Beti used the term "chronicle" and said that he planned to write the last part of the series.

32. See Célérier, "Narration and Commitment in Mongo Beti's *Dzewatama* Novels."

33. In 1963, Wole Soyinka also denounced *L'enfant noir*. He was to tone down his criticism later on.

34. See Eustace Palmer's *An Introduction to the African Novel* (1972), 91–95, Lee's *Camara Laye* (1984), 16–19, Miller's *Theories of Africans* (1990), 122–24, and King's *Rereading Camara Laye* (2002), 18–19. See also Abiola Irele, "In Search of Camara Laye."

35. Excerpts available at http://www.congopage.com/Relire-L-Enfant-noir-de-Camara.

36. Kom confirms that *Main basse sur le Cameroun* was placed on a list of twenty-five censored books published by Maspéro Editions. Other titles on this list included Fanon's *Sociologie d'une révolution* (1959; *A Dying Colonialism*, 1965) and *Les damnés de la terre* (1961). It is only today that Mongo Beti is being recognized for his theoretical articulation of colonialism and neocolonialism.

37. An exception is Thérèse Kuoh Moukoury, who started publishing a few years earlier, with *Rencontres essentielles* (1968; *Essential Encounters*, 2002).

38. In her forthcoming book, *The Nation Writ Small: African Fictions and Feminisms 1958–1988*, Susan Andrade discusses the manners in which Sow Fall writes the political into *La grève des Battù*.

39. Cheikh A. Ndiaye's film, based on the novel, was released in 2008 under the same title. A previous novel by Sow Fall, *La grève des Battù* (1979), was adapted to the screen and filmed by Cheick Oumar Sissoko in 2000, featuring actors Danny Glover and Isaach de Bankolé.

40. Irele identifies some common traits among Kane, Laye, and Birago Diop. According to him, "their themes and . . . attitudes . . . underlie them to the poets of Négritude, and their prose even exhibits this affinity in stylistic traits" (8). In turn, it is interesting to think of Mongo Beti's fierce opposition to traditionalism and those he called "les pittoresquistes" in "Afrique noire, littérature rose."

41. Paper by Romuald Fonkua at a November 14, 2008, conference titled Journée Henri Lopès under the auspices of the Organisation Internationale de la Francophonie (Paris, France).

42. Papa Samba Diop, "Ecriture et décentrement," paper given at the conference Journée Henri Lopès, ibid.

43. Lopès in an interview with Jean-Luc Aka-Evy, *Etudes Littéraires Africaines*, 1997.

44. Available online at http://www.arts.uwa.edu.au/MotsPluriels/MP798jmvinterview1.html.

45. Mongo-Mboussa, "Humour, érotisme, royaume d'enfance: trois stratégies de libération du sujet chez Henri Lopès," Journée Henri Lopès, November 14, 2008, Paris.

46. See Sylvie Kandé's *Lagon Lagunes: Tableau de mémoire* (2000) and Odile Cazenave's "Marginalisation et identité dans la littérature des années 80" (Marginalization and identity in the literature from the 80s).

47. See, for example, Dongala's play, *La femme et le colonel* (2006). We come back to the topic of Dongala's plays in Chapter 3.

48. The internationalist tradition of intellectual commitment was also represented earlier by another journal, that of Abdellatif Laâbi, Abraham Serfati, et al., *Souffles* (1966–1972), in which Mongo Beti and Depestre published.

49. Issue 160 of *Cultures Sud* on "La critique littéraire" is available as a PDF file at http://www.culturesfrance.com/librairie/derniers/index.html.

50. Miller was key in reassessing that epistemological tradition. See, for example, his reading of Camara Laye's *L'enfant noir* in *Theories of Africans: Francophone Literature and Anthropology in Africa* (1990).

51. On the notion of amnesia in French colonial history, also see Bernard Mouralis's *République et colonies: entre histoire et mémoire: la République française et l'Afrique* (Republic and colonies: between history and memory: the French republic and Africa, 1999).

52. Positing the colonial as a contemporary fact, Coquio's *Retours du colonial? Disculpation et réhabilitation de l'histoire coloniale française* (2008) points in the same direction.

53. Furthermore, in his analysis of the function of language, and his choice of Wolof over French, Diop comes back to orality, saying: "Presently, words come back to me from the furthest recesses of the past and if their sound is at once so familiar and so pleasant to me, it is because I intrinsically belong to a culture of orality" (171). This ties back with Irele's argument in *The African Imagination*, according to which "oral literature in Africa . . . stands as a fundamental reference of discourse and of the imaginative mode in Africa . . . it represents the basic intertext of the African imagination" (11).

54. Diop notably protests against Smith's use of "catastrophisme" (Diop, Tobner, and Verschave, 56).

55. Tobner assumed the leadership of the political organization Survie after Verschave passed away in 2005.

56. In 2006, France was still Cameroon's main source of imports.

57. Most particularly, Boni, Nganang, and Raharimanana, who, interestingly, often publish these works in newspapers and periodicals in their respective countries.

58. Quoted in Jean-Luc Douin, "Ecrivains d'Afrique en liberté," *Le Monde,* March 21, 2002, 16.

59. See Boni, "Le poète n'est pas appelé à être militant propagandiste," an interview with Tahar Bekri, *Africultures* 59 (April–June 2004): 157–60.

60. In *The African Imagination*, Irele defines the canon as "a body of texts that have been fixed and set apart, reified as it were, as monuments of a collective sensibility and imagination, expressive of a structure of feeling itself determined by a profound correspondence between experience and imagination" (10). In Chapter 3, we discuss the changes in canon formation.

61. Closing remarks, colloquium on the "Génocide des Tutsi au Rwanda et la reconstruction des savoirs" (The genocide of the Tutsi in Rwanda and the reconstruction of knowledge), July 25, 2008, Kigali, Rwanda. Posted on August 1, 2008, at http://lecreditavoyage.com.

2. THE PRACTICE OF MEMORY

1. Doulaye Konaté, "Une relecture des *Lieux de mémoire* au regard du vécu africain," *Notre Librairie,* 161.

2. "Le Petit Lavisse" refers to a primary school history textbook named after Ernest Lavisse, a professor at the Sorbonne and a member of the Académie Française at the turn of the twentieth century. Lavisse was also the editor of, and contributor to, the twenty-seven volumes of *L'histoire de France,* which came out between 1900 and 1911. This monumental work was followed by the nine volumes of *L'histoire de France contemporaine,* published between 1920 and 1922. Lavisse's goal in producing these works was to transmit "the knowledge of the country."

3. Christiane Taubira is the author of, among other books, *L'esclavage raconté à ma fille* (2002), *Codes noirs de l'esclavage aux abolitions* (with A. Castaldo, 2006), and *Rendez-vous avec la République* (2006).

4. Joffre also was a place of internment of Tsiganes and Spanish Republican refugees, then after the war, of German war prisoners and French collaborators. Following the Evian Accords, the camp housed an estimated 10,000 Harkis (153).

5. Catherine Coquery-Vidrovitch, Gilles Manceron, and Benjamin Stora, "La mémoire partisane du Président," *Libération,* August 13, 2007.

6. Véronique Tadjo, "Sous nos yeux, l'histoire se répète!" *Libération,* August 13, 2007.

7. Essomba does so through children's characters. His most recent novel, *L'enfant aux larmes de sang* (The child who shed tears of blood, 2007) portrays the world of the underground through children's eyes and experience.

8. http://www.mirinet.net.gn/presse/anciens/.

9. Ricoeur, *La mémoire, l'histoire, l'oubli.*

10. Nasrin Qader, "Shadowing the Story-teller," in *Narratives of Catastrophe: Diop, ben Jelloun, Khatibi* (2009).

11. As noted by Qader, through le Cavalier's confusion, "impossible determination of these categories of good and evil, friend and enemy implicates le Cavalier himself in the atrocities. . . . Le Cavalier's dilemma of, on the one hand, searching for universal justice and, on the other hand, being impotent to respond to the singular situation in this time and this place hints toward the ethical aporia that Derrida, following Kierkegaard, has addressed, though in a reversal form. Ethics seems to always be tinged with irresponsibility, which in turn implicates the ethical subject in the failure of ethics" (118).

12. In "Ecris . . . et tais-toi" (in *L'Afrique au-delà du miroir*), Diop writes: "Writing in Wolof is a way to shield oneself from bad blows and spit, to feel a reassuringly firm ground under one's feet. . . . Endeavoring to strengthen the status of African languages is not waging a rearguard battle, but rather to look towards the future. It may not be said enough: the disconnection between the

linguistic and cultural spheres imperils the whole nation. Too often, the formerly colonized dreams of being the Other" (169). He follows up with a more personal analysis of what writing in Wolof has meant to him, insisting on the pleasure of using words that "do not come from school, but from real life" (169).

13. Fanny Pigeaud, "La guerre cachée de la France," *Libération*, September 17, 2008, 38–39.

14. In our text, we chose to use the nonaccented English spelling of "Bamilekes" throughout, but have respected the accented spelling when quoted in French.

15. See Mongo-Mboussa, "Les méandres de la mémoire dans la littérature africaine."

16. See Irène Assiba d'Almeida's 1994 book by this title.

17. See Marie-José Hourantier, Werewere Liking, and Jacques Scherer, *Du rituel à la scène chez les Bassa du Cameroun* (From rituals to stage theater in Bassa region, Cameroon, 1979), where the Hilun is defined as follows: "He is the historian because he is the one to recount what happened, perpetuate and transform it into myth, though his singing and music. Relatively speaking, he is the 'script.' . . . Yet, these two names, the historian and the script, would deprive him of his most important functions, those of leader, instigator, and above all, poet. Because of his great sensibility, his eyes see everything, his ears are like radars" (83).

18. See also the use of that motif by the Nigerian writer, Chimamanda Ngozi Adichie, in her novel, *Half of a Yellow Sun* (2007), to evoke the Biafra war.

19. See Jameson, *The Political Unconscious*.

20. *Oxford American Dictionary*.

21. Alain Ricard, in *L'effet roman: Arrivée du roman dans les langues d'Afrique* (The novel effect: the novel in African languages, 2007), and Chantal Zabus, in *The African Palimpsest: Indigenization of Language in the West-African Europhone Novel* (2007), provide in-depth analyses of the relationship between the novel and African languages.

22. Lénie "speaks"/tells for the first time when she is with Fred and then with Diane (Boni, *Les baigneurs du lac rose*, 109).

23. For a broader context, see Jacques Chevrier's "La littérature francophone et ses héros."

24. "The ocean-child would remain free of any stain, of the injuries men inflicted on one another ceaselessly, of the venom that poisoned their lives, of the evil words that disfigured them" (Tadjo, *Reine Pokou*, 51).

25. See Odile Cazenave in "Par delà une écriture de la douleur et de la violence: Michèle Rakotoson et Ananda Devi" (Writing beyond pain and violence: Michèle Rakotoson and Ananda Devi, 2003) and Françoise Lionnet, "Les romancières contemporaines des Mascareignes" (Contemporary women writers from the Mascareigne Islands, 1994).

26. This journey is also evoked in Rakotoson's *Juillet au pays: chroniques d'un retour à Madagascar* (July at home: chronicle of a return to Madagascar, 2007). In *L'invention du désert* (The invention of the desert, 1987), Tahar Djaout similarly links a personal childhood narrative of a journey through the desert with that of Mohammed Ibn Toumert.

27. Historical periods referred to in the subparts of Raharimanana's *Nour, 1947* are "Vers l'an 970 de l'Hégire," "Attaque des concessions—Mai 1947," "Attaques des églises."

28. To give an idea of the scope of these events, let us say that March 29–30, 1947, marks the first insurrection against the French colonial government after World War II. In 1947, 6,500 colonial troops were stationed in Madagascar, among which were 1,000 Senegalese and 1,500 French officers. In May of the following year, the number of soldiers on the island had risen to 11,500. The insurrection known as "March 1947" in fact lasted three months. The number of victims of the ensuing repression by the French colonial government is estimated at 100,000.

29. A second edition of Lamko's *La phalène des collines* was published by Le Serpent à Plumes in 2002.

30. As Esther Mujawayo remarks in her testimonial narrative: "In any case, in Rwanda, each personal story has become History" (*SurVivantes*, 17).

31. See also Jean-François Forges's *Le travail de mémoire* (1999).

32. See Fest'Africa's 2003 edition in N'Djamena, Chad, and *Africultures* 58.

33. See Bruce Clarke's "Garden of Memory" in Kigali, for instance.

34. See Sonia Lee's notion of *devoir de lecture* articulated in her paper at the 2001 African Literature Association annual conference.

35. See Philippe Joutard, "Le devoir d'oubli—Amnistie et Amnésie sont parfois des passages obligés pour réconcilier un peuple divisé" (The duty of oblivion—amnesty and amnesia may be rites of passage that reconcile a divided people, 2006).

36. But when asked if he would consider writing on what is happening in the Congo (as of now, an estimated four million people have died there) as he had for Rwanda, Diop replied that he does not see himself committed to writing on all wars. He delivered what he had to, as a writer. The rest was the job of the journalists or the historians.

37. See Mongo-Mboussa, "Rwanda 94–2000, entre mémoire et histoire: le savoir des écrivains" (Rwanda: 94–2000, between memory and history: the knowledge of writers, 2006).

38. Boubacar Boris Diop, interview with Catherine Bédarida, "Nos romans sont là pour dire que les victimes ont existé" (Our novels are here to say that the victims existed). Fest'Africa, Kigali, June 2000. See also Bedarida's "Boubacar Boris Diop, l'inconsolable de Murambi" *Le Monde*, January 19, 2001.

In her analysis of *Murambi* and the author's approach to the genocide, Coquio notes the following: "Boris Diop's ideas regarding his new relationship to historical documents, his evolution as a writer, and a witness show that this is no longer a matter of taking an ideological stance. His engagement in this new reality differs from the engagement traditional to the writer as 'witness' of his times" (141–42).

39. See interview with Jean-Marie Volet, "A l'écoute de Boubacar Boris Diop, écrivain," *Mots Pluriels* 9 (February 1999): http://www.arts.uwa.edu.au/MotsPluriels/MP999bbd.html.

40. In C. Bedarida, "Boubacar Boris Diop, l'inconsolable de Murambi."

41. See, for instance, Tadjo's *Le royaume aveugle* (1990), Liking's *L'amour-cent-vies* (1988), Baenga's *Cannibale* (1986), and Effa's *Le cri que tu pousses ne réveillera personne* (2000).

42. The following development borrows elements from an earlier article. See Cazenave, "Writing the Rwandan Genocide," 70–84.

43. Lamko's work asks the same question: "Pelouse hesitated when Vèdaste handed her the big binder with a black cover and canary-yellow binding. What sensible comment could one write in a guestbook after visiting a museum of human carcasses?" (34).

44. See Blight, *Race and Reunion: The Civil War in American Memory.*

45. Available online at www.common-place.org (2, no. 3 [April 2002]).

46. For instance, Hatzfeld's *La stratégie des antilopes.*

47. Two English translations are available for *Dans le nu de la vie: Récits des marais rwandais.*

48. Gil Courtemanche's *Un dimanche à la piscine à Kigali* was first published by Editions Boréal (Montréal, Quebec) in 2000. See also the political essays published in the United States and in Canada, such as Michael Barnett, *Eyewitness to a Genocide: The United Nations and Rwanda* (2002); Roméo A. Dallaire, *Shake Hands with the Devil: The Failure of Humanity in Rwanda* (2003); Nigel Eltringham, *Accounting for Horror: Post-Genocide Debates in Rwanda* (2004).

49. A new edition of *L'inavouable* was published in 2009, with a new preface by Saint-Exupéry. See also Linda Melvern, *Conspiracy to Murder: The Rwanda Genocide* (2005); Coquio, *Rwanda: le réel et le récit;* Colette Braeckman and Human Rights Watch, *Qui a armé le Rwanda? Chronique d'une tragédie annoncée* (Who armed Rwanda? Chronicle of a tragedy foretold, 1994), Les dossiers du GRIP, Institut Européen de Recherche et d'Information sur la Paix et la Sécurité, no. 188 (April 1994), Bruxelles; and Braeckman's *Terreur africaine: Burundi, Rwanda, Zaïre, les racines de la violence* (African terror: Burundi, Rwanda, Zaire, the roots of violence, 1996).

50. Diop's *L'Afrique au-delà du miroir* comes back to this and explicitly addresses the issue of France's responsibility.

51. Bellamy, "Ten Years Later, the Children of Rwanda Are Still Suf-

fering the Consequences of a Conflict Caused Entirely by Adults" (April 6, 2004).

3. LIFTING THE BURDEN?

1. See Jean-Paul Ngoupandé's *L'Afrique sans la France*.

2. In "Sortir des bois" (*Africultures* 59, 47–50), Jean-Luc Rahari-manana's response to Alain Mabanckou's column "L'Amérique noire à N'Djaména," published in *Africultures* 57.

3. For instance in Sony Labou Tansi's *La vie et demie*. See Taoua, *Forms of Protest: Anti-Colonialism and Avant-Gardes in Africa, the Caribbean and France*, chap. 3.

4. For an ironic and original treatment of this question, see Fouad Laroui's *La fin tragique de Philomène Tralala*.

5. Parts of this section build on Patricia Célérier's, "The Discourse of Violence in Contemporary African Literatures," and Odile Cazenave's "Writing, Youth, Children, and Violence into the African Text: The Impact of Age and Gender."

6. Interestingly, Bolya's 2005 essay, *La profanation des vagins: Le viol, arme de destruction massive* (The desecration of vaginas: Rape as a weapon of mass destruction) is a powerful analysis of the pervasiveness of contemporary violence and the ways it affects women in a systematic politics of destruction.

7. Aimé Césaire's *Cahier d'un retour au pays natal* was written in 1938–1939 and published in 1956 by Présence Africaine.

8. In *Afrique: le maillon faible* (Africa, the weak link, 2002), Bolya underlines the long-standing use of child soldiers in war conflicts.

9. This paragraph borrows elements from Cazenave's "Writing Youth, Children, and Violence into the African Text," 59–60.

10. The discussion of *Rêves sous le linceul* is part of an article by Patricia Célérier, titled "Raharimanana: Le viol des douceurs."

11. See Nora and Ageron, *Realms of Memory: The Construction of the French Past* (1996).

12. Reminiscent of Jean-Paul Sartre's famous sentence in *Les mots*: "Longtemps, j'ai pris ma plume pour une épée" (For a long time, I thought that my quill was a weapon).

13. Calixthe Beyala's Parisian novels: *Le petit prince de Belleville, Maman a un amant, Assèze l'Africaine*, and *Les honneurs perdus* hereafter referred to as *Le petit prince, Mam, Assèze*, and *Les honneurs*.

14. Ambroise Kom in *Mots Pluriels* 20 (February 2002). Available at http://www.arts.uwa.edu.au/MotsPluriels/MP2002ak.html.

15. The 2009 Francophone Theater Festival in Limoges included a play addressing this very issue, *Febar*, by the Belgian Michael de Cock. See also

Aminata Traoré's *Ceuta et Melilla: Mais pourquoi partent-ils?* (Ceuta and Melilla: but why are they leaving?, 2008).

16. See Cazenave, "Writing New Identities: the African Diaspora in France," and "Calixthe Beyala's 'Parisian Novels': An Example of Globalization and Transculturation in French Society."

17. See Paul Gilroy, *"There Ain't No Black in the Union Jack": The Cultural Politics of Race and Nation* (1991), *The Black Atlantic: Modernity and Double Consciousness* (1993), and *Small Acts: Thoughts on the Politics of Black Culture* (1993).

18. Fanon, *Les damnés de la terre,* 67.

19. In "La Préférence nationale. La grande supercherie," *Pluriel. Rassembler la jeune gauche* (1): http://pluriel.free.fr /fn.html.

20. See Eric Taieb's analysis, *Immigrés, l'effet générations: rejet, assimilation, intégration, d'hier à aujourd'hui* (Immigrants, the generational effect: rejection, assimilation, integration, from yesterday to today, 1998), in which he explores the dynamic yet double-edged value of sports, particularly soccer, in relation to young Africans' integration to French society.

21. The theme of prostitution can also to be found in anglophone African literature written by women, notably in Amma Darko's *Beyond the Horizon* (1989).

22. Derek Wright, "African Literature and Post-Independence Disillusionment," in *The Cambridge History of African and Caribbean Literature* 2 (2004): 797–808.

23. Michel Laronde, "Représentation du sujet postcolonial et effets d'institution: Les silences de l'Immigré," presènted at the colloquium "Paris and London in the Postcolonial Imagery," Institut Français, London, June 18–19, 2009.

24. See also Patrick Lozès's *Les Noirs sont-ils des Français à part entière?* (2009).

25. Hitherto, only two other francophone African novels are set in the French Caribbean: Lopès's *Sur l'autre rive* (1992) and Mabanckou's *Et Dieu seul sait comment je dors* (2000). In both cases though, the protagonists are from an African country, and the unfolding of the narration is a pretext for a long flashback explaining the circumstances that brought the character to the island. As for the Antillean characters, they remain in the background.

26. The developments on *Hermina* and on Diome's *Le ventre de l'Atlantique* borrow elements from Cazenave's, "Ecrire depuis Paris, depuis la France: nouvelles trajectoires, nouveaux croisements de regards" (forthcoming in 2011).

27. See Higginson's "A Descent into Crime: Explaining Mongo Beti's Last Two Novels."

28. In that regard, Higginson's point on the publishing of *Trop de soleil*

and *Branle-bas* in a serial form by the opposition newspaper, *Le Messager*, is most interesting. Ibid., 389.

29. See Derek Wright's "African Literature and Post-Independence Disillusionment."

30. See Alain Mabanckou's speech at Le Nouveau Congrès des Ecrivains d'Afrique et de ses Diasporas (October 23–31, 2003) in Chad, at a debate on the issue of writing and political commitment, where a number of writers were pressing others to take their pens and write on the violence of AIDS or on the situation in Ivory Coast.

31. Tanella Boni, "Ecritures et savoirs: écrire en Afrique a-t-il un sens?" *Mots Pluriels* (October 8, 1998).

32. And in fact, considering that Rancière's essay came as a response of sorts to the questions of two philosophers, Muriel Combes and Bernard's Aspe, which appeared in their journal, *Alice*, and that from 1997 to 1999, Nimrod was the chief editor of *Aleph*, a journal on arts, philosophy, and literature, his own choice of Alice for the girl's name in his novel may not be coincidental. Through her, he is actually addressing issues of representations of political subjectivity.

33. Kangni Alemdjrodo is the author of four published plays, two volumes of short stories, an essay on Rachid Boudjedra, and several novels, one of which, *Cola Cola Jazz*, was awarded the Grand Prix Littéraire de l'Afrique Noire in 2003. He is also the translator of two books by Ken Saro Wiwa.

34. Yvan Amar: interview with Koffi Kwahulé, *La danse des mots,* Radio France Internationale (August 19, 2006).

35. Ato Quayson's analysis of the use of a narrow epistemological aperture in Athol Fugard's play *Sizwe Bansi Is Dead* (1972) seems particularly fitting here. On the use of photographs, and the type of world one looks at through them, also see Quayson's "Modernism and Postmodernism in African Literature" (2004).

36. See Kangni Alem, "Les petits frères des bêtes sauvages: Prolifération de la vermine et poétique de l'infiniment petit" (The wild beasts' little brothers: proliferation of the vermin and poetics of the infinitely small, 2006).

4. THE FASHIONING OF AN ENGAGING LITERATURE

1. For the 2005 Africa Remix at the Centre Pompidou in Paris see http://www.centrepompidou.fr/education/ressources/ENS-AfricaRemix/ENS-AfricaRemix.htm.

2. Chéri Samba gained international notoriety through a 1989 exhibition at the Centre Pompidou titled Magiciens de la terre.

3. See "La bande dessinée et l'Afrique/Africa, a Breeding Groud for [*sic*] Comic Book" in the bilingual magazine *Afrik'arts. Le magazine des arts visuels,* no. 5 (Dakar, Senegal, April 2007).

4. "Pour une 'littérature-monde' en français," manifesto published in *Le Monde des Livres* (March 16, 2007, 1–3). A PDF file of this manifesto is accessible through Etonnants Voyageurs' website: http://www.etonnants-voyageurs.com/spip.php?article2353.

5. Laura Garcia and Claire Julliard's interview of Daniel Picouly and Mabanckou, "La littérature-monde en français: un bien commun en danger," clarifies the different meanings currently attached to "francophonie." *Libération*, Saturday July 14, 2007; also available online at http://liberation.fr/transversales/weekend/267004.FR.php.

6. Nicolas Sarkozy, "Pour une francophonie vibrante et populaire," *Le Figaro* (March 22, 2007); http://sarko2007.free.fr/articles.php?Ing=fr&pg=1176.

7. Mbembe, "Francophonie et politique du monde"; http://congopage.com/article4594.html.

8. On January 28, 2007, the Festival Temps de Parole welcomed a debate on the topic between Boni and Le Bris. In February 2008, Waberi participated in a conference titled Dénationaliser la langue française, at the University of Toronto, Canada. Paris X-Nanterre organized a two-day conference in September of the same year; the Florida State University in Tallahassee set up a colloquium on the *Littérature-Monde* for February 2009; *The International Journal of Francophone Studies* published an "extra-ordinary special issue" featuring reactions to both manifesto and book during 2009.

9. In "Portraits d'écrivains (5). Dix questions à l'éditeur et agent littéraire Pierre Astier." Available online at http://www.congopage.com/article.php3?id_article=3730.

10. Taking up the topic of publishing from a different point, but echoing Diop's remarks, Jacques Chevrier in his discussion with Yvan Amar (in RFI's program *La danse des mots*, April 16, 2004) characterized the publishing situation in Africa as such: "En Afrique, on écrit beaucoup, mais on lit peu" (In Africa, many books are written, few are read). He stressed that, in most African countries, there is no "politique du livre" and that books remain luxury items. Given the challenging economic situation of most countries on the continent, people actually have less time to read, and those most likely to do so (teachers, for instance) frequently hold more than one job to make ends meet. The literacy rate remains problematic. In Senegal during Senghor's presidency, there was a definite effort to encourage education (30 percent of the budget). Today, only 40 percent of children are schooled, and the literacy rate is only 39.5 percent. To Chevrier's arguments, one needs to add that the increasing Wolofization of the country, including at school, is one further factor to take into consideration.

11. In a 2008 conversation with the authors, Diop underlined that audio cassettes and CDs of Wolof literature can now be found, notably at the Sandaga market in Dakar. Although their quality is not optimum, this marks a new development in production trends.

12. Conference titled "Présences Africaines in Paris," Paris, April 2006.

13. Editions du Rocher was subsequently bought by Editions Privat and integrated into the Groupe Fabre in 2005.

14. For instance, Sami Tchak, who published three novels at Gallimard's Continents Noirs left to join Mercure de France with *Le paradis des chiots* (The puppies' paradise, 2006). His books are thus no longer tied to a specific series.

15. On the other hand, a few more established writers have joined the series, notably Bessora with *Et si Dieu me demande, dites-lui que je dors* (2008).

16. The series has also been publishing essays by critics such as Boniface Mongo-Mboussa (*Désir d'Afrique* and *L'indocilité: Supplément au désir d'Afrique*) as well as texts on and by well-known writers—for example, André Djiffack's compilation of the late Mongo Beti's essays (*Le rebelle*, volumes I and II).

17. Mongo Beti, *Le rebelle: Tome I, Le rebelle: Tome II,* and *Le rebelle: Tome III.*

18. Littell is American and lives in Spain. *Les bienveillantes,* his nine-hundred-page first novel, created a stir in France. Khadra and Huston both reside in Paris and were respectively born in Algeria and Ontario, Canada.

19. "Comment penser l'Afrique? De la famille africaine, des artistes, des intellectuels, de la critique et des évolutions de la création: Entretien d'Achille Mbembe avec Célestin Monga," *Le Messager* (May 4, 2006), in partnership with *Africultures*. Available at http://www.africultures.com/php/index.php?nav=article&no=4406.

20. Carlin Romano, "Ignoring Authentic African Literature Means Ignoring Africans," *The Chronicle of Higher Education: The Chronicle Review* 52, no. 17 (December 16, 2006).

21. See the success of books such as Zakes Mda's *The Heart of Redness* (2002), Helon Habila's *Waiting for an Angel* (2003), Chimamanda Ngozi Adichie's *Purple Hibiscus* (2003), and *Half of a Yellow Sun* (2006), although Chris Abani's *Graceland* (2004) belies this trend.

22. Texts by Simon Njami (*Cercueil and cie* [1985; Coffin & Co., 1987]), Beyala, Mabanckou, Biyaoula, Essomba, and Bessora. See Cazenave's *Afrique sur Seine: Une nouvelle génération de romanciers africains à Paris* (2003; *Afrique sur Seine: A New Generation of African Writers in Paris,* 2005).

23. Chevrier defines this space of alternance as "a third space" which he calls "migritude." In *Black France* (2007), Dominic Thomas expands on this theorizing of transnational negotiations through the concept of "mediation" (5–6).

24. Filmmakers have also paid an important role in this reevaluation.

25. See Pigeaud's "La guerre cachée de la France."

26. See, for example, Yamina Benguigui's current project on the *banlieues*.

27. For example, *L'avenir de la question noire en France: Enjeux et perspectives* (The future of the idea of blackness in France: challenges and perspectives), by Tshiyembe Mwayila, Robert Wazi, et al. (2007).

28. Interestingly, Kesteloot is also one to say: "La question de l'engagement se règle dans la conscience de chacun et n'est pas un critère esthétique . . . " (The question of engagement is answered by each person's conscience and is not an aesthetic criterion) (*Anthologie négro-africaine: Panorama critique des prosateurs, poètes et dramaturges noirs du 20ème siècle*, 10).

29. Mongo Beti's *Perpetua and the Habit of Unhappiness* is currently out of print.

30. In Diop's case, *Murambi, le livre des ossements* (2000) is his only book to have appeared in translation (*Murambi, the Book of Bones*, 2006).

31. See the infamous comment of the then mayor of Paris, Jacques Chirac, about "le bruit et l'odeur" (the noise and the smell), the polemics on Allocations Familiales for foreigners (public subsidies), and so on.

32. Beyala's *Loukoum: The "Little Prince" of Belleville* is also currently out of print.

33. It should be added that anglophone novels, such as Ayi Kwei Armah's *The Beautiful Ones Are Not Yet Born,* are out of print as well.

34. On the topic of "minorization," see Françoise Lionnet and Shu-mei Shih's *Minor Transnationalism* (2005).

35. The French literary establishment created a second Rentrée Littéraire, to take place annually in February, and accordingly a new batch of literary awards.

36. Take, for example, Diome's *Le ventre de l'Atlantique* (2003) that became the novel of the 2003 Fall Rentrée Littéraire. It was as if immigration and the pleas of African women were approached for the first time. Diome persuasively denounces the myth of France as a place where young Senegalese soccer players can become overnight sport stars, and France is synonymous with success. Yet, Mabanckou had also broached the subject with *Bleu blanc rouge* (1998), as had Bessora with *53 cm* (1999), and others.

37. In her most recent novel, *Les Nègres n'iront jamais au paradis* (Negroes will never go to heaven, 2006), Boni has her characters address, critically and ironically, the inner workings of the publishing world as well as its representations of Africa (25–27).

38. For the online announcement of *Dernières nouvelles du colonialisme* (2006) see http://www.ventsdailleurs.com/Titre.php?Livre_ID=56.

39. See Mbembe's article, "La République et l'impensé de la 'race' in *La Fracture coloniale: La société française au prisme de l'héritage colonial*" (2005).

40. See Kesteloot, Mouralis, Chevrier, Kane, Mateso, and Ossito-Midiohouan.

41. See *Africultures* at http://www.africultures.com.

42. See *Afriscope* at http://afriscope.fr.

43. See Mensah's conference, Présences Africaines, at University of Florida in Paris, April 11, 2006.

44. Along the same lines, since 1981, Radio France Internationale has set up the Prix Découvertes RFI, organized in partnership with the Agence Intergouvernementale de la Francophonie, the Ministry of Foreign Affairs, Culturesfrance, and the SACEM. Besides an award of 7,000 euros, the laureate receives a career development fellowship of 12,500 euros allotted by the Ministry of Foreign Affairs, enabling her or him to tour in Africa through Culturesfrance and enjoy a promotional campaign on RFI and its radio partners in the world. This award represents a key element in France's support to artists and groups of Africa, the Caribbean, and the Indian Ocean. Le Prix Découvertes RFI has contributed to the launching of several artists, notably Didier Awadi (Senegal), Tiken Jah Fakoly (Ivory Coast), Rokia Traoré (Mali), Sally Nyolo (Cameroon), Rajery (Madagascar), Habib Koité (Mali), and Beethova Obas (Haiti).

45. La Plume Noire in Paris was created around the same time as Dominique Loubao's initiative, based in Paris, and taking place yearly, over a weekend in mid-October.

46. To name just a few: in the online site of the African literary journal *Chimurenga,* see http://www.chimurenga.co.za/modules.php?name=News &file=article&sid=91; in Algeria-Watch, see "Informations sur la situation des droits humains en Algérie" at http://www.algeria-watch.org/fr/article/pol/france/republique_bete.htm; in Multitudes Web, see http://multitudes.samizdat.net/spip.php?article2213.

47. The website for the group Fabula was started in 1999 by Alexandre Gefen and René Audet. The group gathers researchers from different nationalities and serves as both a research tool around literary theory and an informational site about colloquiums, online articles, new publications, and blogs of interest. Available at http://www.fabula.org.

48. See Thomas Spear's *île en île* at http://www.lehman.cuny.edu/ile.en.ile.

49. See Virginie Coulon's LITAF at http://www.litaf.cean.org.

50. Another element of Ebodé's work that signals new editorial configurations is the fact that a chapter of his novel, *La dette du père* (The father's debt), has appeared online.

51. See websites by Mabanckou, Kangni Alem, Waberi, Boni, Devi, and Léonora Miano: http://www.lecreditavoyage.com; http://togopages.net/blog;http://www.abdourahmanwaberi.com/?page=actu_article&id_article=131; http://tanellaboni.net; http://anandadevi.cinequanon.net/Ananda_Devi/Carnets/Carnets.html; http://www.leonoramiano.com.

52. See Pierre Assouline's *La République des Livres* at http://passouline.blog.lemonde.fr.

53. Binyavanga Wainaina, "Discovering Home," is available at http://www.g21.net.

54. Wainaina's address on receiving the Caine prize is available at http://www.cca.ukzn.ac.za/CCAarchive/TOW/TOW2003bio6a.htm. A number of online literary journals have been created, particularly in East Africa, including Wainaina's *Kwani?*, *Wasafari*, and *Chimurenga*, which offers printed publications three times a year as well as monthly online publications.

55. For another perspective on the issue, see Ambroise Kom, "Oralité, imprimerie et internet: Le livre africain écartelé" (2001).

56. On the issue of technological imbalances, see http://en.wikipedia.org/wiki/Internet_in_Africa.

57. For *Les Dépêches de Brazzaville*, see http://www.brazzaville-adiac.com/index.php?action=theme&them_id=26.

58. Oliver Barlet in "Les Cinq Décennies des cinémas d'Afrique," *Africultures* 73 (May 2008), http://www.africultures.com/php/index.php?nav=article&no=7304.

CONCLUSION

1. Marie Ndiaye, interview with Nellie Kaprielan in *les Inrockuptibles*, available online at http://www.lesinrocks.com/actualite/actu-article/t/1251629881/article/lecrivain-marie-ndiaye-aux-prises-avec-le-monde/?tx_ttnews%5BsViewPointer%5D=1&tx_ttnews%5Btt_content%5D=138&cHash=be53840706.

2. "Eric Raoult s'attaque à Marie Ndiaye et invente un 'devoir de réserve' pour les prix Goncourt," *Service Actu*, November 10, 2009.

3. "De l'étranger[s]," *Notoire*, Antananarivo (November 2008). Available at notoire@wanadoo.fr.

4. Interview with Mabanckou available at http://www.rue-des-livres.com/interviews/13/alain_mabanckou.html.

5. This question came up during a conversation between Patrice Nganang and Patricia Célérier at Vassar College in 2007.

6. Manifestation d'Encre et d'Exil, 8ème Rencontre Internationale des Ecritures d'Exil, "Ahmadou Kourouma et Mongo Beti: deux itinéraires d'exil," December 5–7, 2008, Centre Pompidou in Paris, France.

7. Marie Bénard, "Entretien avec Boubacar Boris Diop." March 5, 2001. Available online at http://aircrigeweb.free.fr/ressources/rwanda/Rwanda-Diop1.html.

Abani, Chris. *Graceland*. New York: Picador, 2004.

Abtan, Benjamin, Souâd Belhaddad, et al. *Rwanda: Pour un dialogue de la mémoire*. Paris: Albin Michel, 2007.

Adichie, Chimamanda Ngozi. *Half of a Yellow Sun*. New York: Anchor Books, 2007.

———. *Purple Hibiscus*. New York: Anchor Books, 2003.

———. *The Thing Around Your Neck*. New York: Knopf, 2009.

Adotevi, Stanislas. *Négritude et négrologues*. Paris: Union Générale d'Editions, 1972.

Agnani, Suni, Fernando Coronil, Gaurav Desai, Mamadou Diouf, Simon Gikandi, Susie Tharu, and Jennifer Wenzel. "Editor's Column: The End of Postcolonial Theory?" *PMLA* 122–23 (May 2007): 633–651.

Alem, Kangni. *Atterrissage*. Bertoua, Cameroon: Editions Ndzé, 2002.

———. *Canailles et charlatans*. Paris: Editions Dapper Littérature, 2005.

———. *Cola Cola Jazz*. Paris: Editions Dapper Littérature, 2002.

———. *Esclaves*. Paris: Jean-Claude Lattès, 2009.

———. *La gazelle s'agenouille pour pleurer* (nouvelles). 2nd ed. Motifs. Paris: Serpent à Plumes, 2003.

———. "La mémoire des traites et de l'esclavage au regard des littératures africaines." *Notre Librairie: Revue des Littératures du Sud* 161 (March–May 2006): 17–22.

———. "Les petits frères des bêtes sauvages: Prolifération de la vermine et poétique de l'infiniment petit." *Notre Librairie* 163 (September–December 2006). Available on line at http://www.culturesfrance.com/librairie/derniers/163/somm163.htm.

———. *Un rêve d'albatros*. Continents Noirs. Paris: Gallimard, 2006.

Almeida, Irène d'. *Francophone African Women Writers: Destroying the Emptiness of Silence*. Gainesville: University of Florida Press, 1994.

Althusser, Louis. "Idéologie et appareils idéologiques d'Etat." In *Positions*. Paris: Editions sociales, 1972. Translated as "Ideology and Ideological State Apparatuses," in *On Ideology* (London/New York: Verso, 2008).

Amin, Samir. *L'empire du chaos*. Paris: L'Harmattan, 1991.

Amselle, J. L. *L'Occident décroché: Enquête sur les postcolonialismes*. Un Ordre d'Idées. Paris: Stock, 2008.

Amselle, J. L., M. Mamdai, S. Njami, M. Diawara, et al., eds. *Africa Remix*. New York: Hatje Cantz, 2005.

Ananisso, Théo. *Lissaholé*. Continents Noirs. Paris: Gallimard, 2005.

Anderson, Benedict. *Imagined Communities: Reflections on the Origin and Spread of Nationalism*. 2nd ed. London: Verso, 1991.

Appiah, Kwame Anthony. *The Ethics of Identity*. Princeton: Princeton University Press, 2007.

———. *In My Father's House*. Oxford: Oxford University Press, 1992.

Appiah, Kwame Anthony, Charles Taylor, Jürgen Habermas, et al., eds. *Multiculturalism: Examining the Politics of Recognition*. Princeton: Princeton University Press, 1994.

Armes, Roy. *Postcolonial Images: Studies in North African Film*. Bloomington: Indiana University Press, 2005.

Arnold, Steven, ed. *Critical Perspectives on Mongo Beti*. Boulder, Colo.: Lynne Rienner, 1998.

———. "Mongo Beti and Négritude: A New Phase in an Old Debate." *Canadian Journal of African Studies/Revue Canadienne des Etudes Africaines* 24, no. 3 (1990): 442–49.

Astier, Pierre. "Les écrivains francophones sont de plus en plus appréciés à l'étranger." Audio file. *Libération*, July 2006.

Atta, Sefi. *Everything Good Will Come*. Northampton, Mass.: Interlink Books, 2005.

Augé, Marc. *Pour quoi vivons-nous?* Paris: Fayard, 2003.

Baenga, Bolya (also see Bolya). *Cannibale*. Lausanne: Pierre-Marcel Favre, 1986.

Balibar, Etienne. *Nous, citoyens d'Europe?: Les frontières, l'état, le peuple*. Paris: La Découverte, 2001. Translated by James Swenson as *We, the People of Europe?: Reflections on Transnational Citizenship* (Princeton: Princeton University Press, 2003).

———. *Très loin et tout près*. Paris: Bayard, 2007.

Balibar, Etienne, and Immanuel Wallerstein. *Race, Nation, Class: Ambiguous Identities*. London and New York: Verso, 1991.

Bancel, Nicholas, Pascal Blanchard, and Françoise Vergès. *La colonisation française*. Toulouse: Editions Milan, 2007.

————. *La République coloniale*. Paris: Hachette, 2006.

Barlet, Olivier. "Les cinq décennies des cinémas d'Afrique." *Africultures* 73 (May 2008). Available online at http://www.africultures.com/php/index. php?nav=article&no=7304.

————. "Grandeur et ambivalences de la révolution numérique." *Africultures* 73 "Festivals et biennales d'Afrique: machine ou utopies" (February 2, 2008). Available online at http://www.africultures.com/index. asp?menu=affiche_article&no=7305.

Barnett, Michael N. *Eyewitness to a Genocide: The United Nations and Rwanda*. Ithaca, N.Y.: Cornell University Press, 2002.

Barry, Mariama. *La petite peule*. Paris: Mazarine, 2000.

Barthes, Roland. "L'effet de réel." In *Le bruissement de la langue: Essais Critiques IV*, 179–87. Paris: Seuil, Essais, 1984.

Bayart, Jean-François, Stephen Ellis, and Béatrice Hibou. *Criminalisation de l'Etat en Afrique*. Brussels: Editions Complexe, 1997. Translated as *The Criminalization of the State in Africa* (Oxford/Bloomington: James Currey/Indiana University Press, 1999).

Belhaddad, Souâd, and Esther Mujawayo. *SurVivantes: Rwanda-histoire d'un génocide*. La Tour d'Aigues: L'Aube, 2004.

Benda, Julien. *La trahison des clercs*. Paris: Grasset, 1927. Translated by Richard Aldington as *The Treason of the Intellectuals* (New Brunswick, N.J.: Transaction, 2006).

Béjannin, Pascal. *Mammo*. Continents Noirs. Paris: Gallimard, 2005.

Bessora. *53 cm*. Paris: Serpent à Plumes, 1999.

————. "Bas prix et compagnie." In *Nouvelles mythologies*. Paris: Seuil, 2007.

————. "Bionic Woman." In *Les balançoires*. Yaoundé: Tropiques, 2006.

————. *Courant d'air aux Galeries*. Fictions. Paris: Eden, 2003.

————. "Le cru et le cuit." In *Dernières nouvelles du colonialisme*. Paris: Editions Vents d'Ailleurs, 2006.

————. *Cueillez-moi, jolis messieurs*. Continents Noirs. Paris: Gallimard, 2007.

————. *Deux bébés et l'addition*. Paris: Le Serpent à Plumes, 2002.

————. *Et si Dieu me demande, dites-Lui que je dors*. Continents Noirs. Paris: Gallimard, 2008.

————. *Petroleum*. Paris: Denoël, 2004.

————. *Les taches d'encre*. Fiction Française. Paris: Serpent à Plumes, 2000.

Beti, Mongo. *Africains, si vous parliez*. Paris: Homnisphères, 2008 (posthumous).

————. "Afrique Noire, littérature rose." *Présence Africaine* 14 (1953): 17–32.

————. *Branle-bas en noir et blanc*. Paris: Julliard, 2000.

————. *Les deux mères de Guillaume Ismaël Dzewatama*. Paris: Buchet-Chastel, 1983.

————. *La France contre l'Afrique, retour au Cameroun*. Paris: La Découverte, 1993.

————. *L'histoire du fou*. Paris: Julliard, 1994. Translated by Elizabeth Darnel as *The Story of the Madman* (Charlottesville: University of Virginia Press, 2001).

————. *Lettre ouverte aux Camerounais ou la deuxième mort de Ruben Um Nyobé*. Rouen: Editions des Peuples Noirs, 1986.

————. *Main basse sur le Cameroun: Autopsie d'une décolonisation*. 2nd ed. Rouen: Editions des Peuples Noirs, 1984.

————. *Mission terminée*. Paris: Buchet/Chastel, 1957. Translated by Peter Green as *Mission to Kala* (London: Heinemann Press, 1958).

————. *Le Pauvre Christ de Bomba*. Paris: Laffont, 1956. Translated by Gerald Moore as *The Poor Christ of Bomba* (Long Grove, Ill.: Waveland Press, 2005).

————. *Perpétue et l'habitude du malheur*. Paris: Buchet-Chastel, 1974. Translated by John Reed and Clive Wake as *Perpetua and the Habit of Unhappiness* (London: Heinemann Educational, 1978).

————. *Le rebelle, tome 1*. Edited by André Djiffack. Preface by Boniface Mongo-Mboussa. Continents Noirs. Paris: Gallimard, 2007.

————. *Le rebelle, tome 2*. Comments by André Djiffack. Preface by Boniface Mongo-Mboussa. Postface by Odile Biyidi. Continents Noirs. Paris: Gallimard, 2007.

———— (with André Djiffack). *Le rebelle, tome 3*. Preface by Boniface Mongo-Mboussa. Continents Noirs. Paris: Gallimard, 2008.

————. *Remember Ruben*. Paris: Union Générale d'Editions (10/18), 1974.

————. *La revanche de Guillaume Ismaël Dzewatama*. Paris: Buchet-Chastel, 1984.

————. *Le roi miraculé*. Paris: Buchet-Chastel, 1958.

————. *La ruine presque cocasse d'un polichinelle*. Rouen: Editions des Peuples Noirs, 1979.

————. *Trop de soleil tue l'amour*. Paris: Julliard, 1999.

————. (Eza Boto). *Ville cruelle*. Paris: Présence Africaine, 1954.

———— (with Odile Tobner). *Dictionnaire de la négritude*. Paris: L'Harmattan, 1989.

Beti, Mongo, and Philippe Bissek. *Mongo Beti à Yaoundé 1991–2001*. Rouen: Editions des Peuples Noirs, 2005.

Beyala, Calixthe. *Amours sauvages*. Paris: Albin Michel, 1999.

———. *Les arbres en parlent encore*. Littérature. Paris: LGF Livre de Poche, 2004.

———. *Assèze l'Africaine*. Paris: Albin Michel, 1994.

———. *C'est le soleil qui m'a brûlée*. Paris: Stock, 1991. Translated by Marjolijn de Jager as *The Sun Hath Looked upon Me* (London: Heinemann Educational, 1996).

———. *Comment cuisiner son mari à l'africaine*. Romans. Paris: J'ai Lu, 2002.

———. *L'homme qui m'offrait le ciel*. Littérature Générale. Paris: Albin Michel, 2007.

———. *Les honneurs perdus*. Paris: Albin Michel, 1996.

———. *Lettre d'une Africaine à ses soeurs occidentales* (essai). Paris: Spengler, 1995.

———. *Lettre d'une Africaine française à ses compatriotes* (essai). Documents. Paris: Mango, 2005.

———. *Maman a un amant*. Paris: Albin Michel, 1993.

———. *La petite fille du réverbère*. Paris: Albin Michel, 1998.

———. *Le petit prince de Belleville*. Paris: Albin Michel, 1992. Translated by de Jager as *Loukoum: The "Little Prince" of Belleville* (London: Heinemann Educational, 1995).

———. *La plantation*. Paris: LGF Livre de Poche, 2007.

———. *Tu t'appelleras Tanga*. Stock Littérature Française. Paris: Stock, 1988. Translated by de Jager as *Your Name Shall Be Tanga* (London: Heinemann Educational, 1996).

Bhabha, Homi. *The Location of Culture*. London: Routledge, 1994.

———, ed. *Nation and Narration*. New York: Routledge and Kegan Paul, 1990.

Bidima, Jean-Godefroy, "Art de la critique et critique de l'art." In *L'art de la philosophie*, 57–66. Saint-Cloud: Editions de l'Ecole Normale Supérieure, 1998.

———. "Le corps, la cour et l'espace public." *Politique Africaine* 77 (2000): 90–106.

———. "De l'humanisme latin: propos sur la Renaissance et les Lumières à l'heure de la globalisation." In *Proceedings of Globalization and Latin Humanism*, 147–57. New York: Cassamarca, 2000.

Bisanswa, Justin. "D'une critique l'autre: La littérature africaine au prisme de ses lectures." *Notre Librairie* 160 (December–February 2006): 65–70.

Biyaoula, Daniel. *Agonies*. Paris: Présence Africaine, 1998.

———. *L'impasse*. Paris: Présence Africaine, 1996.

———. *La source de joies*. Paris: Présence Africaine, 2003.

Bjornson, Richard. *The African Quest for Freedom and Identity: Cameroonian Writing and the National Experience*. Bloomington: Indiana University Press, 1991.

Blight, David W. "Historians and 'Memory.'" *Common-place* 2, no. 3 (April 2002). Available online at http://www.common-place.org/vol-02/no-03/author.

———. *Race and Reunion: The Civil War in American Memory*. Cambridge, Mass.: Belknap Press, 2001.

Bolya (also see Baenga, Bolya). *Afrique: Le maillon faible*. Essais/Documents. Paris: Serpent à Plumes, 2002.

———. *L'Afrique en kimono: Repenser le développement*. Ivry-sur-Seine: Nouvelles du Sud, 2004.

———. *Les cocus posthumes*. Serpent Noir. Paris: Serpent à Plumes, 2001.

———. *La polyandre*. Serpent Noir. Paris: Serpent à Plumes, 1998.

———. *La profanation des vagins: Le viol, arme de destruction massive*. Essais/Documents. Paris: Editions du Rocher, 2005.

Boni, Tanella. *L'atelier des génies*. Abidjan: Editions Acoria, 2001.

———. *Les baigneurs du lac rose*. 2nd ed. Motifs. Paris: Serpent à Plumes, 2002.

———. "L'écrivain et le pouvoir." *Notre Librairie* 98 (July–September 1989): 83.

———. *Matins de couvre-feu*. Fiction Française. Paris: Editions Du Rocher, 2005.

———. *Les nègres n'iront pas au paradis*. Fiction Française Paris: Serpent à Plumes, 2006.

———. "Le regard de la différence: Réflexions autour du mot 'francophonie.'" *Africultures* 65 (October–December 2005): 129–37.

———. "La tolérance: une disposition permanente nécessaire à la construction d'un horizon d'humanité." *Mots Pluriels* 1, no. 4 (1997): 2.

———. *Une vie de crabe*. Abidjan: NEI, 1989.

———. *Que vivent les femmes d'Afrique?* Paris: Editions du Panama, 2008.

———. "Violences familières dans les littératures francophones du Sud." *Notre Librairie* 148 (July–September 2002): 110–15.

Boni-Claverie, Isabelle. *La grande dévoreuse*. Abidjan: NEI, 2000.

Boulaga, Fabien Eboussi. *La crise du Muntu: authenticité africaine et philosophie*. Paris: Présence Africaine, 1977.

Bourdieu, Pierre. "Le champ littéraire." *Actes de la recherche en sciences sociales* 89 (1991): 4–46.

———. *The Field of Cultural Production*. New York: Columbia University Press, 1993.

Boyi, Elisabeth. *Essai sur les cultures en contact: Afrique, Amériques, Europe*. Lettres du Sud. Paris: Karthala, 2006.

———. "Langue volée, langue violée: Pouvoir, écriture et violence dans le roman africain." In *Figure et violence dans les littératures francophones de l'Afrique subsaharienne et des Antilles*, ed. Marcato Falzoni Franca, 1:101–18. Bologna: Cooperative Lib. Univ. Editrice, 1991.

Braeckman, Colette. *Les nouveaux prédateurs: Politiques des puissances en Afrique Centrale*. Paris: Fayard, 2003.

———. *Terreur africaine: Burundi, Rwanda, Zaïre, les racines de la violence*. Paris: Fayard, 1996.

Brière, Eloïse. *Le roman camerounais et ses discours*. Ivry: Editions Nouvelles du Sud, 1993.

Bugul, Ken. *Le baobab fou*. Dakar: NEA, 1983.

———. *Cendres et braises*. Paris: L'Harmattan, 1994.

———. *De l'autre côté du regard*. Paris: Le Serpent à Plumes, 2003.

———. "Ecrire aujourd'hui: Questions, défis, enjeux." *Notre Librairie* 142 (October–December 2000): 6–11.

———. *La folie et la mort*. Paris: Présence Africaine, 2000.

———. *La pièce d'or*. Littérature. Paris: UBU Editions, 2006.

———. *Mes hommes à moi*. Paris: Présence Africaine, 2008.

———. *Riwan ou le chemin de sable*. Paris: Présence Africaine, 1999.

———. *Rue Félix-Faure*. Etonnants Voyageurs. Paris: Editions Hoëbeke, 2005.

Casanova, Pascale. *La République mondiale des Lettres*. Paris: Seuil, 1999.

Casarino, Cesare, and Antonio Negri. *In Praise of the Common*. Minneapolis: University of Minnesota Press, 2008.

Cazenave, Odile. *Afrique sur Seine: Une nouvelle génération de romanciers africains à Paris*. Paris: L'Harmattan, 2003.

———. "Calixthe Beyala's 'Parisian Novels': An Example of Globalization and Transculturation in French Society." *Sites: the Journal of 20th Century/Contemporary French Studies*, special issue "Women/Femmes," edited by Isabelle de Courtivron et al., 3, no. 2 (Spring 2000): 119–27.

———. "Ecrire depuis Paris, depuis la France: Nouvelles trajectoires, nouveaux croisements de regards." In *Afriques-Europe, Regards croisés*. Lille III: Presses Universitaires de Lille, 2009.

———. "Marginalisation et identité dans la littérature des années 80: L'image du métis." *Présence Francophone* 38 (1991): 111–32.

———. "Par-delà une écriture de la violence: Michèle Rakotoson et Ananda Devi." *Interculturel francophonies: Identités, langues, et imaginaires dans l'Océan Indien*, ed. Jean-Luc Raharimanana (November–December 2003): 51–62.

———. "Paroles engagées, paroles engageantes." *Africultures* 59 (April–June 2004): 59–65.

———. "Roman africain au féminin et immigration: dynamisme du devenir." In *Changements au féminin en Afrique noire*, ed. Danielle De Lame and Chantal Zabus, 2:49–69. Paris: L'Harmattan, 1999.

———. "Vingt ans après Mariama Bâ: nouvelles écritures au féminin." *Africultures* 35, "Masculin-Féminin" (February 2001): 7–15.

———. "Writing New Identities: The African Diaspora in France." In *Literature of Immigration in France*, ed. Susan Ireland and Patrice J. Proulx, 153–63. Westport, Conn.: Greenwood Press, 2001.

———. "Writing the Rwandan Genocide: African Literature and the Duty of Memory." In *Reconstructing Societies in the Aftermath of War: Memory, Identity, and Reconciliation*, ed. Flavia Brizio-Skov. Berkeley, Calif.: Bordighera Press, 2004.

———. "Writing Youth, Children, and Violence into the African Text: The Impact of Age and Gender." *Research in African Literatures* 36, no. 2 (Summer 2005): 59–71.

Célérier, Patricia. Afterword and selected bibliography to *The Story of the Madman*, by Mongo Beti. CARAF Book Series. Charlottesville: University of Virginia Press, 2001.

———. "Bessora: De la 'gaulologie' à l'impéritie." *Présence Francophone* 58, "Francophonie, écriture et immigration" (May 2002): 73–84.

———. "Effets de retour: Entretien avec Michèle Rakotoson." *Cultures du Sud* 172, special issue "L'Engagement au féminin" (2009): 57–62.

———. "Engagement et esthétique du cri." *Notre Librairie* 148 (July–September 2002): 60–63.

———. "The Discourse of Violence in Contemporary African Literatures." Under revision for *The French Review*.

———. "The Disorder of Order: Constructions of Masculinity in the Works of Mongo Beti and Calixthe Beyala." *Romance Notes* 36 (Fall 1995): 83–92.

———. "Narration and Commitment in Mongo Beti's Dzewatama Novels." In *Critical Perspectives on Mongo Beti*, ed. Stephen H. Arnold, 251–60. . London/Boulder, Colo.: Three Continents/Lynne Rienner, 1998.

———. "Raharimanana: 'Le viol des douceurs.'" *Présence francophone* 70, "Arts visuels et communication au Sénégal" (Spring 2008): 136–53.

Certeau, Michel de. *Culture in the Plural*. Minneapolis: University of Minnesota Press, 1997.

Césaire, Aimé. *Cahier d'un retour au pays natal.* Paris: Présence Africaine, 1939. Translated by John Berger and Anna Bostock as *Return to My Native Land* (Baltimore: Penguin, 1969).

———. *Discours sur le colonialisme.* Paris: Présence Africaine, 1970. 5th ed. Translated by Joan Pinkham as *Discourse on Colonialism* (New York: Monthly Review Press, 2001).

Chanda, Tirthankar. "Tant que l'Afrique écrira, l'Afrique vivra." *Le Monde Diplomatique* (December 2004): 30–31.

Chatterjee, Partha. *The Nation and Its Fragments: Colonial and Postcolonial Histories.* Princeton: Princeton University Press, 1993.

Chevrier, Jacques. "Des formes variées du discours rebelle." *Notre Librairie* 148 (July–September 2002): 64–70.

———. "La littérature francophone et ses héros." *Esprit* 317 (August–September 2005): 70–85.

Chomsky, Noam. *Failed States.* New York: Holt, 2007.

———. "The Responsibility of Intellectuals." *New York Review of Books* (23 February 1967). Available online at http://www.chomsky.info/articles/19670223.htm.

Coquery-Vidrovitch, Catherine. *Les Africaines: Histoire des femmes d'Afrique Noire du XIXème au XXème siècles.* Paris: Editions Desjonquères, 1994.

Coquery-Vidrovitch, Catherine, Gilles Manceron, and Benjamin Stora. "La mémoire partisane du président." *Libération,* August 13, 2007, 19.

Coquio, Catherine, ed. *L'histoire trouée, négation et témoignage.* Comme Un Accordéon. Paris: Librairie L'Atalante, 2004.

———. *Retours du colonial? Disculpation et réhabilitation de l'histoire coloniale française.* Comme Un Accordéon, Paris: Librairie L'Atalante, 2008.

———. *Rwanda: Le réel et les récits.* Paris: Editions Belin, 2004.

Coquio, Catherine, and Carol Guillaume. *Des crimes contre l'humanité en République française.* Questions Contemporaines. Paris: L'Harmattan, 2006.

Couao-Zotti, Florent. *Le cantique des cannibales.* Paris: Serpent à Plumes/ Du Rocher, 2004.

———. *Charly en guerre.* 2nd ed. Au Bout du Monde. Paris: Editions Dapper, 2001.

———. *Les Fantômes du Brésil.* Paris: UBU, 2006.

———. *Poulet-Bicyclette et Cie.* Continents Noirs. Paris: Gallimard, 2008.

———. *Notre pain de chaque nuit.* Paris: Editions J'ai Lu, 1998.

Courtemanche, Gil. *Un dimanche à la piscine à Kigali.* Paris: Denoël, 2003.

Translated by Patricia Claxton as *A Sunday at the Pool in Kigali* (Edinburgh: Canongate, 2003).

Coussy, Denise. *La littérature africaine moderne au sud du Sahara.* Paris: Karthala, 2000.

Cusset, François. *French Theory: Foucault, Derrida and Cie et les mutations de la vie intellectuelle aux Etats-Unis.* 2nd ed. Paris: La Découverte/Poche, 2005

Dabla, Sewanou, J. J. *Nouvelles écritures africaines: Romanciers de la seconde génération.* Paris: L'Harmattan, 1986.

Dadié, Bernard Binlin. *Un nègre à Paris.* Paris: Présence Africaine, 1959. Translated by Karen C. Hatch as *An African in Paris* (Urbana: University of Illinois Press, 1994).

Dallaire, Roméo A. *Shake Hands with the Devil: The Failure of Humanity in Rwanda.* 2nd ed. New York: Da Capo Press, 2004.

Davies, Carole Boyce. *Black Women, Writing, and Identity: Migrations of the Subject.* London: Routledge, 1994.

Davidson, Basil. *The Black Man's Burden: Africa and the Curse of the Nation-State.* New York: Three Rivers Press, 1992.

Dehon, Claire. *Le réalisme africain: Le roman francophone en Afrique subsaharienne.* Paris: L'Harmattan, 2002.

———. *Le roman camerounais d'expression française.* Birmingham, Ala.: SUMMA, 1989.

Denis, Benoît. *Littérature et engagement: de Pascal à Sartre.* Points Essais. Paris: Du Seuil, 2000.

Depestre, René. *Bonjour et adieu à la Négritude.* Paris: Editions Robert Laffont, 1980.

Des Forges, Allison. *Leave None to Tell The Truth: Genocide in Rwanda.* Human Rights Watch, 1999.

Devi, Ananda. *Pagli.* Continents Noirs. Paris: Gallimard, 2001.

———. *Soupir.* Continents Noirs. Paris: Gallimard, 2002.

Diabaté, Massa Makan. *L'aigle et l'épervier ou la geste de Soundjata.* Paris: Editions Oswald, 1975.

———. *Comme une piqûre de guêpe.* Paris: Présence Africaine, 1980.

———. *Le lion à l'arc.* Paris: Hatier, 1986.

Diallo, Aïda Mady. *Kouty, mémoire de sang.* 2nd ed. Série Noire. Paris: Gallimard, 2002.

Diarra, Ousmane. *Vieux lézard.* Continents Noirs. Paris: Gallimard, 2006.

Diawara, Manthia. *African Cinema: Politics and Culture.* Bloomington: Indiana University Press, 1992.

———. *In Search of Africa.* Cambridge, Mass.: Harvard University Press, 1998.

Diome, Fatou. *Inassouvies, nos vies*. Fiction Française. Paris: Flammarion, 2008.

———. *Kétala*. Paris: Flammarion, 2006.

———. *La préférence nationale*. Paris: Présence Africaine, 2001.

———. *Le ventre de l'Atlantique*. Paris: Editions Anne Carrière, 2003. Translated by Lulu Norman and Ros Schwartz as *The Belly of the Atlantic* (London: Serpent's Tail, 2006).

Diop, Boubacar Boris. *L'Afrique au-delà du miroir* (essai). Documents. Paris: Philippe Rey, 2007.

———. *Le cavalier et son ombre*. Paris: Stock, 1997.

———. *Doomi Golo*. Dakar: Editions Papyrus, 2003.

———. *Kaveena*. Paris: Philippe Rey, 2006.

———. *Et les menteurs se tairont: pamphlet politique*. Dakar: Les Editions du Groupe Promotion, 1999.

———. "Mongo Beti et nous." In *Remember Mongo Beti*, ed. Ambroise Kom, 87–99. Bayreuth, Germany: Bayreuth African Studies 67, 2003.

———. *Murambi, le livre des ossements*. Paris: Stock, 2000. Translated by Fiona McLaughlin as *Murambi: The Book of Bones* (Bloomington: Indiana University Press, 2006).

———. "Ousmane Sembène ou l'art de se jouer du destin." *Le Quotidien*, June 11, 2008, Document/Hommage-An I de la mort de l'Aîné des anciens.

———. *Reubeuss! ou, l'expérience de la foi: Tout sur la mégalomanie des puissants, l'impuissance du journaliste, ses procès, ses embastillements, l'éclatement de sa foi incomprise: l'exégèse de celle-ci valait un livre*. Dakar: Ed. Spéciale, 1990.

———. *Les tambours de la mémoire*. Paris: L'Harmattan, 1990.

———. *Le temps de Tamango*. Paris: L'Harmattan, 1981.

———. *Les traces de la meute*. Paris: L'Harmattan, 1993.

Diop, Boubacar Boris, Odile Tobner, and François-Xavier Verschave. *Négrophobie*. Paris: Les Arènes, 2005.

Diop, Cheikh M'Backé. *Cheikh Anta Diop: L'homme et l'œuvre*. Paris: Présence Africaine, 2003.

Diouf, Abdou. "La Guerre de Cent Ans." *Le Monde*, Point de Vue, March 19, 2007.

Djaout, Tahar. *L'invention du désert*. Paris: Seuil, 1987.

Djedanoum, Nocky. *Nyamirambo*. Bamako/Paris: Le Figuier/Fest'Africa, 2000.

Djiffack, André. *Mongo Beti: La quête de la liberté*. Paris: L'Harmattan, 2000.

Donadey, Anne. *Recasting Postcolonialism*. Portsmouth, N.H.: Heinemann, 2001.

Donadey, Ann, and Adlai H. Murdoch, eds. *Postcolonial Theory and Francophone Literary Studies*. Gainesville: University Press of Florida, 2005.

Dongala, Emmanuel. "Appel aux intellectuals africains." *Le Monde*, June 8, 1977, 10.

———. "Coucou, revoilà les tirailleurs sénégalais." *PN-PA* 5 (September–October 1978): 51–59.

———. *La femme et le colonel* (théâtre). Ivry-Sur-Seine: Editions A3, 2006.

———. *Le feu des origines*. Motifs. Paris: Alphée/Serpent à Plumes, 2004. Translated by Lillian Corti as *The Fire of Origins* (Chicago: Lawrence Hill Books, 2001).

———. *Un fusil dans la main, un poème dans la poche*. Motifs. Paris: Du Rocher/Serpent à Plumes, 2005.

———. *Jazz et vin de palme*. Monde Noir Poche. Paris: Hatier, 1982.

———. *Johnny chien méchant*. Paris: Le Serpent à Plumes, 2002. Translated by Maria Louise Ascher as *Johnny Mad Dog* (New York: Farrar, Straus and Giroux, 2005).

———. "Littérature et société: ce que je crois." *PN-PA* 9 (May–June 1979): 58–64.

———. *Les petits garçons naissent aussi des étoiles*. Paris: Le Serpent à Plumes, 1998. Translated by Joël Réjouis and Val Vinokur as *Little Boys Come from the Stars* (New York: Anchor Books, 2001).

Drame, Kandioura. *The Novel as Transformation Myth: A Study of the Novels of Mongo Beti and Ngugi Wa Thiong'o*. Syracuse, N.Y.: Maxwell School of Citizenship and Public Affairs, Syracuse University, 1990.

Du Bois, W. E. B. "Criteria of Negro Art." *The Crisis* 32 (October 1926): 290–97.

———. *The Souls of Black Folk*. New York: Blue Heron, 1953.

Eagleton, Terry. *Sweet Violence: The Idea of the Tragic*. Malden, Mass./Oxford, UK: Blackwell, 2003.

Ebodé, Eugène. *La divine colère*. Continents Noirs. Paris: Gallimard, 2003.

———. *Silikani*. Continents Noirs. Paris: Gallimard, 2006.

———. *Tout sur mon maire*. Documents. Paris: Editions Demopolis, 2008.

———. *La transmission*. 2nd ed. Continents Noirs. Paris: Gallimard, 2002.

Edem. *Port-Mélo*. Continents Noirs. Paris: Gallimard, 2006.

Effa, Gaston-Paul. *Cheval-Roi*. Paris: Editions du Rocher, 2001.

———. *Le cri que tu pousses ne réveillera personne*. Paris: Gallimard, 2000.

———. *Mâ*. Paris: Grasset, 1999.

———. *Nous, enfants de la tradition*. Paris: Editions Anne Carrière, 2008.

———. *Quand le ciel se retire*. Paris: L'Harmattan, 1995.

———. *La saveur de l'ombre*. Paris: L'Harmattan, 1993.

———. *Tout ce bleu*. Paris: Grasset, 1998. Translated by Anne-Marie Glesheen as *All That Blue* (London: Black Amber Books, 2002)

———. *A la vitesse d'un baiser sur la peau*. Paris: Editions Anne Carrière, 2007.

———. *Voici le dernier jour du monde*. Paris: Edition Le Rocher, 2005.

Efoui, Kossi. *La fabrique des cérémonies*. Paris: Seuil, 2001.

———. *La polka*. Paris: Seuil, 1998.

———. *Solo d'un revenant*. Cadre Rouge. Paris: Seuil, 2008.

Ela, Jean-Marc. *Cheikh Anta Diop ou l'honneur de penser*. Paris: L'Harmattan, 1989.

Eltringham, Nigel. *Accounting for Horror: Post-Genocide Debates in Rwanda*. London: Pluto Press, 2004.

Essomba, J. R. *Une blanche dans le noir*. Paris: Présence Africaine, 2001.

———. *Le dernier gardien de l'arbre*. Paris: Présence Africaine, 2000.

———. *Le destin volé*. Paris: Présence Africaine, 2003.

———. *Les lanceurs de foudre*. Paris: L'Harmattan, 1995.

———. *Les larmes de sang*. Paris: Présence Africaine, 2007.

———. *Le paradis du Nord*. Paris: Présence Africaine, 1996.

Farah, Nurrudin. *Yesterday, Tomorrow: Voices from the Somali Diaspora*. London: Cassell, 2000.

Fanon, Frantz. *Les damnés de la terre*. 3rd ed. Folio/Actuel. Paris: Gallimard, 1991.

———. *Les damnés de la terre*. Paris: Maspero, 1961. Translated by Constance Farrington as *The Wretched of the Earth* (New York: Grove Press, 1963).

———. *Peau noire: Masques blancs*. Points/Essais. Paris: Du Seuil, 1952.

Fantouré, Alioum. *Le cercle des tropiques*. Paris: Présence Africaine, 1972. Translated as *Tropical Circle,* CARAF Book Series (Charlottesville: University of Virginia Press, 1989)

Ferro, Marc, ed. *Le livre noir du colonialisme*. Paris: Laffont, 2002.

Fisher, Dominique. "The Blank Spaces of Interculturality." *Research in African Literatures* 28, no. 4 (Winter 1997): 85–100.

Fonkoua, R. "Comment appréhender la 'sagesse des barbares.'" In "La Critique Litéraire," *Notre Librairie* 160 (December 2005–February 2006): 4–5.

Fonkoua, R., and P. Halen, eds. *Les champs littéraires africains*. Paris: Karthala, 2001.

Forges, Jean-François. *Le travail de mémoire: une nécessité dans un siècle de violence*. Paris: Editions Autrement, 1999.

Franche, Dominique. *Rwanda: Généalogie d'un génocide*. Les Petits Livres. Paris: Editions des Mille et une Nuits, 1997.

Gadjigo, Samba. *Ousmane Sembène: Une conscience africaine: Genèse d'un destin hors du commun*. Lattitudes Noires. Paris: Homnisphères, 2007.

Galeano, Eduardo. *Memoria del fuego*. Mexico: Siglo Veintiuno Editores, 1999–2001. Translated by Cedric Belfrage as the *Memory of Fire* trilogy (New York: Norton, 1998).

Garnier, Xavier, and Alain Ricard, eds. *L'effet roman: arrivée du roman dans les langues d'Afrique*. Paris: L'Harmattan, 2006.

Gellner, Ernest. *Nations and Nationalism (New Perspectives on the Past)*. Ithaca, N.Y.: Cornell University Press, 1983.

Gikandi, Simon. *Reading the African Novel*. London: Heinemann, 1987.

Gilroy, Paul. *The Black Atlantic: Modernity and Double Consciousness*. Cambridge, Mass.: Harvard University Press, 1993.

———. *Small Acts: Thoughts on the Politics of Black Cultures*. London: Serpent's Tail, 1993.

———. *"There Ain't No Black in the Union Jack": The Cultural Politics of Race and Nation*. Chicago: University of Chicago Press, 1991.

Glickberg, Charles. *The Literature of Commitment*. London: Associated University Presses, 1976.

Glissant, Edouard. *Tout-Monde*. Folio. Paris: Gallimard, 1995.

Glissant, Edouard, and Patrick Chamoiseau. *L'intraitable beauté du monde*. Essais, Paris: Editions Galaade/Institut du Tout-Monde, 2009.

Glissant, Edouard, and Patrick Chamoiseau. *Quand les murs tombent-L'identité nationale hors la loi?* Documents. Paris: Editions Galaade/Institut du Tout-Monde, 2007.

Gnali, Aimée Mambou. *Beto na Beto: Le poids de la tribu*. Continents Noirs. Paris: Gallimard, 2001.

Gourevitch, Philip. *We Wish to Inform You That Tomorrow We Will Be Killed with Our Families: Stories from Rwanda*. New York: Picador/Farrar, Straus and Giroux, 1998.

Goyemidé, Etienne. *Le dernier survivant de la caravane*. Paris: Serpent à Plumes, 2002.

Gugler, Joseph. "Fiction, Fact, and the Critic's Responsibility: *Camp de Thiaroye, Yaaba*, and *The Gods Must Be Crazy*." In *Focus on African Films*, ed. Françoise Pfaff, 69–85. Bloomington: Indiana University Press, 2004.

Hale, A. Thomas. "Busting the Seams: New Dimensions for African Literature in the 21st Century." In *New Directions in African Literature*, ed. Ernest Emenyonu, 10–21. Oxford: James Currey, 2006.

Hall, Stuart. "The Local and the Global: Globalization and Ethnicity." In *Dangerous Liaisons: Gender, Nation, and Postcolonial Perspectives*, ed. Anne McClintock, Aamir Mufti, and Ella Shobat, 173–87. Minneapolis: University of Minnesota Press, 1997.

Hardt, Michael, and Antonio Negri. *Empire*. Cambridge, Mass.: Harvard University Press, 2001.

———. *Multitude: War and Democracy in the Age of Empire*. 2nd ed. New York: Penguin/New Classics, 2005.

Harrow, Kenneth. *Less Than One and Double: A Feminist Reading of African Women's Writing*. Portsmouth, N.H.: Heinemann, 2002.

Hatzfeld, Jean. *Dans le nu de la vie: Récits des marais rwandais*. Paris: Seuil, 2000. Translated by Linda Coverdale as *Life Laid Bare: The Survivors in Rwanda Speak* (New York: Other Press, 2007) and by Gerry Feehily as *Into the Quick of Life: The Rwandan Genocide—The Survivors Speak* (Transatlantic Publications, 2005).

———. *Une saison de machettes*, Paris: Seuil, 2003. Translated by Linda Coverdale as *Machete Season: The Killers in Rwanda Speak* (New York: Farrar, Straus and Giroux, 2005).

———. *La stratégie des antilopes*. Fiction et Cie. Paris: Seuil, 2007. Translated by Coverdale as *The Antelope's Strategy: Living in Rwanda after the Genocide* (New York: Farrar, Straus and Giroux, 2009).

Higginson, Pim. "A Descent into Crime: Explaining Mongo Beti's Last Two Novels." *International Journal of Francophone Studies* 10, no. 3 (2007): 377–91.

———. "Mayhem at the Crossroads: Francophone African Fiction and the Rise of the Crime Novel." *Yale French Studies*, "Crime Fictions" 108 (2005): 160–76.

———. "Tortured Bodies, Loved Bodies: Gendering African Popular Fiction." *Research in African Literatures* 39, no. 4 (Winter 2008): 133–46.

Hirsh, Herbert. "History as Memory" and "The Manipulation of Memory and Political Power." In *Genocide and Politics of Memory*, 16–42. Chapel Hill: University of North Carolina Press, 1995.

Hitchkott, Nicki. *Calixthe Beyala: Performance of Migration*. Liverpool, Eng.: Liverpool University Press, 2006.

Hobsbawm, E. J. *Nations and Nationalism since 1870: Programme, Myth, Reality*. 2nd ed. Cambridge: Cambridge University Press, 1992

Huston, Nancy. *Lignes de faille*. Paris: Editions Actes Sud, 2006. Translated by Huston as *Fault Lines* (New York: Black Cat, 2006).

Ilboudo, Monique. *Le mal de peau*. Paris: Serpent à Plumes, 2001; Imprimerie Nationale du Burkina-Faso, 1992.

———. *Murekatete*. Bamako/Paris: Le Figuier/Fest'Africa, 2000.

Ireland, Susan, and Patrice Proulx, eds. *Immigrant Narratives in Contemporary France*. Westport, Conn.: Greenwood Press, 2001.

Irele, Abiola. *The African Experience in Literature and Ideology*. Bloomington: Indiana University Press, 1990.

———. *The African Imagination: Literature in Africa and the Black Diaspora*. Oxford, UK/New York: Oxford University Press, 2001.

———. "In Search of Camara Laye." *Research in African Literature* 37, no. 1 (Spring 2006): 110–27.

———. *Lectures Africaines: A Prose Anthology of African Writing in French*. London: Heinemann, 1969.

Irele, Abiola, and Simon Gikandi, eds. *The Cambridge History of African and Caribbean Literature*. Cambridge, UK/New York: Cambridge University Press, 2004.

Iweala, Uzodinma. *Beasts of No Nation*. New York: Harper Collins Publishers, 2005.

Jameson, Fredric. "The Ideology of the Text." In *The Ideologies of Theory, Essays 1971–1986*, 1:17–71. Minneapolis: University of Minnesota Press, 1988.

———. *The Political Unconscious*. Ithaca, N.Y.: Cornell University Press, 1981.

Jeannet, Frédéric-Yves, "Jean-Marie Le Clézio ou le Nobel Immérité." Débats, *Le Monde*, October 19–20, 2008, 18.

Jefferess, David. "Postcolonialism's Ethical (Re)Turn: An Interview with Simon Gikandi." *Postcolonial Text* 2, no. 1 (2006). Available online at http://www.postcolonial.org/index.php/pct/article/view/464/165.

Jefferess, David, Julie McGonegal, and Sabine Milz. "Introduction: The Politics of Postcoloniality." *Postcolonial Text* 2, no. 1 (2006). Available online at http://postcolonial.org/index.php/pct/article/viewArticle/448/162.

Jothiprakash, R. *Commitment as a Theme in African American Literature: A Study of James Baldwin and Ralph Ellison*. Bristol, Ind.: Wyndham Hall Press, 1994.

Joutard, Philippe. "Entre histoire et mémoire. Espérer une Méditérranée plurielle." *La Pensée de Midi* 3 (2003): 6–9.

———. "Le devoir d'oubli: Amnistie et amnésie sont parfois des passages obligés pour réconcilier un peuple divisé." *L'Histoire* (July–August 2006).

Jules-Rosette, Benetta. *Black Paris: The African Writers' Landscape*. Urbana: University of Illinois Press, 1998.

Kabou, Axelle. *Et si l'Afrique refusait le développement?* Paris: L'Harmattan, 1991.

Konaré, Ba Adame, Pierre Boilley, and Elikia M'Bokolo. *Petit précis de re-*

mise à niveau sur l'histoire africaine à l'usage du président Sarkozy. Paris: La Découverte, 2008.

Khadra, Yasmina. *L'attentat*. Paris: Julliard, 2005. Translated by John Cullen as *The Attack* (New York: Random House, 2006).

Kane, Cheikh Hamidou. *L'aventure ambigüe*. Paris: Julliard, 1961. Translated by Katherine Woods as *Ambiguous Adventure* (London: Heinemann, 1972).

———. *Les gardiens du temple*. Paris: Stock, 1997.

Kane, Mahamadou. *Sur l'histoire littéraire africaine*. Rabat: Institut des Etudes Africaines, 1992.

Kandé, Sylvie. *Lagon Lagunes: Tableau de mémoire*. Continents Noirs. Paris: Gallimard, 2000.

Kayimahe, Vénuste. *France-Rwanda: les coulisses d'un génocide: témoignage d'un rescapé*. Paris: Dagorno, 2002.

Kayitesi, Annick. *Nous existons encore*. Paris: Michel Lafon, 2004.

Keïta, Fatou. *Et l'aube se lèvera*. Paris/Abidjan: Présence Africaine/NEI, 2007.

———. *Rebelle*. Paris/Abidjan: Présence Africaine/NEI, 1998.

Kesteloot, Lilyan. *Anthologie négro-africaine: panorama critique des prosateurs, poètes et dramaturges noirs du XXe siècle*. Verviers: Les Nouvelles Editions Marabout, 1978.

———. *Les écrivains noirs de langue française: Naissance d'une littérature*. Bruxelles: Université Libre de Bruxelles, 1963, 1967, 1974.

———. *Histoire de la littérature négro-africaine*. Paris: Karthala-Agence Universitaire de la Francophonie, 2001, updated in 2004.

———. *Intellectual Origins of the African Revolution*. Dimensions of the Black Intellectual Experience. Washington, D.C.: Black Orpheus Press, 1972.

———. "Observations sur la nouvelle génération d'écrivains africains." *Ethiopiques. Revue négro-africaine de littérature et de philosophie* 78 (first semester 2007): 65–74.

Kesteloot, Lilyan, and Bassirou Dieng. *Les épopées d'Afrique noire*. Paris: Karthala/UNESCO, 1997.

King, Adèle. *Rereading Camara Laye*. Lincoln: University of Nebraska Press, 2002.

King, Russell, John Connell, and Paul White, eds. *Writing across Worlds: Literature and Migration*. New York/London: Routledge, 1995.

Ki-Zerbo, Joseph. *A quand l'Afrique? Entretien avec René Holenstein*. Paris: Editions de l'Aube/Editions d'En Bas, 2003.

Kom, Ambroise, ed. *La littéraire africaine à la croisée des chemins*. Yaoundé: Editions CLE, 2004.

———. "Littérature africaine: l'avément du polar." *Notre Librairie* 136 (1999): 14–25.

———. *La malédiction francophone: Défis culturels et condition postcoloniale en Afrique.* Hamburg: LIT, 2000.

———. "Mongo Beti-40 ans d'écriture, 60 ans de dissidence." *Présence Francophone* 42 (1993): 1–159.

———. "Mongo Beti and the Responsibility of the African Intellectual." *Research in African Literatures* 34, no. 4 (Winter 2003): 42–56.

———. *Mongo Beti parle: Interview réalisée et éditée par Ambroise Kom.* Bayreuth, Germany: Bayreuth African Studies Series 54, 2002.

———. "Mongo Beti, prophète de l'exil." *Notre Librairie* 99 (October–December 1989): 129–34.

———. "Oralité, imprimerie et internet: Le livre africain écartelé." *littérature africaine à la croisée des chemins.* Yaoundé: Editions CLE, 2001.

———. "Pays, exil et précarité chez Calixthe Beyala, Daniel Biyaoula et Mongo Beti." *Notre Librairie* 138–39 (September 1999–March 2000): 42–55.

———, ed. *Remember Mongo Beti.* Bayreuth, Germany: Bayreuth African Studies Series 67, 2003.

Konaté, Doulaye. "Une relecture des Lieux de mémoire au regard du vécu africain." *Notre Librairie/Revue des Littératures du Sud* 161 (March–May 2006). Available online at http://www.culturesfrance.com/librairie/derniers/161/somm161.htm.

Konaté, Moussa. *Une aube incertaine.* Paris: Présence Africaine, 1985.

———. *L'empreinte du renard.* Fayard Noir. Paris: Fayard, 2006.

———. *Les enquêtes du commissaire Habib: L'assassin du Banconi suivi de: L'honneur de la tribu.* Série Noire. Paris: Gallimard, 2002.

———. *Fils du chaos.* Encres Noires. Paris: L'Harmattan, 1986.

———. *Mali: Ils ont assassiné l'espoir.* Points de Vue. Paris: L'Harmattan, 2000.

———. *L'or du diable.* Paris: L'Harmattan, 1985.

———. *Le prix de l'âme.* Ecrits. Paris: Présence Africaine, 1981.

Kourouma, Ahmadou. *Allah n'est pas obligé.* Paris: Stock, 2000. Translated by Frank Wynne as *Allah Is Not Obliged* (London: Heinemann, 2006).

———. *En attendant le vote des bêtes sauvages.* Paris: Seuil, 1998. Translated by Frank Wynne as *Waiting for the Wild Beasts to Vote* (London: Heinemann, 2001) and by Carrol F. Coates as *Waiting for the Vote of the Wild Animals* (Charlottesville: University of Virginia Press, 2001).

———. *Le chasseur, héros africain.* Paris: Editions Grandir, 1999.

———. *Le diseur de vérité.* Paris: Acoria, 1998.

———. *Le griot, homme de paroles*. Hommes D'Afrique. Nîmes: Editions Grandir, 1999.

———. *Je témoigne pour l'Afrique*. Grigny: Editions Paroles de l'Aube, 1998.

———. *Monnè, outrages et défis*. Paris: Seuil, 1990.

———. *Quand on refuse, on dit non*. Paris: Seuil, 2004.

———. *Les soleils des indépendances*. Paris: Seuil, 1976. Translated by Adrian Adams as *The Suns of Independence* (New York/London: Holmes and Meier, 1997).

———. *Yacouba, le chasseur africain*. Paris: Gallimard Jeunesse, 1998.

Kwahulé, Koffi. *Babyface*. Continents Noirs. Paris: Gallimard, 2006.

———. *Misterioso-119/Blue-s-cat*. Repert Contempo. Paris: Théâtrales, 2005.

Labou Tansi, Sony. *L'anté-peuple*. Cadre Rouge. Paris: Seuil, 1987.

———. *L'état honteux*. Cadre Rouge. Paris: Seuil, 1981.

———. *La parenthèse de sang*. Monde Noir Poche. Paris: Hatier, 1993.

———. *Les sept solitudes de Lorsa Lopez*. Cadre Rouge. Paris: Seuil, 1985.

———. *La vie et demie*. Cadre Rouge. Paris: Seuil, 1979.

———. *Les yeux du volcan*. Cadre Rouge. Paris: Seuil, 1981.

Lacassin, Francis. *Mythologie du roman policier*. Paris: U.G.E./10–18, 1974.

Lamko, Koulsy. *La phalène des collines*. 2nd ed. Motifs. Paris: Le Serpent à Plumes, 2000.

Landry, Donna, and Gerald MacLean, eds. *The Spivak Reader: Selected Works of Gayatri Chakravorty Spivak*. New York/London: Routledge, 1996.

Laroui, Fouad. *La fin tragique de Philomène Tralala*. Paris: Julliard, 2003.

Laye, Camara. *L'enfant noir*. Paris: Plon, 1953. Translated by James Kirkup and Ernest Jones as *The Dark Child: The Autobiography of an African Boy* (New York: Farrar, Straus and Giroux, 1954).

Lazarus, Neil, ed. *The Cambridge Companion to Postcolonial Literary Studies*. Cambridge, UK/New York: Cambridge University Press, 2004.

———. "Ideologies of National Liberation in African Literature." *French Review* 67, no. 1 (1993): 113.

———. *Penser le postcolonial. Une introduction critique*. Paris: Editions Amsterdam, 2006.

———. *Resistance in Postcolonial African Fiction*. New Haven: Yale University Press, 1990.

Le Bris, Michel, and Jean Rouand, eds. *Pour une littérature-monde*. Hors Série. Paris: Gallimard, 2007.

Leclair, Bertrand. *Théorie de la déroute*. Paris: Editions Verticales/Le Seuil, 2001.

Lee, Sonia. *Camara Laye*. Boston: Twayne, 1984.

Levi, Primo. *Se questo è un uomo*. Milan: Einaudi, 2006. Translated by Stuart Woolf as *Survival in Auschwitz* (New York: Touchstone, 1996).

Levi, Primo, Anna Bravo, and Federico Cereja. *Le devoir de mémoire*. Paris: Editions Mille et Une Nuits, 1997.

Liking, Werewere. *L'amour-cent-vies*. Paris: Publisud, 1988. Translated by Marjolijn de Jager as *Love-across-a-Hundred-Lives* (Charlottesville: University of Virginia Press, 2000).

————. *Elle sera de jaspe et de corail (Journal d'une misovire . . .): Chant-roman*. Encres Noires. Paris: Editions L'Harmattan, 1983. Translated by de Jager as *It Shall Be of Jasper and Coral* (Charlottesville: University of Virginia Press, 2000).

————. *La mémoire amputée: Mères Naja et Tante Roz. Chant-roman*. Abidjan: Nouvelles Editions Ivoiriennes, 2004. Translated by de Jager as *The Amputated Memory: A Song Novel* (New York: Feminist Press at the City University of New York, 2007).

————. *Orphée-Dafric*. Encres Noires. Paris: L'Harmattan, 1981.

————. *Puissance de Um*. Abidjan: CEDA, 1979.

Lionnet, Françoise. *Postcolonial Representations: Woman, Literature, Identity*. Ithaca, N.Y.: Cornell University Press, 1995.

————. "Les romancières contemporaines des Mascareignes. Lyrisme, témoinage et subjectivité féminine." *Notre Librairie*, "Nouvelles Ecritures féminines," 2–113 (1994): 86–90.

Lionnet, Françoise, and Shu-Mei Shih, eds. *Minor Transnationalism*. Durham, N.C.: Duke University Press, 2005.

Littell, Jonathan. *Les Bienveillantes*. Paris: Gallimard, 2006. Translated by Charlotte Mandell as *The Kindly Ones* (New York: Harper Collins, 2009).

Lopès, Henri. *Dossier classé*. Cadre Rouge. Paris: Seuil, 2002.

————. *Le chercheur d'Afriques*. Cadre Rouge. Paris: Seuil, 1990.

————. *Le lys et le flamboyant*. Cadre Rouge. Paris: Seuil, 1997.

————. *Le pleurer-rire*. Paris: Présence Africaine, 1982. Translated by Gerald Moore as *The Laughing Cry: An African Cock and Bull Story* (New York: Readers International, 1987).

————. *Ma grand-mère bantoue et mes ancêtres les Gaulois*. Continents Noirs. Paris: Gallimard, 2003.

————. "My Novels, My Characters, and Myself." *Research in African Literatures* 24, no. 1 (Spring 1993).

————. *Sur l'autre rive*. Paris: Seuil, 1992.

————. *Sans tam-tam*. Yaoundé: CLE, 1977.

———. *Tribaliques.* 2nd ed. Paris: Présence Africaine, 1972.

Ly, Ibrahima. *Toiles d'araignées.* 2nd ed. Babel. Paris: Actes Sud, 1997.

Lyotard, Jean-François. *The Postmodern Condition: A Report on Knowledge.* Minneapolis: University of Minnesota Press, 1984.

Mabanckou, Alain. *African psycho.* Paris: Le Serpent à Plumes, 2003. Translated by Christine Schwartz-Hartley as *African Psycho: A Novel* (Brooklyn: Soft Skull Press, 2007).

———. *Au jour le jour.* Paris: Maison Rhodanienne, 1993.

———. *Black Bazaar.* Paris: Seuil, 2009.

———. *Bleu blanc rouge.* Paris: Présence Africaine, 1998.

———. *Et Dieu seul sait comment je dors.* Paris: Présence Africaine, 2001.

———. "L'Amérique noire à N'Djaména." *Africultures* 57 (January 23, 2004).

———. *Les arbres aussi versent des larmes.* Paris: L'Harmattan, 1997.

———. "La Francophonie, oui, le ghetto: non!" *Le Monde,* March 19–20, 2006, 14–15.

———. *La légende de l'errance.* Paris: L'Harmattan, 1995.

———. *Lettre à Jimmy à l'occasion du vingtième anniversaire de ta mort.* Rentrée Littéraire. Paris: Fayard, 2007.

———. *Les petits-fils nègres de Vercingétorix.* Paris: Le Serpent à Plumes, 2002.

———. *L'usure des lendemains.* Paris: Nouvelles du Sud, 1995.

———. *Mémoires de porc-épic.* Paris: Seuil, 2006.

———. *Verre cassé.* Paris: Seuil, 2005. Translated by Helen Stevenson as *Broken Glass* (London: Serpent's Tail, 2009).

Mamdani, Mahmood. *Citizen and Subject.* Princeton: Princeton University Press, 2002.

———. *When Victims Become Killers: Colonialism, Nativism and the Genocide in Rwanda.* Princeton: Princeton University Press, 2002.

Marx, John. "Postcolonial Literature and the Western Literary Canon." *The Cambridge Companion to Postcolonial Literary Studies* (2004): 83–96.

Mbembe, Achille. "Comment penser l'Afrique? De la famille africaine, des artistes, des intellectuels, de la critique et des évolutions de la création: Entretien d'Achille Mbembe avec Célestin Monga." *Africultures* (May 4, 2006). Available online at http://www.africultures.com/index. asp?menu=affiche_article&no=4406.

———. *De la postcolonie: essai sur l'imagination politique dans l'Afrique contemporaine.* Paris: Karthala, 2000. Translated by A. M. Berrett, Janet Roitman, Murray Last, Steven Rendall, and Mbembe as *On the Postcolony* (Berkeley/Los Angeles/London: University of California Press, 2001).

————. "La France et l'Afrique: décoloniser sans s'auto-décoloniser." *Histoire et colonies: La France et son passé colonial* (LDH-Toulon). Available online at http://www.ldh-toulon.net/spip.php?article905.

————. *La politique par le bas en Afrique noire: Contributions à une problématique de la démocratie.* Paris: Karthala, 1992.

————. "La république et sa bête." *Africultures* 65 (November 8, 2005).

————. *Les jeunes et l'ordre politique en Afrique noire.* Paris: L'Harmattan, 1985.

Mbembe, Achille, J. F. Bayart, and C. Toulabor. *Afriques indociles: Christianisme, pouvoir et Etat en société postcoloniale.* Paris: Karthala, 1988.

M'Bokolo, Elikia. "Le Panafricanisme au 21ème siècle." *La diaspora africaine: tribune culturelle panafricaine* 13, Special Printemps (2006): 7.

McClintock, Anne, et al., eds. *Dangerous Liaisons: Gender, Nation and Postcolonial Perspectives.* Minneapolis: University of Minnesota Press, 1997.

Melone, Thomas. *Mongo Beti: L'homme et le destin.* Paris: Présence Africaine, 1971.

Melvern, Linda. *Conspiracy to Murder: The Rwanda Genocide.* London: Verso, 2005.

Mercer, Kobena. "Black Art and the Burden of Representation." In *Welcome to the Jungle: New Positions in Black Cultural Studies.* New York: Routledge, 1994.

Meredith, Martin. *The Fate of Africa: A History of Fifty Years of Independence.* New York: Public Affairs, 2005.

Miano, Léonora. *Afropean soul et autres nouvelles.* GF Etonnants Classiques. Paris: Flammarion, 2008.

————. *Contours du jour qui vient.* Paris: Plon, 2006.

————. *Les aubes écarlates "Sankofa cry."* Paris: Plon, 2009.

————. *L'intérieur de la nuit.* Paris: Plon, 2005.

————. *Soulfood équatoriale.* Exquis d'Ecrivain. Paris: NIL, 2009.

————. *Tels des astres éteints.* Paris: Plon, 2008.

Midiohouan, Guy Ossito. "Le devoir de penser: Mongo Beti et la passionante aventure de *Peuples noirs-Peuples africains.*" In *Remember Mongo Beti,* ed. Ambroise Kom, 205–14. Bayreuth, Germany: Bayreuth African Studies Series 67, 2003.

————. *Ecrire en pays colonisé: Plaidoyer pour une nouvelle approche des rapports entre la littérature négro-africaine d'expression française et le pouvoir colonial.* Paris: L'Harmattan, 2002.

————. *L'idéologie dans la littérature négro-africaine d'expression française.* Paris: L'Harmattan, 1986.

————. *La nouvelle d'expression française en Afrique Noire.* Paris: L'Harmattan, 1999.

Miller, Christopher L. *Blank Darkness: Africanist discourse in French*. Chicago/London: University of Chicago Press, 1985.

———. *The French Atlantic Triangle: Literature and Culture of the Slave Trade*. Durham, N.C.: Duke University Press, 2008.

———. *Nationalists and Nomads: Essays on Francophone African Literature and Culture*. Chicago: University of Chicago Press, 1998.

———. *Theories of Africans: Francophone Literature and Anthropology in Africa*. Chicago/London: University of Chicago Press, 1990.

Mondzain, Marie-José, "Quelle éthique, esthétique et politique de la représentation?" In *Le Théâtre des idées: 50 penseurs pour comprendre le XXIème siècle*, ed. Nicholas Truong, 368–82. Paris: Flammarion, 2008.

Monénembo, Tierno. *L'aîné des orphelins*. Paris: Seuil, 2000. Translated by Monique Fleury Nagem as *The Oldest Orphan* (Lincoln: University of Nebraska Press, 2004).

———. *Un attiéké pour Elgass*. Paris: Seuil, 1993.

———. *Cinéma*. Paris: Seuil, 1997.

———. *Les crapauds-brousse*. Paris: Seuil, 1979. Translated by James Kirkup as *The Bush Toads* (Harlow, Essex, Eng.: Longman, 1983).

———. *Les écailles du ciel*. Paris: Seuil: 1986.

———. *Pelourinho*. Paris: Seuil, 1995.

———. *Peuls*. Paris: Seuil, 2004.

———. *Un rêve utile*. Paris: Editions du Seuil, 1991.

———. *Le roi de Kahel*. Paris: Seuil, 2008.

———. *La tribu des gonzesses*. Paris: Cauris Editions, 2006.

Monga, Célestin. *Anthropologie de la colère: Société civile et démocratie en Afrique Noire*. Paris: L'Harmattan, 1994. Translated by Linda L. Fleck and Monga as *The Anthropology of Anger: Civil Society and Democracy in Africa* (Boulder, Colo.: Lynne Rienner, 1996).

———. *Un Bantou à Washington* suivi de *Un Bantou à Djibouti*. Paris: Presses Universitaires de France, 2007.

———. "Economie d'une créance impayée." In *Remember Mongo Beti*, ed. Ambroise Kom, 151–68. Bayreuth, Germany: Bayreuth African Studies 67, 2003.

Mongo-Mboussa, Boniface. *Désir d'Afrique*. Continents Noirs. Paris: Gallimard, 2002.

———. *L'indocilité: Supplément au désir d'Afrique*. Continents Noirs. Paris: Gallimard, 2005.

———. "L'inutile utilité de la littérature." In "L'engagement de l'écrivain africain." *Africultures* 59 (April–June 2005): 5–11.

———. "La littérature en miroir: création, critique et intertextualité." *Notre*

Librairie: Revue des Littératures du Sud 160 (December 2005–February 2006): 48–54.

———. "Les méandres de la mémoire dans la littérature africaine." *H&M* 1228 (November–December 2000): 68–79.

———, ed. "Rwanda 2000: Mémoires d'avenir." *Africultures* 30 (September 2000).

———. "Rwanda 94–2000, entre mémoire et histoire: le savoir des écrivains." *Africultures* 30, *Rwanda 2000: mémoires d'avenir* (September 2000): 5–6.

Moudileno, Lydie. "Le droit d'exister: trafic et nausée postcoloniale." *Cahiers d'Etudes Africaines* 165 (2002): 83–98.

———. "Literature and Postcolony." *Africultures* 28 "Postcolonialisme: inventaire et débats" (May 1, 2000): 9–13. Available at http://www.africultures.com/index.asp?menu=revue_affiche_article&no=5446&rech=1.

———. *Littératures africaines francophones des années 1980 et 1990. Document de travail.* Dakar: CODESRIA, 2003.

Mouffe, Chantal, ed. *On the Political.* London/New York: Routledge, 2005.

Moura, Jean-Marc. *Exotisme et lettres francophones.* Paris: PUF, 2003.

———. *Littératures francophones et théorie postcoloniale.* Ecritures Francophones. Paris: PUF, 1999.

Mouralis, Bernard. *L'Europe, l'Afrique et la folie.* Paris: Présence Africaine, 1993.

———. *Littérature et développement: Essai sur le statut, la fonction et la représentation de la littérature négro-africaine d'expression française.* Paris: Agence de Coopération Culturelle et Technique, 1984.

———. *L'oeuvre de Mongo Beti.* Issy-Les-Moulineaux, France: Editions Les Classiques Africains, 1981.

———. "Qu'est-ce qu'un classique africain?" *Notre Librairie: Revue des Littératures du Sud* 160 (December 2005–February 2006): 34–39.

———. "Réflexions sur le champ littéraire dans la période 1988–1998: Enjeux et perspectives de la production littéraire francophone." In *Littéraire africaine à la croisée des chemins,* ed. Ambroise Kom. Yaoundé: Editions CLE, 2004.

———. *République et colonies: entre mémoire et histoire: la République française et l'Afrique.* Paris: Présence Africaine, 1999.

Mukasonga, Scholastique. *Inyenzi ou les cafards.* Continents Noirs. Paris: Gallimard, 2006.

Mudimbe, V. Y. *The Idea of Africa.* Bloomington: Indiana University Press, 1994.

———, ed. *The Invention of Africa: Gnosis, Philosophy and the Order of Knowledge.* Bloomington: Indiana University Press, 1988.

Mujawayo Esther, and Souâd Belhaddad. *La fleur de Stéphanie*. Paris: Flammarion, 2006.

———. *SurVivantes: Rwanda, 10 ans après le génocide*. Paris: Editions de L'Aube, 2004.

Mukagasana, Yolande. *La mort ne veut pas de moi*. Paris: Fixot, 1997.

———. *N'aie pas peur de savoir*. Paris: J'ai Lu, 2000.

Mukasonga, Scholastique. *La femme aux pieds nus*. Continents Noirs. Paris: Gallimard, 2008.

Mulvern, Linda. *Conspiracy to Murder: The Rwandan Genocide*. London: Verso, 2005.

Mwayila, Tshiyembe, Robert Wazi, et al. *L'avenir de la question noire en France: Enjeux et perspectives*. Etudes Africaines. Paris: L'Harmattan, 2007.

Naudillon, Françoise. "Black polar." *Présence francophone* 60 (2002): 96–110.

Ndiaye, Marie. *Trois femmes puissantes*. Paris: Gallimard, 2009.

Ndiaye, Pap. *La condition noire: Essai sur une minorité ethnique*. Paris: Editions Calmann-Lévy, 2008.

Ndione, Abasse. *La vie en spirale*. Série Noire. Paris: Gallimard, 1998.

———. *Ramata*. Série Noire. Paris: Gallimard, 2000.

N'Djehoya, Blaise. *Le nègre Potemkine*. Paris: Lieu Commun, 1988.

———. *Un regard noir*. Paris: Autrement, 1984.

Negri, Antonio. *The Politics of Subversion: A Manifesto for the Twenty-first Century*. Cambridge: Polity, 2005.

Nganang, Alain Patrice. "Ecrire sans la France." *Africultures* 60 (November 21, 2004). Available online at http://www.africultures.com/index.asp?menu=affiche_article&no=3610.

———. *Elobi*. Paris: Editions Saint-Germain-des-Prés, 1995.

———. *La joie de vivre*. Paris: Le Serpent à Plumes, 2003.

———. *La promesse des fleurs*. Paris: L'Harmattan, 1997.

———. *Le principe dissident*. Yaoundé: Editions Interlignes, 2005.

———. *L'invention du beau regard: contes citadins*. Continents Noirs. Paris: Gallimard, 2005.

———. *Manifeste d'une nouvelle littérature africaine: Pour une écriture préemptive*. Lattitudes Noires. Paris: Homnisphères, 2007.

———. *Temps de chien*. Paris: Le Serpent à Plumes, 2001. Translated by Amy Reid as *Dog Days: An Animal Chronicle* (Charlottesville: University of Virginia Press, 2006).

Ngoupandé, Jean-Paul. *L'Afrique sans la France: Histoire d'un divorce consommé*. Paris: Albin Michel, 2002.

N'goye, Achille. *Agence Black Bafoussam*. Paris: Le Serpent à Plumes, 1996.

―――. *Ballet Noir à Chateau-Rouge*. Série Noire. Paris: Gallimard, 2001.

―――. *Sorcellerie à bout portant*. Série Noire. Paris: Gallimard, 1998.

―――. *Yaba terminus*. Paris: Le Serpent à Plumes, 1999.

Ngugi, Wa Thiongo. *Decolonizing the Mind: The Politics of Language in African Literature*. Nairobi, Kenya/London, UK/Portsmouth, N.H., U.S.A.: Heinemann/James Currey, 1986.

Niang, Sada, and Samba Gadjigo. "Interview with Ousmane Sembène." *Research in African Literatures* 26, no. 3, "African Cinema" (Autumn 1995): 174–78.

Nimrod. *Le départ*. Paris: Actes Sud, 2005.

―――. *Les jambes d'Alice*. Les Afriques. Paris: Actes Sud, 2001.

―――. *La nouvelle chose française*. Paris: Actes Sud, 2008.

Nizan, Paul. *Les chiens de garde*. New ed. Marseille: Agnon, 1998. Translated by Paul Fittingoff as *Watchdogs: Philosophers of the Established Order* (New York: Monthly Review Press, 1971).

Njami, Simon. *African gigolo*. Paris: Seghers, 1999.

―――. *Cercueil et compagnie*. Paris: Lieu Commun, 1985.

―――. *James Baldwin ou le devoir de violence*. Paris: Seghers, 1991.

Njami, Simon, et al. *The African Sniper Reader*. Zurich: J.R.P./Ringier/Migros Museum, 2005.

Njami, Simon, A. Akin Biyi, Kan-Si, and Y. Konaté. *Africas: The Artist and the City: A Journey and an Exhibition*. New York, U.S.A./Barcelona, Spain: Actar, 2002.

Njami, Simon, B. Jules-Rosette, and E. Mbokolo. *Anthology of African Art*. Paris: D.A.P. Editions/Revue Noire, 2002.

Njami, Simon, L. Firstenberg, S. Hassan, et al. *Looking Both Ways*. Ghent: Snoeck Publishers, 2004.

Nkashama, Pius Ngandu. *Le fils de la tribu*. Dakar: NEA, 1983.

―――. *Le pacte de sang*. Paris: L'Harmattan, 1984.

―――. *Ruptures et écritures de la violence. Etudes sur le roman et les littératures africaines contemporaines*. Paris: L'Harmattan, 1997.

―――. *Vie et mœurs d'un primitif en Essonne, 91*. Encres Noires. Paris: L'Harmattan, 2000.

Nora, Pierre, and Charles-Robert Ageron, Dir. *Les lieux de mémoire: Tomes 1, 2 and 3*. Paris: Gallimard, Quarto, 1997. Translated by Arthur Goldhammer as *Realms of Memory: The Construction of the French Past* (New York: Columbia University Press, 1996).

Ntonfo, André. *Football et politique du football au Cameroun*. Douala: Editions du CRAC et André Ntonfo, 1994.

Okonkwo, Chidi. *Decolonization Agonistics in Postcolonial Fiction.* New York: Palgrave, 1999.

Osofisan, Femi. "Warriors of a Failed Utopia: West African Writers Since the 70s." 1997. Available online at www.PostExpressWire.com.

Ouologuem, Yambo. *Le devoir de violence.* Paris: Le Serpent à Plumes, 2003. Translated by Ralph Manheim as *Bound to Violence* (London: Heinemann, 1983).

———. *Lettre à la France nègre.* Paris: Seuil, 1969.

Oyeyemi, Helen. *The Icarus Girl.* New York: Anchor Books, 2005.

Oyono, Ferdinand. *Le vieux nègre et la médaille.* Paris: Julliard, 1956. Translated by John Reed as *The Old Man and the Medal* (London: Heinemann, 1989).

———. *Une vie de boy.* Paris: Julliard, 1956. Translated by Reed as *Houseboy* (Oxford: Heinemann, 1995).

Palmer, Eustace. *An Introduction to the African Novel: A Critical Study of Twelve Books by Chinua Achebe, James Ngugi, Camara Laye, Elechi Amadi, Ayi Kwei Armah, Mongo Beti and Gabriel Okara.* New York: Africana Publishing, 1972.

Péan, Pierre. *Le monde selon K.* Paris: Fayard, 2009.

———. *Noires fureurs, Blancs menteurs: Rwanda 1990–1994.* Paris: Mille et Une Nuits, Enquête, 2005.

Pfaff, Françoise. *The Cinema of Ousmane Sembène: A Pioneer of African Film.* Westport, Conn.: Greenwood, 1984.

———, ed. *Focus on African Film.* Bloomington: Indiana University Press, 2004.

Pigeaud, Fanny. "La guerre cachée de la France." *Libération,* September 17, 2008, 38–39.

Prunier, Gérard. *The Rwandan Crisis: History of a Genocide.* New York: Columbia University Press, 1995.

Qader, Nasrin. *Narratives of Catastrophe: Diop, ben Jelloun, Khatibi.* New York: Fordham University Press, 2009.

Raharimanana, Jean-Luc. *L'arbre anthropologique.* Paris: Editions Joelle Losfeld/ Gallimard, 2004.

———, ed. *Dernières nouvelles du colonialisme* (collectif.). La Roque d'Anthéron, France: Vents d'Ailleurs, 2006.

———. *Dernières nouvelles de la Françafrique.* Ouagadougou, Burkina Faso: Sankofa/La Roque d'Anthéron, France: Editions Vents d'ailleurs, 2003.

———. *Lucarne.* Paris: Le Serpent à Plumes, 1995.

———. *Nour, 1947.* Paris: Le Serpent à Plumes, 2001.

————. *Rêves sous le linceul*. Paris: Le Serpent à Plumes, 1998.

————. *Za*. Paris: Editions Philippe Rey, 2008.

Rakotoson, Michèle. *Le bain des reliques*. Lettres du Sud. Paris: Karthala, 1988.

————. *Henoÿ—fragments en écorce*. Belgique: Editions Luce Wilquin, 1998

————. *Juillet au pays: Chroniques d'un retour à Madagascar*. Bordeaux: Elytis, 2007.

————. *Lalana*. La Tour d'Aigues: Editions de l'Aube, 2002.

Rancière, Jacques. "L'entretien avec Jacques Rancière." *Télérama* 3074 (December 10, 2008): 17–20.

————. *Le partage du sensible*. Paris: La Fabrique, 2000. Translated by Gabriel Rockhill as *The Politics of Aesthetics: The Distribution of the Sensible* (London/New York: Continuum, 2004).

————. *Politique de la littérature*. Paris: Galilée, 2007.

————. *Le spectateur émancipé*. Paris: La Fabrique, 2008.

Renan, Ernest. "Qu'est-ce qu'une nation?" Available online at http://ourworld.compuserve.com/homepages/bib_lisieux/nation01.htm.

Rérolle, Raphaëlle, "Un exotisme de cape et d'épée." *Le Monde des Livres,* November 14, 2008, 4.

Ricoeur, Paul. *La mémoire, l'histoire, l'oubli*. Paris: Seuil, 2000.

Robin, Régine. *La mémoire saturée*. Paris: Stock, 2003.

Romano, Carlin. "Ignoring Authentic African Literature Means Ignoring Africans." *The Chronicle of Higher Education: The Chronicle Review* 52, no. 17 (December 16, 2005). Available online at http://chronicle.com/weekly/v52/i17/17b01301.htm.

Rosello, Mireille. *Declining the Stereotype: Ethnicity and Representation in French Cultures*. Hanover, N.H.: University Press of New England, 1998.

Rurangwa, Jean-Marie. *Au sortir de l'enfer*. Preface by Boubacar Boris Diop. Ecrire l'Afrique. Paris: L'Harmattan, 2007.

————. *Le génocide des Tutsi expliqué à un étranger*. Bamako/Paris: Le Figuier/Fest'Africa, 2000.

————. *Un Rwandais sur les routes de l'exil*. Paris: L'Harmattan, 2005.

Rushdie, Salman. *Imaginary Homelands: Essays and Criticism 1981–1991*. 11th ed. New York: Penguin Books, 1991.

Sadji, Addoulaye. *Nini, mulâtresse du Sénégal*. Paris: Présence Africaine, 1954.

Said, Edward W. *Culture and Imperialism*. New York: Alfred A. Knopf, 1994.

————. *Des intellectuels et du pouvoir*. Essais. Paris: Du Seuil, 1996.

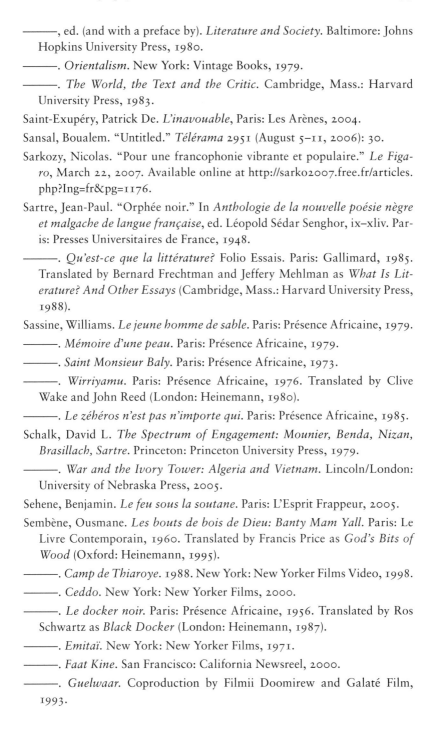

———, ed. (and with a preface by). *Literature and Society*. Baltimore: Johns Hopkins University Press, 1980.

———. *Orientalism*. New York: Vintage Books, 1979.

———. *The World, the Text and the Critic*. Cambridge, Mass.: Harvard University Press, 1983.

Saint-Exupéry, Patrick De. *L'inavouable*, Paris: Les Arènes, 2004.

Sansal, Boualem. "Untitled." *Télérama* 2951 (August 5–11, 2006): 30.

Sarkozy, Nicolas. "Pour une francophonie vibrante et populaire." *Le Figaro*, March 22, 2007. Available online at http://sarko2007.free.fr/articles. php?Ing=fr&pg=1176.

Sartre, Jean-Paul. "Orphée noir." In *Anthologie de la nouvelle poésie nègre et malgache de langue française*, ed. Léopold Sédar Senghor, ix–xliv. Paris: Presses Universitaires de France, 1948.

———. *Qu'est-ce que la littérature?* Folio Essais. Paris: Gallimard, 1985. Translated by Bernard Frechtman and Jeffery Mehlman as *What Is Literature? And Other Essays* (Cambridge, Mass.: Harvard University Press, 1988).

Sassine, Williams. *Le jeune homme de sable*. Paris: Présence Africaine, 1979.

———. *Mémoire d'une peau*. Paris: Présence Africaine, 1979.

———. *Saint Monsieur Baly*. Paris: Présence Africaine, 1973.

———. *Wirriyamu*. Paris: Présence Africaine, 1976. Translated by Clive Wake and John Reed (London: Heinemann, 1980).

———. *Le zéhéros n'est pas n'importe qui*. Paris: Présence Africaine, 1985.

Schalk, David L. *The Spectrum of Engagement: Mounier, Benda, Nizan, Brasillach, Sartre*. Princeton: Princeton University Press, 1979.

———. *War and the Ivory Tower: Algeria and Vietnam*. Lincoln/London: University of Nebraska Press, 2005.

Sehene, Benjamin. *Le feu sous la soutane*. Paris: L'Esprit Frappeur, 2005.

Sembène, Ousmane. *Les bouts de bois de Dieu: Banty Mam Yall*. Paris: Le Livre Contemporain, 1960. Translated by Francis Price as *God's Bits of Wood* (Oxford: Heinemann, 1995).

———. *Camp de Thiaroye*. 1988. New York: New Yorker Films Video, 1998.

———. *Ceddo*. New York: New Yorker Films, 2000.

———. *Le docker noir*. Paris: Présence Africaine, 1956. Translated by Ros Schwartz as *Black Docker* (London: Heinemann, 1987).

———. *Emitaï*. New York: New Yorker Films, 1971.

———. *Faat Kine*. San Francisco: California Newsreel, 2000.

———. *Guelwaar*. Coproduction by Filmii Doomirew and Galaté Film, 1993.

————. *Mandabi*. Comptoir Français du Film Production, 1968.

————. *Le Mandat*. Paris: Présence Africaine, 1965. Translated by Clive Wake as *The Money Order* with *White Genesis* (London: Heinemann Educational, 1997).

————. *Molaade*. New York: New Yorker Video, 2007.

————. *O pays, mon beau peuple!* Paris: Presses Pocket, 1957.

————. *Xala*. Films Domireew, 1975.

————. *Xala*. Paris: Présence Africaine, 1973. Translated by Clive Wake (Chicago: Lawrence Hill Books, 1976).

Semprun, Jorge. *L'écriture ou la vie*. Folio. Paris: Gallimard, 1996. Translated by Linda Coverdale as *Literature or Life* (New York: Penguin, 1998).

Semprun, Jorge, and Elie Wiesel. *Se taire est impossible*. Paris: Mille et Une Nuits/Arte Editions, 1995.

Semujanga, Josias. *Récits fondateurs du drame rwandais, discours social, idéologies et stéréotypes*. Etudes Africaines. Paris: L'Harmattan, 2000.

Seyhan, Azade. *Writing Outside the Nation*. Princeton: Princeton University Press, 2000.

Simone, Abdou Maliq. *Mutations urbaines en Afrique*. Dakar: CODESRIA, 1997. Translated as *Urban Process and Change in Africa* (Oxford, UK: African Books Collective, 1998).

Smith, Stephen. *Négrologie: Pourquoi l'Afrique meurt*. Paris: Calmann-Lévy, 2003.

Solis, René. "Francophonies, les plaies ouvertes." *Libération*, September 29, 2008, 24.

Sontag, Susan. *Regarding the Pain of Others*. New York: Picador, 2004.

Sow Fall, Aminata. *L'appel des arènes*. Dakar: NEA, 1982.

————. *Douceurs du bercail*. Abidjan: NEI, 1998.

————. *L'ex-Père de la Nation*. Paris: L'Harmattan, 1987.

————. *Festins de la détresse*. Terres D'Ecriture. Nyons: L'Or des Fous Editeur, 2005.

————. *Un grain de vie et d'espérance*. Saveurs de la Réalité. Paris: François Truffaut Editions, 2002.

————. *La grève des battù*. Dakar: NEA, 1979. Translated by Dorothy S. Blair as *The Beggars' Strike, or, The Dregs of Society* (Harlow, Essex: Longman, 1986).

————. *Le jujubier du patriarche*. Khoudia: CAEC, 1993.

————. *Le revenant*. Dakar: NEA, 1976.

————. "Sur le flanc gauche du Belem." Arles: Actes Sud, 2002.

Soyinka, Wole. *The Burden of Memory: The Muse of Forgiveness*. New York: Oxford University Press, 1999.

———. *Myth, Literature, and the African World*. Cambridge: Cambridge University Press, 1990.

———. *The Open Sore of a Continent: A Personal Narrative of the Nigerian Crisis*. New York: Oxford University Press, 1996.

———. *You Must Set Forth at Dawn*. New York: Random House, 2007.

Spivak, Gayatri Chakravorty. *A Critique of Postcolonial Reason: Toward a History of the Vanishing Present*. Cambridge, Mass.: Harvard University Press, 1999.

———. *The Post-Colonial Critic: Interviews, Strategies, Dialogues*. Edited by Sarah Harasym. New York/London: Routledge, 1990.

Steger, Manfred B. *Globalization: A Very Short Introduction*. Oxford: Oxford University Press, 2003.

Stratton, Florence. *Contemporary African Literature and the Politics of Gender*. London: Routledge, 1994.

Suleiman, Susan Rubin. *Authoritarian Fictions: The Ideological Novel as a Literary Genre*. Princeton: Princeton University Press, 1983.

———. *Subversive Intent: Gender, Politics, and the Avant-Garde*. Cambridge, Mass./London: Harvard University Press, 1990.

Tadjo, Véronique. *Champs de bataille et d'amour*. Paris/Abidjan: Présence Africaine/NEI, 1999.

———. *Latérite*. Monde Noir Poche. Paris: Hatier, 1984.

———. *A mi-chemin*. Paris: L'Harmattan, 2000.

———. *L'ombre d'Imana: Voyages jusqu'au bout du Rwanda*. Paris: Actes Sud, 2000. Translated by Véronique Wakerly as *The Shadow of Imana*, African Writers Series (Portsmouth, N.H.: Heinemann, 2002).

———. *Reine Pokou: Concerto pour un sacrifice*. Arles, France: Actes Sud, 2004. Translated by Amy Baram Reid as *Queen Pokou: Concerto for a Sacrifice* (Banbury, UK: Ayebia Clarke, 2009).

———. *Le royaume aveugle*. Encres Noires. Paris: L'Harmattan, 1990. Translated by Janis A. Mayes as *The Blind Kingdom* (Banbury, UK: Ayebia Clarke, 2008).

———. "Sous nos yeux, l'histoire se répète." *Libération*, August 13, 2007.

———. *A vol d'oiseau*. Encres Noires. Paris: L'Harmattan, 1986.

Taieb, Eric. *Immigrés, l'effet générations: rejet, assimilation, intégration, d'hier à aujourd'hui*. Paris: Editions de l'atelier, 1998.

Taoua, Phyllis. *Forms of Protest: Anti-Colonialism and Avant-Gardes in Africa, the Caribbean, and France*. Portsmouth, N.H.: Heinemann, 2002.

Taubira, Christiane. "Mémoires universelles." In *Rwanda: Pour un dialogue des mémoires*, by Benjamin Abtan, Souâd Belhaddad, et al.,147–64. Paris: Albin Michel, 2007.

Tcha-Koura, Sadamba (Sami Tchak). *Femme infidèle*. Lomé: Nouvelles Editions Africaines, 1988.

Tchak, Sami. *La fête des masques*. Continents Noirs. Paris: Gallimard, 2004.

———. *Filles de Mexico*. Paris: Mercure de France, 2008.

———. *Hermina*. Paris: Gallimard, 2003.

———. *Le paradis des chiots*. Paris: Mercure de France, 2006.

———. *Place des fêtes*. Paris: Gallimard, 2001.

Thackway, Melissa. *Africa Shoots Back: Alternative Perspectives in Sub-Saharan Francophone African Film*. Bloomington: Indiana University Press, 2003.

Thomas, Dominic. *Black France. Colonialism, Immigration, and Transnationalism*. Bloomington: Indiana University Press, 2007.

———. "Intertextuality, Plagiarism, and Recycling in Ousmane Sembène's *Le docker noir (Black Docker)*." *Research in African Literatures* 37, no. 1 (Spring 2006): 72–90.

———. *Nation-Building, Propaganda, and Literature in Francophone Africa*. Bloomington/ Indianapolis: Indiana University Press, 2002.

Tine, Alioune. "Wolof ou français: Le Choix de Sembène." *Notre Librairie* 81, "Littérature sénégalaise" (1989): 43–50.

Towa, Marcien. *Léopold Sedar Senghor: Négritude ou servitude?* Yaoundé: CLE, 1971.

Todorov, Tzvetan. *Les abus de la mémoire*. Paris: Arléa, 1998.

Traoré, Aminata. *L'Afrique sacrifiée*. Paris: Fayard, 2008.

———. *Ceuta et Melilla: Mais pourquoi partent-ils?* Œil du Cyclone, Paris: Les Perséides, 2008.

———. *L'étau: L'Afrique dans un monde sans frontières*. Paris: Actes Sud, 1999.

———. *Le viol de l'imaginaire*. Paris: Actes Sud/Fayard, 2002.

Traoré, Aminata, and Cheikh Hamidou Kane. *L'Afrique humiliée*. Littérature Générale. Paris: Fayard, 2008.

Uvin, Peter. *Aiding Violence: The Development Enterprise in Rwanda*. West Hartford, Conn.: Kumarian Press, 1998.

Verschave, François-Xavier. *La Françafrique*. Paris: Stock, 1998.

Vieyra, Cécile. *Une odeur aigre de lait rance*. Paris: Présence Africaine, 1999.

Waberi, Abdourahman. *Aux Etats-Unis d'Afrique*. Paris: Editions Jean-Claude Lattès, 2006.

———. *Balbala*. Paris: Serpent à Plumes, 1997.

———. *Cahier nomade*. Motifs. Paris: Serpent à Plumes, 1999.

———. "Les enfants de la postcolonie: Esquisse d'une nouvelle génération d'écrivains francophones d'Afrique Noire." *Notre Librairie* 135 (September–December 1998): 8–15.

———. *Le pays sans ombre*. Motifs. Paris: Serpent à Plumes, 1995.

———. *Moisson de crânes: Textes pour le Rwanda*. Paris: Serpent à Plumes, 2000.

———. "Mongo Beti, si près si loin." In *Remember Mongo Beti*, ed. Ambroise Kom, 109–16. Bayreuth, Germany: Bayreuth African Studies 67, 2003.

———. *Rift*. Paris: Gallimard, 2001.

———. *Transit*. Continents Noirs. Paris: Gallimard, 2003.

Wainaina, Binyavango. "How to Write about Africa? Some Tips: Sunsets and Starvation Are Good." *Granta* 92, "The View from Africa" (Winter 2005). Available online at http://www.granta.com/Magazine/92/How-to-Write-About-Africa.

Waintrater, Régine. *Sortir du génocide, témoigner pour réapprendre à vivre*. Paris: Payot, 2003.

Weldon Johnson, James. "The Dilemma of the Negro Author." *American Mercury* (December 1928): 467.

Wood, James. *The Broken Estate: Essays on Literature and Belief*. New York: Farrar, Straus and Giroux, 2000.

Wright, Derek. "African Literature and Post-Independence disillusionment." *Cambridge History of African and Caribbean Literature* 2 (2004): 797–808.

Young, Robert. *White Mythologies: Writing, History, and the West*. 2nd ed. New York: Routledge, 2004.

Zabus, Chantal. *African Palimpsest*. Amsterdam: Cross/Cultures, 1991.